Mapping For§

GW01402659

Mapping Forgiveness

Edited by

Malika Rebai Maamri

Inter-Disciplinary Press

Oxford, United Kingdom

© Inter-Disciplinary Press 2012
http://www.inter-disciplinary.net/publishing/id-press/

The *Inter-Disciplinary Press* is part of *Inter-Disciplinary.Net* – a global network for research and publishing. The *Inter-Disciplinary Press* aims to promote and encourage the kind of work which is collaborative, innovative, imaginative, and which provides an exemplar for inter-disciplinary and multi-disciplinary publishing.

British Library Cataloguing in Publication Data. A catalogue record for this book is available from the British Library.

Inter-Disciplinary Press, Priory House, 149B Wroslyn Road, Freeland, Oxfordshire. OX29 8HR, United Kingdom.
+44 (0)1993 882087

ISBN: 978-1-84888-152-5
First published in the United Kingdom in Paperback format in 2012. First Edition.

Table of Contents

Introduction   vii
Malika Rebai Maamri

Part 1:   **Forgiveness as a Transformational Process**

The Art of Forgiving: Conditions of Perspective   3
and Transformation
Richard Kyte

Empirical Studies of Forgiveness as an Altruistic Response: 15
Relationships with Rumination, Suppression of Negative
Emotions and Benefit-Focused Reappraisal
Charlotte vanOyen Witvliet

Healing and Forgiveness after Traumatic Events: The Case   33
of Holocaust Survivors from the Fortunoff Archives
Clara Mucci

Part 2:   **Does Religiosity Foster Forgiveness?**

Forgiveness and Religion: Update and Current Status   53
Daryl R. Van Tongeren, Everett L. Worthington, Jr.,
Don E. Davis, Joshua N. Hook, Aubrey L. Gartner,
David J. Jennings II, Chelsea L. Greer and Todd W. Greer

Anger toward God: A New Frontier in the Study   71
Julie J. Exline

Radical Forgiveness and Feminist Theology   85
Elisabeth Gedge

Part 3:   **The Practice of Peace and Reconciliation**

Memorials as Sites of National Conscience   99
Cayo Gamber

Algerian President's Peace Plan: Political and   121
Psychological Perspectives
Malika Rebai Maamri

Forgiveness and Hope: Re-building Fractured Communities   141
James Arvanitakis

Part 4:   Interpretations of Forgiveness in Literary Studies

Poetry as a Medium of Forgiveness in the Light of   157
Czesław Miłosz's Oeuvre
Anna M. Szczepan-Wojnarska

Hemans Hosting the Poetic Absolution in   169
'Anguish with Delight'
Maryam Farahani

Levinasian Ethics and the Failure to Forgive in   193
Jean-Paul Sartre's *The Flies*
Canan Şavkay

Mapping Forgiveness: Conclusion   213
Malika Rebai Maamri

Introduction

Malika Rebai Maamri

'To err is human; to forgive, divine.'
-Alexander Pope

Conflict has plagued humankind for centuries. Mistrust, hatred and violence have constantly built into explosive experiences that have become justifications for various human responses of holding grudges and/or outright actions of revenge. As current conflicts rage across the globe, the need for innovative strategies to resolve conflict is greater than ever. Consequently, human beings have developed many paradigms for achieving what they consider to be resolutions to their problems of pain and outright injury inflicted on them by others. The problems facing human society today, I would argue, demand a global response and require a 'magic alchemy,' (Anthony Emmett) as we re-examine the way we relate to each other. Globalisation is considered *the* antidote to societal fragmentation. As a vital step toward both a more stable world and better life for the people, it should contribute to establishing harmony and removing not only cultural barriers, but also many of the negative dimensions of culture. Globalisation should bring together people and nations for the common good. However, the gates of the world are groaning shut. Human history and the everyday experiences of the world's peoples do not provide a glowing picture of the Self/Other relationship, because the growing globalisation has a two-sided effect: it has the power of binding and dividing at the same time. Indeed, if globalisation nowadays seems to re-unite societies under the same objectives and realities, we cannot ignore the new challenges that are defying nation-states around the world. The events happening in different parts of the globe nowadays have seriously impaired the notion of a multi-cultural or multi-religious society. To re-establish multilateralism, a genuine individual and collective willingness to try to release the hurts of the past, accompanied by hope and determination to start anew can be argued to be a starting point in this process. Multilateralism creates a framework that sustains common action, and the reconstruction of a new world based on multilateralism can survive only if carried out through dialogue, respect of the identities of each culture, and forgiveness. Increasingly, we live indeed in a world where forgiveness is demanded, granted, or withheld. Forgiveness however remains a contested concept. While psychologists tend to emphasize the intrapersonal aspects of the phenomenon, theologians, philosophers and sociologists see an important correlation between forgiveness and reconciliation due to relational factors. Culture further complicates the study of forgiveness in that it questions the universality of dominant understandings of the concept. All in all, forgiveness offers a broader perspective and deeper engagement with the world. It is 'the touchstone of our humanity,'[1] a catalyst for human growth. In Derrida's words, 'forgiveness must rest on a *human possibility*.'[2]

Specifically, forgiving someone who has brutalized you may help toward his/her becoming more human. Moreover, 'To forgive is not just altruistic; it is the best form of self-interest. What dehumanizes you inexorably dehumanizes me.'[3]

Moreover, many of those who explored the nature of forgiveness pointed out that true forgiveness can only come after things have been set right and justice rendered. Scholarship on conflict resolution has indeed been too much focused on the mechanisms for reconciliation viewed from the perspective of judge or victim. Though appealing, the concept of retributive justice is not totally clear because if it refers merely to punishing offences, this sense of justice, which recalls the Old Testament 'eye for an eye, tooth for a tooth' version of justice, seems to me incompatible both with forgiveness and reconciliation between victim and perpetrator. If forgiving means renouncing blind hatred and feelings of revenge, then why seek punishment of the offender? In his advocacy of truth and reconciliation, Desmond Tutu (1999) makes it clear that forgiveness and reconciliation are incompatible with retributive justice. He rather assesses the moral value of forgiveness in terms of restorative justice because it fosters dialogue between victim and offender. For the process of restorative justice to be effective, it must be committed to by both parties. Restorative justice rests on three key ideas: First, the understanding that both the victim and the nearby community have been affected by the offender's action thus, rehabilitation is necessary; second, the offender's duty to help repair the harm he/she has caused by making amends with both the victim and the involved community; third, the most important process of restorative justice is the notion of 'healing' of both parties. It instils safety back into the victim's life and provides help for the offender in order to avoid recidivism. In line with Desmond Tutu, Linda Radzik opts for this alternative response to wrongdoing.[4] She believes that it is the wrongdoer's moral obligation to address the harm and take action, even while recognizing that the past cannot be erased and that some damage is irreversible. From the point of view of the perpetrator, who experiences guilt from harming another, making reparation to the victim for the deed through an apology is necessary for the burden of guilt to be released. It should be noted however, that in some contexts, forgiveness may be granted without any expectation of restorative justice, and without any response on the part of the offender. Both apology and forgiveness thus, reflect the constructive ways in which the victimizer and the victimized in an intractable strife can come to grips with the pain and suffering the conflict engendered.

Accordingly, from the mid-1980s, the world began to witness an explosion of public, representative apologies for past wrongs, the first of which came from the leaders of European nations in reference to the Shoah. Apologies also came from many nations across the world for systematic violations against indigenous peoples. In all the scenes of repentance, confession, forgiveness, or apology which have proliferated on the geopolitical scene since the last war, and escalated in the past few years, one has seen not only individuals, but also whole communities, professional bodies, the representatives of ecclesiastical hierarchies, monarchs, and heads of state ask for forgiveness. Social relationships are restored and a sense of justice is rendered indeed if the offending person apologizes or asks for forgiveness.

As its title indicates, this volume maps different experiences of forgiveness. It explores the fundamental issues of forgiving in the wake of profound victimization, and the why, how and when a victim may forgive a transgressor for wrongdoing; in other words, what it means to forgive, what calls for forgiveness, who calls for, and who calls upon forgiveness. The authors of this volume have tried to answer these questions using different approaches. Collaborative scholarly endeavour, discussions and contributions from all corners of the globe and from many disciplines resulted in a kind of 'globalisation' of forgiveness. Although for Jacques Derrida, forgiveness originally belongs 'to a religious heritage,'[5] which connotes Judaism, Christianity, and Islam, the authors of this volume's interpretation of forgiveness goes beyond these religions and tends to efface the traditionalistic assumption in the course of 'globalisation,' or what Derrida calls 'internationalisation.' These chapters presented at the third annual global conference on *Forgiveness: Probing the Boundaries*, held at Mansfield College, University of Oxford, convey the dilemma: the distinction between theological – a matter between god and the believer – and human – between victim and perpetrator – conceptions of forgiveness. This open-ended framework provides a wide-ranging scope for this book, which deals with philosophical, ethical, sociological, political, and religious approaches to post-violence politics and societies. It also explores the role of literature in reinforcing cultural connections and boundaries. Part 1 concerns the many emotional changes induced by forgiveness. It focuses on ways traumatized people might first go through to become strong enough to begin forgiving. This part also includes a discussion of essential elements in forgiving. Empathy, humility and compassion are explored in this context. Part 2 discusses forgiveness from a religious perspective. Part 3 highlights the fact that reconciliation, which encompasses much more than getting along with those who once injured people, may effectively be achieved by humans. The impact of memorial rituals as well as the importance of forgiveness in an individual's life as inescapably bound up with the community, are discussed in the next chapters that constitute this third part. Given the growing rhetoric of forgiveness in international politics, these authors seek to articulate a model of political forgiveness. The closing part analyses forgiveness through literary texts. The writers of the fourth and last part of the volume reveal what creative works can bring to secular debates on forgiveness and conflict resolution.

Part 1: Forgiveness as a Transformational Process
    In his chapter, Richard Kyte draws attention to the two movements that constitute forgiving: a 'stepping out,' or the degree of emotional detachment

maintained toward a person, group of people, or event, and a 'stepping in.' While the former puts the injury in a larger context and enables a kind of cleansing of negative emotions and effects a change in the way one views the wrongdoer, the latter is meant to restore a relationship with the offender. Drawing on Edward Bullough's work on *Psychical Distance in Art and Aesthetic Principle*,[6] Kyte applies his metaphor of 'distance,' which describes a personal relation, to the compelling art of forgiving. Kyte defends four important points: (1) some preliminary work is necessary to produce an emotional transformation in the victim, (2) the capacity to separate oneself from events is a psychological achievement, (3) detachment is not the result of a 'decision' in any straightforward sense, and (4) forgiving resists justification because the distanced perception results in a change of meaning that is unlikely to be acknowledged by sympathetic observers. This transformational process of forgiveness is carried further in Charlotte vanOyen Witvliet's thought-provoking chapter.

Psychotherapists have worked to help their patients to forgive and some have written extensively about the importance of forgiveness. However, until recently the scientific literature has not had much to say about the effect of resentment and forgiveness. Witvliet's study brings together theoretical understandings of forgiveness with empirical experimentation. The real import and value of her work revolves around the fact that forgiveness is important in healing. In her three programmatic experiments, Witvliet examined the implications of reliving interpersonal hurts in contrast to compassionate responding. Each experiment revealed changes within the participants. In the first experiment, in which seventy one undergraduates (36 males, 35 females) participants had been instructed to ruminate about the hurtful offence, she recorded both physiological and emotional changes within the participants. Her next experiment aimed at extending her understanding of forgiveness as a compassionate response to the offender, and trying to see what sort of changes occurred within individuals when they adopted the various responses of rumination, suppression of negative affect, or compassionate reappraisal of their offender, which she defines as thinking of one's offender 'as a human being.'[7] Her third and final experiment investigated forgiveness as compassion-focused reappraisal in contrast to benefit-focused reappraisal. The psychologist concluded that this altruistic-oriented approach to forgiveness helps in transforming negative feelings caused by hurtful offence memories or grudge-holding into more positive ones. Forgiveness can even lead to feelings of understanding, empathy and compassion for the perpetrator. This compassionate response allows the victim's healing. The boost to one's health from forgiveness indeed includes lower blood pressure and heart rates, a reduction in chronic pain and fewer symptoms from anxiety, depression or stress.

Clara Mucci's clinical study of forgiveness also offers interesting insights into the challenges faced by the demand for forgiveness. Her treatment of traumatized patients has resonance with Kyte's first claim about forgiving, i.e. that some initial work is necessary before forgiving. Mucci's research on trauma is informed by some confrères' works such as Judith Herman, Ilde Grubrich-Simitis and Dori Laub in treating victims of traumas of the Shoah or incest survivors. The psychoanalyst stresses the necessity of re-building the historical reality of the traumatic event and the emotions and feelings involved with its happening, before starting any work. Re-discovering the truth and proclaiming the truth within oneself are prerequisites for the restoration of social order and the healing of the victim. Mucci's second phase in the treatment of her traumatized patients has to do with what the French psychoanalyst, Michèle Bertrand, terms a 'triple acknowledgment' whereby 1) the victim asks for the social recognition of the harm done to her/him; 2) she/he asks for a recognition on behalf of the transgressor; 3) the victim asks for the acknowledgement of the truth of her/his words. After this stage, the patient tries to overcome his/her anger by letting go of resentments and the desire for revenge. It is at this point only that a true sense of love can be achieved and that reconciliation with the other is initiated, argues the psychoanalyst. Mucci also provides various testimonies from the Fortunoff Archives at Yale University. The people she interviewed embraced the offender with a multitude of acts of forgiveness, and strongly agreed that the tragedy that had befallen on them deepened their understanding of life. This fact along with the stated belief that forgiveness is indeed possible, beneficial and an important element in their healing would indicate that forgiveness is transforming for the forgiver.

Part 2: Does Religiosity Foster Forgiveness?

Daryl R. Van Tongeren, et al. attempted a scientific study of forgiveness and religion within psychology. Because all religions place great emphasis on the need for humans to practise forgiveness of one another, religious individuals might say that they are more forgiving. In practice however, they may not actually forgive more. The writers' experiments in this chapter, were aimed at finding answers to three main questions: 1) which religion is 'best' at offering forgiveness? 2) Are religious people hypocritical when it comes to forgiveness? 3) How does spirituality affect forgiveness? The conclusion they reached is that most world religions include teachings on the nature of forgiveness and value forgiveness, though in quite different ways. They suggested some interesting points: that the victim's humility, which may be related to his/her religious beliefs, may impact on his/her forgiving. Indeed as it relates to their spirituality, this increased self-understanding and self-control allow the victims to better monitor their own struggles, as well as be aware of their reactions toward God and to the people around them. As an openness of mind and heart, humility provides a framework to an improved life. More importantly, in interpersonal relations, humility and empathy provide a way to conflict resolution. Daryl R. Van Tongeren, et al.'s second important argument concerns the impact of cultural differences on the victim's experience of forgiveness.

Julie J. Exline continues the thematic investigation of religion and forgiveness by attempting criticism of a new source. Exline discusses some challenging issues revolving around the assessment of anger toward God. Much of the emphasis in her chapter has been to demonstrate the similarity between anger toward God and interpersonal anger. In time of distress, people may feel resentment at God and hold Him for being responsible for their hardships. Believing God to be righteous and incapable of wrongdoing, suffering thus ignites an avalanche of anger, bitterness and recrimination. Consequently, people feel frustration, rage and even mistrust. 'Some might also feel abandoned or rejected by God, triggering responses related to shame and loss,' adds Exline. 'How might a person then resolve anger toward God, and how does it affect mental health?' she asks. Exline proposes that the core element of any genuine act of forgiveness is the overcoming of anger toward God. Yet she does so specifically in relation to recent research in psychology. Exline also proposes some techniques that could help people come to terms with this type of anger. She draws her recommendations from descriptive studies, two experimental imagery exercises presented at the annual meeting of the American Psychological Association, Toronto, Ontario, CA, August 6, 2009, and Everett L. Worthington, Jr.'s 'Pyramid Model of Forgiveness.'[8]

A similar kind of alignment informs Elisabeth Gedge's account of radical forgiveness as the virtue for controlling anger, and a component in the healing of individual 'soul suffering.' Gedge's analysis of 'Radical Forgiveness and Feminist Theology' provides substance to the intuitive assumption that forgiveness must be part of our faith in God. To make her case, she relies on 'the Lord's prayer'[9] and the parable of the ungrateful servant,[10] which suggest that the individual's practice of forgiveness should be modelled on God's forgiveness, which is radical. Against such a schema, Gedge induces the unconditionality of forgiveness. The author further explores the claim made in Beverly Lanzetta's *Via Feminina*,[11] 'engaging in radical forgiveness without compromising personal dignity, political solidarity, or hope in Divine vindication.' Gedge's second argument is that problems with radical forgiveness are further exacerbated when viewed from the perspective of feminist politics. God's forgiveness sometimes violates important considerations of justice: in this case, 'demanding radical forgiveness might render God complicit in reinforcing damaging stereotypes and unreasonable moral demands of women and other subordinates,'[12] she notes. Insofar as radical forgiveness operates as part of a contemplative ethic aimed at reducing segregation and exclusion, it nonetheless offers a remedy for structural injustice. At this juncture, it would be interesting to see if radical forgiveness is possible in the case of Holocaust survivors.

Part 3: The Practice of Peace and Reconciliation

Memorials also stand for inner peace and forgiveness and suggest a greater public awareness of the dark past. Concurrently, the impact of memorial rituals cannot be underestimated because they honour the dead with memories of shared moments of great joy and great sorrow. Analysing Simon Wiesenthal's *The Sunflower: on the Possibilities and Limits of Forgiveness*, Cayo Gamber discusses how national memorials, such as Kollwitz's Mourning the Fallen, Duszenko and Haupt's Stones of Treblinka, Hoheisel's Aschrott's Fountain, Eisenman's Monument to the Murdered Jews, and Lin's Vietnam Veterans Memorial, function as sites of national conscience. Although developing and including forgiveness rituals may operate a larger social transformation in that there is a sense of shared purpose and intent, a gathering of friends and neighbours to grieve, would it be really possible for these memorials to facilitate the transformation of grief from anger to acceptance, retribution to forgiveness? Can they really promote social recovery? Do they not sometimes crystallize a sense of victimization, injustice, discrimination, and the desire for revenge?

While memorials to the Holocaust insist upon the impossibility of clemency, Malika Rebai Maamri stresses that amnesty constitutes one of the many tools of reconciliation. Although potentially problematic, this concept of reconciliation is perhaps the closest to the evolution of an institutional framework that encourages the possibility of forgiveness. Rebai Maamri focuses on the Algerian President's platform for a political and peaceful solution to the question of terrorism in Algeria in the 1990s. As a background to the guerrilla war, the author examines the contemporary phenomenon of political Islam in order to show clearly how this ideology operates as a barrier to forgiveness. Based upon her analysis, one is able to claim that the fundamentalists deploy violence as a political weapon to force through their own desire to belong by destroying similar claims of belonging by the victims. Rebai Maamri's chapter draws extensively on Jacques Derrida's notion of forgiveness as being without 'limit[s] and *measure*,'[13] echoing thus Elizabeth Gedge's notion of radical forgiveness. Through compelling examples, Rebai Maamri argues that true forgiveness consists in forgiving the unforgivable. She also discusses the relationship between forgiveness and reconciliation and tries to demonstrate that the Algerian President holds forgiveness as a high virtue and one to rely on in all matters of conflict. Such thoughts capture the ethos underlying the dominant forms of Islam. She also explains that while the restitution of social order and human dignity is paramount, the Head of the Algerian State believes that crime should carry consequences. Rebai Maamri further maintains that the Algerian President's charter is not a charter for amnesia, but involves accepting the promise that the future can be more than dwelling on memories of past injury. It is a part of social reconstruction, an act of rehabilitation based on Islamic precepts.

Despite the controversy over the application of the Civil Harmony law, Rebai Maamri concludes that the great bulk of families of the victims of terrorism have accepted the government's demand to forgive the perpetrators not because of their dependence on the government, but because they believed that forgiveness holds great promise as one approach to conflict resolution and violence cessation and could be achieved only by learning to live together and reconciling the victim and the offender.

The question surrounding community and forgiveness also informs James Arvanitakis's chapter. Arvanitakis expands the process of forgiveness from a personal experience to a broader societal experience. It is indeed evident that violence does not just affect the direct victims and their families but draws the entire community into the grieving process. Arvanitakis analyses the far-reaching effects of the Civil War in Bougainville, Papua New Guinea, a war which opposed not only the native population to the PNG Defence Force but also turned local people against each other, in order to highlight both the role of forgiveness and hope in bringing fractured communities together. The author, who had been supporting a community project in Papua, challenges us to reconsider our definitions of community. He investigates the ways in which the Bougainville community demonstrated its support immediately after the violent event. This reaction of the people was not simply intended to show solidarity for the victim and their families and friends, but it was also an expression of a greater need for the larger community to restore a sense of safety and unity as was the case in Algeria. Arvanitakis consistently maintains that forgiveness is both required and provides the foundation for a new community of hope. His closing thesis is that communities can be united in tragedy through love.

Part 4: Interpretations of Forgiveness in Literary Studies

Looking beyond the African cultural boundaries, the writers of the final part of the volume reveal that creative production and interpretation can play a vital role in practices of forgiveness. Developing a model of poetry as a form of penance through Czesław Miłosz's work, Anna M. Szczepan-Wojnarska demonstrates that, according to the Polish poet, poetry has the capacity to mediate forgiveness without merging into it. Moreover, as a form of penance, poetry consists of two core elements: recognizing the guilt and carrying out tasks by putting some effort into compensating the unwanted results of the committed crime. Echoing somehow Michèle Bertrand's 'triple acknowledgment,' and Clara Mucci's psychoanalytic prerequisite of re-discovering the truth and proclaiming the truth within oneself, Szczepan-Wojnarska explains that in Miłosz's oeuvre, forgiveness can be accorded only to the one who is aware of the harm done, asks for forgiveness, and realizes the collapse of his world after committing the hideous crime. Michel Foucault also explained, though in a quite different context, that 'The more we discover the truth about ourselves, the more we have to renounce ourselves, and the more we want to renounce ourselves, the more we need to bring to light the reality of ourselves.'[14]

In this regard, Miłosz's poetry might be described as an ambivalent attempt to bring to light the suspected reality of the unacknowledged self. Maryam Farahani charts new territory. Her chapter explores the theme of forgiveness in the well-known Romantic female poet, Felicia Hemans's *Records of Woman*, (1828) which chronicles the lives of women. Because as Hemans stated in a letter to Mary Russel Mitford, a close friend of hers: '[She had] put [her] heart and individual feelings into [her poetry] more than anything else...,'[15] to some male readers, she seemed to offer a lyricism consonant with Victorian sentimentality. This biased male perception made her stature as a poet gradually decline. Why the continuing resistance to women authors when overwhelming evidence shows that women published prolifically during the Romantic era? We have learned that women shaped Romantic-era discourse under the guise of sentimental, yet revolutionary literature. This gendered classification of women's writings as emotional underpins Farahani's text.

In her study of 'Records of Woman,' Farahani maintains that Hemans's poetry 'provides a means of showcasing (un)forgiveness as a step towards understanding the sublime, the self, and the origin of sublimity.' Though the main focus in this chapter is on how Hemans achieves the juxtaposition of 'anguish with delight,' Farahani's work also reads as a sort of 'vindication of the rights of woman.'[16] The author takes the gender controversy in Romanticism and Romantic studies in a new direction. In investigating the relationship between male and female authors, Farahani seems to render justice to Hemans. Her work constitutes an extended, provocative, and thoughtful response to male dismissal of Hemans.

While the writers of the preceding chapters highlight forgiveness as the virtue of virtues, Canan Salkay's chapter reveals the problematic nature of forgiveness in Jean Paul Sartre's *The Flies*, a re-writing of Aeschylus's tragedy, *The Oresteia*. While the failure to forgive fosters debilitating attitudes of resentment and rage in the Greek play, Sartre gives it a twist. In *The Oresteia* indeed, the possibility to forgive is totally absent. Orestes had to avenge his father's murder. The Greek playwright emphasizes the fact that 'those who forgive... share the sinner's guilt.'[17] In *The Flies*, however, Sartre gives Orestes the chance to leave Argos without committing the hideous deed. Analysing Sartre's play from Levinas's concept of the dwelling and hospitality, Salkay also draws attention to Orestes's feeling of homelessness due to his inability to establish a psychic space of his own, which leads him to violence because he fails to reconcile the two sides in him. In *The Flies*, moreover, Sartre identifies revenge with masculine characteristics and endows forgiveness with traits that are generally regarded as feminine. The topics of revenge and forgiveness are also tackled differently in the two plays through the representation of Clytemnestra's dilemma. In the Greek tragedy, because he represents masculine authority, and because justice is based on masculine force and violence, Clytemnestra is expected to forgive her husband. Elizabeth Gedge's perplexing query: 'Does forgiveness not represent a reinforcement of traditional patterns of behaviour for women?' seems quite relevant to Salkay's argument. According to Salkay, however, Sartre's play suggests that the option to forgive could have saved Clytemnestra and as such, it would have been a moral action.

As can be seen in the twelve chapters that follow, multidisciplinary analysis by a group of scholars coming from all continents, offers important insights on the most critical challenge facing human existence today: how to overcome hostilities and live together in peace.

Notes

[1] Diana Medlicott, 'Forgiveness after Torture: Narratives of Grief and Grace', in *Forgiveness: Promise, Possibility and Failure*, edited by Geoffrey Karabin and Karolina Wigura (Oxford: Inter-Disciplinary Press, 2011), 241.

[2] Jacques Derrida, *On Cosmopolitanism and Forgiveness*, trans. M. Dooley and M. Hughes (Routledge: London and New York, 1997), 52.

[3] Desmond Tutu, *No Future without Forgiveness* (Image Books: New York, 2000), 31.

[4] See Linda Radzik, *Making Amends: Atonement in Morality, Law, and Politics* (Oxford: University Press, 2009).

[5] Derrida, *On Cosmopolitanism and Forgiveness*, 31.

[6] See Edward Bullough, 'Psychical Distance as a Factor in Art and an Aesthetic Principle,' *British Journal of Psychology* 5 (1912): 87-118.

[7] Charlotte van Oyen Witvliet, 'Understanding and Approaching Forgiveness as Altruism: Relationships with Rumination, Self-Control, and a Gratitude-Based Strategy', in *A Journey through Forgiveness*, edited by Malika Rebai Maamri, Nehama Verbin and Everett L. Worthington, Jr. (Oxford: Inter-Disciplinary Press, 2011), 103, Accessed May 20, 2011, http://www.inter-disciplinary.net/wp-content/uploads/2011/01/forgiveness3ever19122010.pdf.

[8] Everett L. Worthington Jr., 'Pyramid Model of Forgiveness: Some Interdisciplinary Speculations about Unforgiveness and the Promotion of Forgiveness', in *Dimensions of Forgiveness*, ed. Everett L. Worthington, Jr. (Philadelphia: Templeton, 1998).

[9] Matthew 6: 12.

[10] Matthew 18: 23-35. Also Colossians 3:13.

[11] See Beverly Lanzetta, *Radical Wisdom: A Feminist Mystical Theology* (Minneapolis: Fortress Press, 2005).

[12] See Elisabeth Gedge, 'Radical Forgiveness and Feminist Theology', in this volume.

[13] Derrida, *Cosmopolitanism*, 27.

[14] Michel Foucault, 'Sexuality and Solitude', in *On Signs*, edited by Marshall Blonsky (John Hopkins Univ. Press: Baltimore, 1985), 368.
[15] Susan J. Wolfson, *Felicia Hemans: Selected Poems, Letters, Reception Material* (Princeton: Princeton Univ. Press, 2001), 498.
[16] Mary Wollstonecraft, *A Vindication of the Rights of Woman, with Strictures on Political and Moral Subjects*, Boston: Peter Edes for Thomas and Andrews, Faust's statue, no. 45, Newbury-street, MDCCXCII. [1792], 1999, viewed 12 August 2011, Bartleby.com. http://www.bartleby.com/144/.
[17] Aeschylus, *The Oresteian Trilogy* (London: Penguin, 1959), 56.

Bibliography

Aeschylus. *The Oresteian Trilogy*. London: Penguin, 1959.

Bullough, Edward. 'Psychical Distance as a Factor in Art and an Aesthetic Principle'. *British Journal of Psychology* 5 (1912): 87-118.

Derrida, Jacques. *On Cosmopolitanism and Forgiveness*. Translated by M. Dooley and M. Hughes. Routledge: London and New York, 1997.

Foucault, Michel. 'Sexuality and Solitude'. In *On Signs*, edited by Marshall Blonsky. John Hopkins Univ. Press: Baltimore, 1985.

Gedge, Elisabeth. 'Radical Forgiveness and Feminist Theology'. In this volume.

Lanzetta, Beverly. *Radical Wisdom: A Feminist Mystical Theology*. Minneapolis: Fortress Press, 2005.

Medlicott, Diana. 'Forgiveness after Torture: Narratives of Grief and Grace'. In *Forgiveness: Promise, Possibility and Failure*, edited by Geoffrey Karabin and Karolina Wigura. Oxford: Inter-Disciplinary Press, 2011.

Radzik, Linda. *Making Amends: Atonement in Morality, Law, and Politics*. Oxford: University Press, 2009.

Tutu, Desmond. *No Future without Forgiveness*. Image Books: New York, 2000.

Witvliet, Charlotte vanOyen. 'Understanding and Approaching Forgiveness as Altruism: Relationships with Rumination, Self-Control, and a Gratitude-Based Strategy'. In *A Journey through Forgiveness*, edited by Malika Rebai Maamri, Nehama Verbin and Everett L. Worthington, Jr. Oxford: Inter-Disciplinary Press, 2011. Accessed May 20, 2011, http://www.inter-disciplinary.net/wp-content/uploads/2011/01/forgiveness3ever19122010.pdf.

Wolfson, Susan J. *Felicia Hemans : Selected Poems, Letters, Reception Material*. Princeton: Princeton Univ. Press, 2001.

Wollstonecraft, Mary. *A Vindication of the Rights of Woman, with Strictures on Political and Moral Subjects*. Boston: Peter Edes for Thomas and Andrews, Faust's statue. no. 45. Newbury-street, MDCCXCII. [1792], viewed 12 August 2011. Bartleby.com, http://www.bartleby.com/144/.

Worthington, Everett L. Jr. 'Pyramid Model of Forgiveness: Some Interdisciplinary Speculations about Unforgiveness and the Promotion of Forgiveness'. In *Dimensions of Forgiveness*, edited by Everett L. Worthington, Jr. Philadelphia: Templeton, 1998.

Part 1:

Forgiveness as a Transformational Process

The Art of Forgiving: Conditions of Perspective and Transformation

Richard Kyte

Abstract
If we look at stories of forgiveness, we see that forgiving consists of two movements: a 'stepping out' which places the injury in a broader context and a 'stepping in' whereby an attempt is made to re-establish some sort of relationship with the person who caused the injury. The process of stepping out is generally described as a change in perspective or point of view. Using Edward Bullough's notion of 'psychical distance,' this chapter will propose an explanation of the human capacity for separating oneself from events while still retaining a type of emotional interest. Based on that, the chapter will then set forth and defend four claims about forgiving: (1) that forgiving requires a certain type of preliminary work that effects an emotional transformation in the person who has been injured, (2) that the capacity for attaining distance is a psychological achievement, (3) that distancing is not the result of a 'decision' in any straightforward sense, and (4) that forgiving resists justification because the distanced perception results in a change of meaning that is unlikely to be acknowledged by sympathetic observers.

Key Words: Forgiveness, psychical distance, catharsis.

*****

Note too that a faithful study of the liberal arts humanizes character and permits it not to be cruel.
-Ovid[1]

[A]rt is not nature, but is nature transformed by entering into new relationships where it evokes a new emotional response.
-John Dewey[2]

A puzzling and significant question for those attempting to understand the psychology of forgiveness is: what kind of transformation allows the person who suffers injury to forgive the wrongdoer? It is puzzling because forgiving, especially in cases of serious injury, involves a transformation that is not entirely within one's control. It is significant because that transformation involves emotions which are central to one's identity and happiness.

Forgiveness involves two general steps: a 'stepping out' which places the injury in a broader context and a 'stepping in' whereby an attempt is made to re-establish some sort of relationship with the person who caused the injury. The first step is a condition of forgiving; the second the act of forgiving.

1. Stepping Out

The process of stepping out is generally described as a change in perspective or point of view. Charlotte vanOyen Witvliet terms this process 'compassionate reappraisal' and describes it as thinking of one's offender 'as a human being.'[3] Joanna North follows Robert Enright and others in describing the process as one of 'reframing,' and defines it as 'a process whereby the wrongdoer is viewed in context in an attempt to build up a complete picture of the wrongdoer and his actions.'[4] Likewise, Jean Hampton describes the process as 'overcoming a point of view,' but later, in a more complete statement, she says:

> The forgiver who previously saw the wrongdoer as someone bad or rotten or morally indecent to some degree has a change of heart when he 'washes away' or disregards the wrongdoer's immoral actions or character traits in his ultimate moral judgement of her, and comes to see her as still *decent, not* rotten as a person, and someone with whom he may be able to renew a relationship.[5]

There is some tension in the use of the metaphor here. A perspective or point of view is something that we can take up, get in position for. We can occupy one point of view and then another. But a change of heart is deeper, more central to our identity than perspectival change. When I move from anger to love, there is a sense in which *I* am changed. When I move from one point of view to another, I stay the same, only my position has changed. I suspect that the metaphor of perspective has misled North when she claims, for example, that 'when we forgive another person we have to move from our own perspective, of initial hurt and internal suffering, to that of the wrongdoer, the context of his wrong and his motivation for it as well as his present situation.'[6] For, of course, it is not the wrongdoer's *perspective* that we must adopt; rather, we must come to some *understanding* of the wrongdoer's actions, which frequently requires going beyond the wrongdoer's own perception of events and circumstances. The metaphor of perspective seems to mislead Hampton again when she says, against the tenor of her essay, that forgiveness is 'the decision to see a wrongdoer in a new, more favourable light.' Once we begin thinking of forgiveness as a change in perspective, it is natural to think of it as the result of a decision, like choosing to view a statue from the right side or the left.

Witvliet's research on the physiology of forgiveness is compelling in part because she distinguishes the relatively direct approach of emotional suppression from the less direct process of perspectival transformation and discovers that only the latter leads to genuine forgiveness. This distinction is important because even though one may learn, with practice, how to effectively suppress negative emotions, deep and lasting emotional change is not so amenable to one's will.

Another way of thinking about the process of 'stepping out' would be that of coming to see one's injury in a detached or impersonal manner. Yet that is problematic also, for it suggests that the condition of forgiving is 'forgetting,' losing all personal interest or emotional stake in the events of the past. Stoic philosophers such as Epictetus recommended taking such an attitude toward personal insult, for example. But whatever one might think of Stoic advice in general, detachment does not seem to be a condition of forgiveness, because it does not prepare one for re-establishing relationships with those who have wronged us. Rather, it seems to devalue relationships altogether.[7]

Still, there are ways of thinking about detachment which may be significant for forgiveness. It is possible to be detached from something in a certain respect while still maintaining a kind of connection. This ability is what Immanuel Kant tried to describe in setting forth the idea of 'disinterested interest' in his *Critique of Judgment*. Following Kant, the British psychologist, Edward Bullough, used the term 'psychical distance' to describe the capacity to separate oneself from events while still retaining a type of emotional interest.[8] He defines 'distance' as a *'personal* relation, often highly emotionally coloured, but *of a peculiar character.* Its peculiarity lies in that the personal character of the relation has been filtered, so to speak.'[9] And he adds: 'One of the best-known examples is to be found in our attitude towards the events and characters of the drama: they appeal to us like persons and incidents of normal experience, except that that side of their appeal, which would usually affect us in a directly personal manner, is held in abeyance.'[10] Without the ability to 'distancing' ourselves from the events depicted in a story, on stage, or in a painting, we would not be able to enjoy the work as a work of art. In fact, what it *means* to enjoy something as a work of art is to regard it in a properly 'distanced' manner. If we are too close, we cannot maintain our status as observers. On the other hand, if we are too far away, it cannot engage our interest.

Psychical distance is a capacity that makes art possible, because art is something intended to be perceived aesthetically. But anything, potentially, can be perceived aesthetically because natural objects as well as human artifacts can be viewed in a distanced manner. One of the most frequently quoted passages from Bullough in which he draws attention to the contrast between our ordinary manner of perceiving events and the distanced manner reads as follows:

> Imagine a fog at sea: for most people it is an experience of acute unpleasantness. Apart from the physical annoyance and remoter forms of discomfort such as delays, it is apt to produce feelings of peculiar anxiety, fears of invisible dangers, strains of watching and listening for distant and unlocalised signals. The listless movements of the ship and her warning calls soon tell upon the nerves of the passengers; and that special, expectant, tacit anxiety and nervousness, always associated with this experience, make a

fog the dreaded terror of the sea (all the more terrifying because of its very silence and gentleness) for the expert seafarer no less than for the ignorant landsman.

Nevertheless, a fog at sea can be a source of intense relish and enjoyment. Abstract from the experience of the sea fog, for the moment, its danger and practical unpleasantness…and the experience may acquire, in its uncanny mingling of repose and terror, a flavour of such concentrated poignancy and delight as to contrast sharply with the blind and distempered anxiety of its other aspects.[11]

Given this example, it may not be apparent what relevance the notion of psychical distance has for the understanding of forgiveness. I am certainly not suggesting that a feeling of 'poignancy and delight' at the remembrance of an injury is a prerequisite of forgiveness. Rather, I would like to use Bullough's notion of psychical distance to suggest that the process of 'stepping out,' which is preliminary to forgiving, may be characterized as a kind of detachment which makes room for a new kind of personal interest. We will then be in a position to understand how 'stepping out' can prepare the way for re-establishing relationships on the basis of such interest.

2. Psychical Distance as an Acquired Ability

The state of psychical distance is not the state of our ordinary experience, nor would we want it to be. Bullough says,

[a]s a rule, experience constantly turns the same side toward us, that which has the strongest practical force of appeal. We are not ordinarily aware of those aspects of things which do not teach us immediately and practically, nor are we generally conscious of impressions apart from which our own self is impressed.[12]

As we grow up, the number of things in the world which assume practical significance increases steadily, so that by the time we are adults, our daily experience is one of passing through a series of practically directed perceptions. When we then encounter, say, a particularly striking sunset on our drive home from work, we may, in our enjoyment of beauty, feel like children again, as if we are seeing freshly, with eyes of innocence and wonder. Such experiences suggest that psychical distance is a natural capacity which is gradually lost over time.[13] But it would be a mistake to think of psychical distance merely as a way of looking at things with a child's eyes. Psychical distance may seem to be a natural ability because it involves shedding certain perceptual tendencies that are due to accumulated practical concerns and anxieties, but it does not consist merely in the *lack* of prejudicial concerns. Rather, it implies the possession of an interest which one may learn to take in view of certain kinds of objects or events in the world. When parents read stories to their children, they are teaching them how to regard with interest characters and events which do not have an immediate, personal bearing on their own lives. Proper enjoyment of all the arts – poetry, music, painting, drama – requires development of the capacity for distance with regard to certain types of objects and events.

Bullough speaks of a 'distance-limit,' a limit 'which marks the minimum at which [one's] appreciation can maintain itself in the aesthetic field.'[14] There are certain themes, often having to do with morality, religion, or political matters, which are dealt with in a work of art. For some people, however, including many artists, the distance-limit is considerably higher than for others, and almost anything can be looked at aesthetically and without disturbance.[15] For those in whom the distance-limit is relatively low, the range of things which afford an opportunity for aesthetic *appreciation* is severely restricted. What this means for forgiveness is that the ability to 'step out' is a general capacity which can be developed. However, even those who have developed this capacity to a high degree may have difficulty in achieving distance with regard to certain types of offences.

3. Gestures as Prompts to Psychical Distance

Institutional art relies upon certain gestures or markers to let us know when to view something in a 'distanced' manner. Paintings are not only framed, but also set apart from other objects and hung on walls designated for the purpose. Pottery is set upon a stand or enclosed in a glass case. When we go to see a play, we buy tickets, enter a special room, sit in assigned seats, look at a program and a curtain opens. Such cues serve to prepare us to view the event in a certain way. When the gestures are not used, or used unexpectedly, confusion results. Orson Welles sends radio listeners across the United States into a panic over an alien invasion. A dinner guest puts his cigarette out in a sculpture.[16] When we enter a museum, we are directed by certain cues to modify our perception – to look at objects without immediate practical interest.

We may also develop our own private gestures as a way of prompting a change of attitude toward something or someone. Marion Milner, writing under the pseudonym of Joanna Field, describes, in her book *A Life of One's Own,* how she learned to discern two kinds of attention: narrow attention, which is 'the authentic one, the kind of attention which my mind gave to everyday affairs when it was left to itself' and wide attention, which occurs when we are able to 'attend to something and yet want nothing from it.'[17] She developed an inner gesture to prompt a change from one mode of attention to the other. 'Once when I was lying, weary and bored with myself, on a cliff looking over the Mediterranean, I had said, 'I want nothing, and immediately the landscape dropped its picture-postcard garishness and shone with a gleam from the first day of creation, even the dusty weeds by the roadside.'[18] She found that if she repeated those words – 'I want nothing' – in other circumstances, a similar perceptual/emotional change would occur.

A private gesture often used by those who seek a change of heart leading to forgiveness is prayer. And though the forms that such prayers take may differ a great deal, they generally serve to broaden one's attention by arresting, temporally, one's exclusively personal interests.

4. Psychical Distance Changes Meanings

Bullough notes the way in which psychical distance may be achieved suddenly 'like a momentary switching on of some new current.'[19] It is as if the whole scene changes, with no transition from one perception to the next. One can move forth and back, from one's ordinary, or proximate perception to distance, but one cannot perceive in both ways at once.[20] This is referred to as a gestalt shift.

When one apprehends meaning in a picture, one does not necessarily notice the details of the composition. When one reads a word on a page, one does not necessarily notice the colour of the print or the style of font. What one remarks is the meaning of the word. Or again, when one reads somebody's facial expression, one does not necessarily notice that the brow is furrowed, or that the corners of the mouth are turned down. What one notes first, or directly, is that so-and-so is angry. For these reasons, what we often call 'perception' is never merely perception. It is always also the apprehension of meaning.

In a little known essay titled 'A Lecture on the Notion of Reading,' Simone Weil describes how the meanings of perceived objects come to us directly, without mediation, without interpretation:

> If one evening, on a solitary path, I think that I see a man lying in ambush, instead of a tree, a threatening human presence imposes itself on me, and … it makes me shudder before I even know what is going on. I get closer and suddenly everything is different; I do not shudder anymore; I read a tree and not a man. There is not an appearance plus an interpretation. A human presence had reached my soul through my eyes, and now suddenly it is the presence of a tree.[21]

The implication of Weil's observation about reading for understanding forgiveness is significant. In most cases, a wronged person does not reflect upon how to regard the wrongdoer – her response is immediate. And the person who forgives may have an equally direct response to the wrongdoer. That is so because 'stepping out,' or the process of coming to see the wrongdoer in a new light, does not consist in logically re-evaluating the wrongdoer's behaviour. It is instead a process of changing the way one *reads* the wrongdoer. Similarly, if one comes to see beauty in a painting by Cezanne, that perception does not result from a line of reasoning about the worthiness of the painting. To be sure, one may say to oneself: 'This painting is universally admired by critics. It is the product of a great artist at the height of his ability. Surely, it is a beautiful painting.' Such reasoning may encourage one to keep trying, perhaps to sit down for a while in front of the painting, to be patient before it, to do the sorts of things that may somehow prompt a perception of its beauty. In the case of the wrongdoer, one may say to oneself something like the following: 'This man also is a child of God. I am commanded to love my enemies. Surely, I ought to forgive him.' Such reasoning may encourage one to keep trying to effect a change of perception by doing the sorts of things that are likely to change how one reads a person. But the reasoning itself will not bring about the change one seeks.

In this vein, Marietta Jaeger, speaking of the man who kidnapped and murdered her daughter, says: 'I realized I ...wanted to reach out and help this man.'[22] Her realization, I would contend, resulted from what she read in the very appearance of that particular man, and though she worked to achieve it, by continually praying for him over a period of months, it came as a surprise to her, and to him. That is why forgiveness is often perplexing or unintelligible to onlookers, even to the person being forgiven. It defies understanding, just as a written message defies understanding to one who cannot read. To the person who is incapable of attaining a distanced perception, forgiving always seems inexplicable, and therefore unjustified.

To sum up the findings of this essay, we could say that attending to the relationship between forgiving and aesthetic experience has produced the following four observations:

- Forgiving requires a certain type of preliminary work that effects an emotional transformation in the person who has been injured. The kind of transformation that takes place is of the same sort that one undergoes in aesthetic experience. It is a temporary, perceptual change, but it may have lasting consequences on one's behaviour and attitudes.
- The capacity for attaining distance is a psychological *achievement*. It is, therefore, a generally desirable characteristic, even though it is not a state that we would want to be in continually because it would deprive us of our ability to participate practically in the events of the world. In short, it is good to have the capacity to forgive even though not all wrongdoings should be forgiven.
- Distance is not the result of a 'decision' in any straightforward sense. I cannot simply decide to see the person who injured me as worthy of love any more than I can

decide to see beauty in one of Cezanne's paintings. However, there are strategies we can employ such as prayer and other gestures to prompt a distanced perception.

- Forgiving resists justification because the distanced perception which makes it possible is a way of reading. It is not something that results from deliberation or argument, though the initial effort to try to prompt the distanced perspective may result from a decision based on deliberation.[23]

5. Stepping In

Up to this point, I have merely tried to show that aesthetic experience and the process of stepping out preliminary to forgiving are similar. This suggests that the same psychological capacities are employed in both cases, thus placing forgiveness within a wider range of human phenomena. However, in this final section of the chapter, I would like to put forth a stronger and more controversial thesis, namely that the artist and the forgiver are attempting to do essentially the same thing. They are trying to realize a certain kind of perception of the world. It is a perception made possible through the operation of psychical distance and characterized by love.

When we are injured, our natural tendency is to narrow our perceptual field and withdraw practically from the world. If we acknowledge the extent to which our lives consist of a series of injuries, some small, some large, some real, and other imagined then, we may recognize that we are inclined toward continual and gradual retreat from the world, becoming increasingly narrow in our focus and isolated in our relations. Forgiveness allows us to reverse that natural tendency, to widen our focus and to become more fully engaged in the world. In other words, forgiveness allows us to love again. However, we often cannot accomplish that directly. Sometimes it is too difficult to address the sources of our pain head on, so we employ a variety of techniques, which frequently involve art of one kind or another.

Art, in part constituted by the gestures we employ to promote aesthetic perception,[24] may thus serve the same function as the suggestive strategies employed in psychoanalysis to relax the patient and prompt the memory of traumatic events. In psychoanalysis the goal is catharsis, an emotional transformation brought about by the imaginative re-enactment of events which led to repression.[25] Psychoanalysis, in general, may be understood as an attempt to help a person resume an emotional development that has been arrested. In tragic art, catharsis serves the same function.[26] This insight may allow us to answer, at least partially, a question which has puzzled those who have tried to explain the power of tragic art since Aristotle: why is it that human beings take pleasure in the depiction of suffering? Aristotle's answer was to say that we take pleasure in a tragic performance because it induces a catharsis, the Greek term for 'washing away' or 'cleansing.' Aristotle's meaning has been notoriously difficult to comprehend in any satisfactory way. However, if we regard catharsis not as a purgation of negative emotions but as an emotional transformation in which attitudes of fear or anger, as it were, dissolve and are replaced by an attitude of love or acceptance, we can see how the experience is felt to be pleasurable.

If we can depict the circumstances of our injuries in such a way that the injuries no longer block out the perception of beauty in the world, then we are able to depict the world in such a way that allows for love.[27] Fear and anger stand in the way of love in the same way that emotions of anxiety and expectation obscure the perception of beauty. Some kinds of art, such as tragic drama for instance, afford us the opportunity of looking at events without the kind of fear and anger those events would produce if they actually occurred in our own lives, or at least without being debilitated by those emotions. We take pleasure in a tragic performance because it transforms us; it brings us, through identification with the characters, to a state of fear, and then allows us to replace that fear with love. An aspect of the world which was lost to us is recovered, and we feel ourselves to be ennobled, lifted up and the world to be grander and more beautiful.

Psychical distance, then, may be thought of as a form of catharsis. It is a cleansing or washing away of debilitating emotions. But in order for them to be washed away, we must first be brought into the state of experiencing them in such a way that they may be supplanted by love. Forgiveness is the resumption of love. To forgive is to reclaim a part of the world which has been lost to us.

Notes

[1] Ovid, *Epistulae ex Ponto*, II, ix, 47.

[2] John Dewey, *Art as Experience* (New York: Minton, Balch & Company, 1934), 82.

[3] See 'Understanding and Approaching Forgiveness as Altruism: Relationships with Rumination, Self-Control, and a Gratitude-Based Strategy', in *A Journey through Forgiveness*, ed. Malika Rebai Maamri, Nehama Verbin and Everett L. Worthington, Jr. (Oxford: The Inter-Disciplinary Press, 2011), 103, Accessed May 20, 2011, http://www.inter-disciplinary.net/wp-content/uploads/2011/01/forgiveness 3ever19122010.pdf.

[4] Robert Enright and Joanna North, *Exploring Forgiveness* (Madison: University of Wisconsin Press, 1998), 24.

[5] Jeffrie G. Murphy and Jean Hampton, *Forgiveness and Mercy* (Cambridge: Cambridge University Press, 1988), 83.

[6] Enright and North, *Exploring Forgiveness*, 29.

[7] 'From the start, then, work on saying to each harsh appearance, 'You are an appearance, and not at all the thing that has the appearance.' Then examine it and assess it by these yardsticks that you have, and first and foremost by whether it concerns the things that are up to us or the things that are not up to us. And if it is about one of the things that is not up to us, be ready to say, 'You are nothing in relation to me.' Epictetus, *The Handbook*, trans. Nicolas P. White (Indianapolis: Hackett Publishing Company, 1983), 12.

[8] Bullough derived the notion of 'psychical distance' from Immanuel Kant's description of 'disinterested interest' in his *Critique of Judgment*. See Edward Bullough, 'Psychical Distance as a Factor in Art and as an Aesthetic Principle', *British Journal of Psychology* (1912): 87-118.

[9] Ibid., 91.

[10] Ibid., 91.

[11] Ibid., 95.

[12] Ibid., 89.

[13] One may recall Mark Twain's description of how he lost the ability to see beauty in a sunset, as he learned the skills of a riverboat navigator. See Mark Twain, *Life on the Mississippi* (New York: Library of America, 2009), 64-69.

[14] Bullough, 'Psychical Distance as a Factor in Art and as an Aesthetic Principle', 95.

[15] A host of controversies between artists and the communities in which they work can be elucidated by noticing differences in their respective distance-limits.

[16] Much of what is called 'postmodern' in art consists of work that intentionally draws attention to rather than simply employs gesture which we have become accustomed to rely upon to prompt our attention.

[17] Joanna Field, *A Life of One's Own* (Los Angeles: J. P. Tarcher, 1981), 107-108.

[18] Ibid., 109.

[19] Bullough, 'Psychical Distance as a Factor in Art and as an Aesthetic Principle', 89.

[20] Artists and critics alike rely upon their facility at moving back and forth between proximate and distanced perception to create their work.

[21] Simone Weil, 'Essai sur la notion de lecture,' *Etudes Philosophiques*, (January-March 1946): 14.

[22] Quoted in Enright and North, *Exploring Forgiveness*, 13.

[23] The only sense in which one can be said to have a 'duty' to forgive is in the sense of having a duty to try to prompt a distanced perspective.

[24] According to some theories, such as George Dickie's 'institutional theory of art,' art is constituted by such gestures. An object is a work of art because it is contextually placed in such a way as to prompt a certain type of perception. See George Dickie, *Aesthetics: An Introduction* (Cambridge: Pegasus, 1971), 101.

Marcel Duchamp's 'readymades' demonstrated that it is, sometimes at least, enough to change an object's context in order for it to become 'art.'
[25] Jonathan Lear, 'Catharsis: Fantasy and Reality', in *Love and Its Place in Nature: A Philosophical Interpretation of Freudian Psychoanalysis* (New York: Farrar, Straus, and Giroux, 1990), 29-68.
[26] See Sigmund Freud, 'Psychopathic Characters on the Stage', in *The Standard Edition of the Complete Psychological Works of Sigmund Freud*, vol. 7, ed. James Strachey (London: Hogarth Press, 1981), 305-310.
[27] My thanks to Lynne Tirrell for her helpful comments at the Third Global Conference on Forgiveness, which led me to rephrase this sentence in order to avoid the unwelcome suggestion that one's perception of injury is itself transformed so that one comes to see it as an object of beauty.

Bibliography

Bullough, Edward. 'Psychical Distance as a Factor in Art and as an Aesthetic Principle'. *British Journal of Psychology* (1912): 87-118.

Dewey, John. *Art as Experience*. New York: Minton, Balch & Company, 1934.

Dickie, George. *Aesthetics: An Introduction*. Cambridge: Pegasus, 1971.

Enright, Robert and North, Joanna. *Exploring Forgiveness*. Madison: University of Wisconsin Press, 1998.

Epictetus. *The Handbook*. Translated by Nicolas P. White. Indianapolis: Hackett Publishing Company, 1983.

Field, Joanna. *A Life of One's Own*. Los Angeles: J. P. Tarcher, 1981.

Freud, Sigmund. *The Standard Edition of the Complete Psychological Works of Sigmund Freud*. Edited and translated by James Strachey. London: Hogarth Press, 1981.

Lear, Jonathan. *Love and Its Place in Nature: A Philosophical Interpretation of Freudian Psychoanalysis*. New York: Farrar, Straus, and Giroux, 1990.

Murphy, Jeffrie G., and Hampton, Jean. *Forgiveness and Mercy*. Cambridge: Cambridge University Press, 1988.

Ovid. *Epistulae ex Ponto*. The Latin Library. Accessed June 28, 2011. http://www.thelatinlibrary.com/ovid/ovid.ponto2.shtml.

Twain, Mark. *Life on the Mississippi*. New York: Library of America, 2009.

Weil, Simone. 'Essai sur la notion de lecture'. *Etudes Philosophiques* (January-March 1946): 13-19.

Witvliet, Charlotte vanOyen. 'Understanding and Approaching Forgiveness as Altruism: Relationships with Rumination, Self-Control, and a Gratitude-Based Strategy'. In *A Journey through Forgiveness*, edited by Malika Rebai Maamri, Nehama Verbin and Everett L. Worthington, Jr., 99-107. Oxford: The Inter-Disciplinary Press, 2011. Accessed May 20, 2011. http://www.inter-discipli nary.net/wp-content/uploads/2011/01/forgiveness3ever19122010.pdf.

Richard Kyte is a Professor of Philosophy and Director of the D. B. Reinhart Institute for Ethics in Leadership at Viterbo University, La Crosse, Wisconsin.

Empirical Studies of Forgiveness as an Altruistic Response: Relationships with Rumination, Suppression of Negative Emotions, and Benefit-Focused Reappraisal

Charlotte vanOyen Witvliet

Abstract

Conceptualizations of forgiveness need to engage features of both justice and grace as the forgiver responds to the truth of the injustice while transforming his/her response toward the offender. An altruistically forgiving response ought to have as full and accurate an understanding of the offender and offence as possible. Then altruistic forgiveness transforms destructive responses and outcomes into constructive and prosocial ones. This chapter addresses granting *altruistically oriented interpersonal forgiveness*, which cultivates compassion for the blameworthy offender, a human being who has clearly demonstrated the need to experience positive transformation. Three within-subjects experiments had been conducted to understand the implications of altruistic forgiveness in comparison to alternative responses. A foundational study showed that empathy and prosocial forgiveness significantly reduced the negative emotion and physiological stress of rumination and grudge-holding, while also increasing positive emotion. A subsequent experiment compared compassionate reappraisal of the offender to suppression of negative emotion and to rumination about the hurtful transgression. Both coping approaches decreased aroused and negative emotion. Only compassionate reappraisal increased empathy for the offender, the decisional commitment to forgive, emotional forgiveness as a change of heart toward the offender, and increased activity at the smile muscle. In the third experiment, we compared a compassion-focused reappraisal of the offender to benefit-focused reappraisal, in which the victim focused on lessons learned, insights gained, or strengths shown in the face of interpersonal transgression. Compared to offence rumination, both positive reappraisals reduced emotional arousal, negative emotion, and facial muscle tension at the brow. Both positive reappraisals also increased happiness and positive emotion in ratings and written narratives. Only compassion stimulated the greatest empathy, prompted the most forgiving and social language, calmed tension under the eye, and slowed the cardiac cycle. The findings of these three experiments are considered in the light of altruistic approaches to forgiveness, and the themes of truth-telling and transformation at the heart of altruistically oriented forgiveness.

Key Words: Forgiveness, rumination, suppression, reappraisal, altruism, compassion, physiology, facial electromyography, heart rate variability.

*****

1. Introduction to Altruistically Oriented Forgiveness

Before addressing altruistic approaches to forgiveness, we first examine forgiveness definitions in the psychological literature. As can be seen in the work of psychologically oriented contributors to this volume, researchers have some shared understandings about the nuances that characterize forgiveness. We distinguish forgiveness from forgetting, condoning, justifying, excusing, exonerating, accepting, seeing justice served, and reconciling. These alternatives must be different from forgiveness in part because forgiveness is concerned with both truth-telling and with transformation that has particular attendant boundary conditions.

Forgiveness cannot be confused with disregarding or minimizing the injustice because it demands truthfulness and hinges on a clear-eyed understanding of the offence and its implications. Distinguishing forgiveness from forgoing justice by excusing or exonerating are important clarifications because of the importance of ensuring safety and respect to both victim and community. When forgiveness is mistakenly fused with reconciliation in ways that confuse justice or trust, victims may be at increased risk of subsequent harm. It is important to support the victims' spiritual, psychological, and physical well-being and safety. One way to do this is by attending to their self-differentiation, which promotes spiritual stability, mental health, and well-being, as explained in Steven J. Sandage's chapter.[1] Furthermore, forgiveness does not merely accept what happened or move on by distracting oneself from it; rather, it transforms one's response, and replaces negative and destructive behaviour with positive emotions and constructive thoughts. Altruistically oriented forgiveness is concerned not just with regulating one's emotional responses for the sake of oneself. Rather, it embodies compassion for the blameworthy offender whose transgression provides clear evidence of his/her need to experience positive transformation. The victim can see particular ways in which the offender can grow, change, heal or learn. This insight can be the pivot *point away* from hateful, bitter, and dehumanizing responses that totalize the offender, and *toward* compassionate, humanizing hope for that person's transformation. Responsible compassion can promote one's capacity for self-understanding, differentiation from the offender, maturity, and virtue while maintaining boundaries.

Other important features of interpersonal forgiveness vary based on the nature of the offence and the relationship between victim and offender. A broad array of offences and relational factors raise critical philosophical, theological, and psychological questions and concerns. Mark S. Rye's chapter for instance, addresses psychological and relational challenges and consequences of forgiveness after divorce.[2] Likewise, features of forgiveness in relationship to justice are explored in alternative dispute resolution settings,[3] and restorative justice models as explained respectively in Geraldine Neal's and Jack Armstrong's chapters.[4] The global and historical arena broadens our view further. Karolina Wigura raises philosophical and theological questions about forgiveness after the Shoah.[5] And Clara Mucci complements Wigura's view in her study of psychological issues for healing and forgiveness in Holocaust survivors.[6] Psychological and political questions about forgiveness are also highlighted in Malika Rebai Maamri's treatment of Algerian history,[7] and James Arvanitakis's exploration of social forgiveness in Bougainville, Papua New Guinea.[8] Beyond these, chapters on literature and poetry challenge us further to realize that each approach to forgiveness has its fingerprint shaped by the writers' philosophical and theological frameworks, as well as the socio-historical contexts in which the particular transgressions occurred. Across contexts, forgiveness hinges on a clear understanding of the offence and its implications. Only then, can forgiveness transform responses in constructive ways that promote maturity and flourishing.

Even though transgressions, and thus unforgiving and forgiving responses, occur in relational contexts, states of interpersonal forgiveness involve a transformative process within the forgiver. Obviously, reconciliation is impossible with the deceased and it is unwise to reconcile with a repetitive abuser. One can see further comments on why forgiveness and reconciliation need to be conceptually distinguished in Elizabeth Gedge's chapter.[9] Everett Worthington et al's theorizing also distinguishes between two types of forgiveness: sometimes forgiveness involves a decisional commitment (*decisional forgiveness*), but it can also be experienced as emotional change (*emotional forgiveness*).[10] Both involve truth-telling and transformation to be genuine. The transformation of decisional forgiveness may be evidenced most in one's cognitions, motivations, and civil behaviours in reference to the offender. The change involved in emotional forgiveness will include shifts in affective cognition and behaviour. Even so, the nature of the offence and one's relational history with the offender guide the process and the longitudinal outcomes. Even conceptualizations of forgiveness that focus on emotional replacement of negative unforgiving responses with positive and prosocial responses note that this transformation may be either part of the process *or* a result of emotional forgiveness.

The perspective offered in this chapter is that forgiveness starts with holding an offender responsible for a hurtful offence, and it then, seeks to respond to injustice with goodness. Forgiveness can be understood as multi-dimensional, involving the victim's cognitive, affective, behavioural, spiritual, and interpersonal responses to a perceived injustice that causes personal pain. It is a process through which the victim reduces his/ her negative other-diminishing responses, often by cultivating positive other-regarding responses of compassion toward an undeserving transgressor.

The three experiments presented in this chapter address many questions: what is it like to pursue forgiveness altruistically, with compassion for the humanity of the offender? What subjective emotions do victims have when they take the offence seriously and cultivate compassion for a blameworthy offender? What physical changes occur when a victim focuses on the offender and gives the gift of forgiveness?

Forgiveness is a concept engaged by diverse people with varied core beliefs, values, and faiths. Some may advance the idea that forgiveness is a good choice because it has emotional and physical benefits for the forgiver: forgive for you. However, we examine here the experimental outcomes of adopting forgiving responses that focus on giving compassion to the offender, rather than feeling better for the sake of oneself. An altruistic approach to forgiving places the emphasis on showing compassion and graciousness toward a blameworthy offender, a human being who has just demonstrated his/her clear need to experience a positive transformation. Such an altruistic approach can be genuine even in circumstances in which further contact with the offender is impossible, unsafe, or unwise.

2. Experiment I: Empathic Perspective: Taking and Pro-Social Forgiveness Compared to Offence Rumination and Grudge-Holding

In their everyday lives after an offence, people think about their offenders as they ruminate about hurts and imagine different responses, including forgiveness. In the laboratory, we used a paradigm that connects with these real-world experiences. We studied seventy one undergraduates (36 males, 35 females).[11] In this experiment, each person identified another individual offender they held responsible for causing personal hurt due to a transgression. Throughout the experiment, each participant focused on responding to this one real-life offender. Participants engaged in four distinct responses to that offender: rumination, grudge-bearing, empathy, and forgiveness. They did so multiple times in randomly assigned, counterbalanced orders. During imagery, continuous measures of sweat (skin conductance) levels, heart rate, blood pressure, muscle tension (electromyography; EMG) above the brow (corrugator muscle, responsive to negative emotion) and under the eye (orbicularis oculi muscle, responsive to emotional arousal) had been recorded. After several trials, the participants had the opportunity of making ratings about the emotional responses for each unforgiving and forgiving condition. This approach allowed us to see changes within the person in physiology and in self-reported emotion, highlighting the implications of adopting various responses toward one's offender.

In this study, participants 1) ruminated about the hurtful offence as if it were really happening; 2) remembered or thought about the desire to have the offender feel bad for causing the hurtful offence against them; 3) engaged in empathic perspective-taking that emphasized the human qualities of the offender and also acknowledged that in the past the victim has also hurt others, even unintentionally; 4) identified a way to give a gift of mercy and goodwill, even on a small scale, as they released the negative feelings of hurt and revenge to grant forgiveness to the blameworthy offender. In individual two-hour sessions, each participant completed every condition eight times in carefully counter-balanced orders, with multiple relaxation task periods in between the sixteen-second offence-related response trials. Physiological reactivity reflected changes from relaxation periods to active offender response trials of each type.

Empathic perspective-taking and forgiveness as giving goodwill toward the offender were both contrasted with ruminating about a hurtful offence and nursing a grudge against the offender. When focused on unforgiving responses of hurt rumination and grudge-bearing, the participants' blood pressure surged up from pre-trial relaxation levels, heart rates increased, high sweat levels persisted, brow muscles tensed, and negative feelings escalated. All of these responses were significantly higher than when participants were empathic and forgiving toward the offender. By contrast, the empathic and forgiving responses induced more positive subjective feelings, greater perceived control, and calmer physical responses for the facial muscles, sweat, blood pressure, and heart rate.

These data are important for our conceptualizations of the victim's responses after interpersonal transgressions, when people remembered being hurt, experienced subjective distress and physiological stress. Follow-up analyses showed that by shifting one's focus to how the offender ought to suffer (grudge/revenge), reduced fear and sadness from rumination levels, and increased perceptions of control and joy. Grudge and revenge fantasies may be reinforced by this emotional relief. However, the data also showed that grudge and revenge thoughts kept subjective anger and physiological stress levels high. Shifting one's response from the victim to the aggressor did not resolve the problem.

By contrast, empathic perspective-taking did significantly subdue anger, other negative and aroused emotions, and physiological stress while also cultivating perceptions of control and joy. However, the highest levels of perceived control and joy, along with the lowest levels of negative emotions, emotional arousal, and calmest sweat, heart rate, blood pressure, and facial muscle measures were found for the prosocial forgiveness condition.

This study was conducted to better understand the types of transformation that would occur measurably in victims when they adopted empathic and prosocial forgiveness responses. The positive affective changes across subjective feelings and continuous physiology are transformational implications of other-oriented forgiveness that still takes seriously the truth of the offender's culpability.

3. Experiment II: Forgiveness as Compassionate Reappraisal versus Suppression of Negative Emotion

The next experiment was conducted to partially replicate and extend our understanding of forgiveness as a compassionate response to the offender.[12] It contrasted compassionate reappraisal with offence rumination, and also examined a self-oriented regulation strategy designed to decrease one's own negative emotions. In this way, we hoped to learn more about how a prosocial, altruistic type of response to one's offender would compare to a strategy that would merely down-regulate one's own negative emotion.

In the face of being hurt through an interpersonal transgression, people may pursue forgiveness in different ways. Efforts to forgive may look like self-control that restrains or suppresses one's hurt, angry, hostile, and bitter feelings and urges. Forgiveness may also involve an altruistic reappraisal of the offender. We studied both responses in contrast to rumination, as informed by James Gross's research on suppression and reappraisal.[13]

The participants in our research, fifty four undergraduates (26 males, 28 females), had been instructed to use different emotional responses to a specific situation in which a person hurt them in the past. Those responses were *offence rumination, suppression,* and *compassionate reappraisal*. In the first type of response, the participants had to dwell on the negative feelings the situation and offender brought up. In the second type, they had been asked to think about the offence, but inhibit and conceal any negative emotions or expressions. In the third type, the participants had to think of their offender as a 'human being' who behaved badly. The participants had been guided to genuinely wish that this person would experience something positive or healing even if the relationship could not be restored. The difficulty of the task was also acknowledged while encouraging participants to focus their thoughts and feelings on giving a gift of mercy or compassion.

Half of the participants (blocked by gender) had been randomly assigned to proceed from offence rumination to compassionate reappraisal and then from offence rumination to emotion suppression. The other half had been randomized to proceed from offence rumination to emotion suppression and then from offence rumination to compassionate reappraisal. Each relaxation and offender response condition lasted two minutes. We compared the effect of each coping response (suppression or compassionate reappraisal) to the effect of rumination. We also compared the change from rumination that each strategy caused, to see which approach out-performed the other.

What difference does it make within individuals when they adopt the various responses: rumination, suppression of negative affect, or compassionate reappraisal of their offender? The participants in this study provided many of the same ratings as in Experiment I, similar physiological measures plus a cardiovascular measure of the parasympathetic nervous system's regulatory calming responses, and additional written descriptions after each condition. Specifically, they typed, into a computer, their responses to these questions, which had been then analysed: What/how were you feeling, thinking, physically responding? And what would you like to do or say to your offender?

Rumination about the hurtful transgression and its implications increased the participants' negative subjective emotional experiences and their typed responses, and their physiological responses relative to the other coping strategies. Physically, rumination activated more intense negative emotion expressions on the face, a faster cardiac cycle, and impaired the measure of the body's calming system – the parasympathetic nervous system, which we measured with spectral analysis of heart rate variability. Notably, within only two minutes of dwelling on the hurtful aspects of one's past experience with an interpersonal offence, the participants activated their negative, aroused responses and also decreased the actions of the calming system. By dwelling on past hurts, people could perpetuate their harm. Is there a way to honestly deal with these hurts while transforming them in ways that are constructive?

Compassionate reappraisal views the offender as a complex human with limitations and flaws (e.g. past hurts, immaturity, undeveloped virtue, and/or psychopathology) and uses that insight to cultivate mercy. This perspective may aid in genuinely desiring that person's growth, learning, healing, and/or transformation, even if reconciliation does not occur. Compassion can create an alternative way to navigate between the extremes of devaluing and idealizing the offender.

How did compassionate reappraisal compare to the negative emotion suppression strategy? Both alternative coping strategies were equally effective at decreasing the negative emotion aroused by ruminations about the offender and offence. However, only reappraisal was effective at increasing positive emotion, as well as empathy, the commitment to forgive, the experience of heartfelt forgiveness for the offender, and the most activity at the zygomatic cheek muscle involved in smiling. Both reappraisal and suppression calmed the orbicularis oculi muscle under the eye associated with affective arousal. Only suppression decreased tension at the corrugator muscle (that furrows the brow), which was consistent with suppressing facial expressions of negative emotion. The cardiac measure of parasympathetic nervous system's calming response showed that rumination impaired parasympathetic activity compared to a relaxing baseline. However, both coping strategies were equivalent to the relaxation baseline.

Considering suppression in relation to forgiveness warrants reflection. In terms of promoting forgiveness, this experiment showed that emotion suppression was ineffective. Although emotion suppression was associated with higher empathy ratings than in rumination, that increase was significantly smaller than the empathy increase prompted by compassionate reappraisal. In fact, linguistic analyses showed that suppression moved people away from using forgiveness-relevant language in an assessment that mimics human knowledge representations. Analyses that rely on word counts in the narratives showed that suppression and rumination prompted the same number of forgiveness references, and both were significantly lower than compassionate reappraisal. Suppression also failed to increase the participants' ratings of decisional forgiveness and emotional forgiveness, whereas compassionate reappraisal increased both forgiveness ratings.

Use of forbearance may restrain negative emotions and expressions in the short term, but it is unlikely to resolve or transform offence-related negative responses.

Compassionate reappraisal offered a more transformative experience within the individual. Compassion increased positive and prosocial responses and decreased negative responses. This had been demonstrated across ratings, linguistic analyses, and physiology. Compassionate reappraisal cultivated significant increases in decisional and emotional forgiveness ratings, and in forgiveness word usage in written narratives. Compassionate reappraisal also uniquely increased the use of social words, positive ratings and word use, and activity at the *zygomatic* muscle associated with smiling expressions.

Caution about compassion is still warranted in the effort to engage both truth-telling and transformation after interpersonal offences. While compassion has many positive features, some individuals and relational contexts may carry risks. It is wise to recall the importance of maturity and self-differentiation that allows victims to resist polarized responses that devalue or over-idealize the offender. Compassion needs to be considered along with power and justice concerns so that the victim's safety is assured. The maturation and flourishing of all parties are best cultivated when the dimensions of forgiveness, justice, and power are managed in relation to each other.

4. Experiment III: Forgiveness as Compassionate Reappraisal Compared to Another Positive Reappraisal

This final experiment investigated forgiveness as compassion-focused reappraisal in comparison to another positive strategy, benefit-focused reappraisal.[14] We tested seventy one undergraduates (38 females, 33 males) using a within-subjects experimental design with multiple two-minute periods for relaxation and offence-related response conditions, similar to Experiment II. Compassion-focused reappraisal emphasized the offender's humanity, and interpreted the transgression as evidence of the offender's need for positive transformation. Benefit-focused reappraisal emphasized insights gained or strengths shown in facing the offence. This within-subjects experiment (i.e., each participant experienced all the different conditions) tested whether each positive reappraisal strategy was more effective for well-being than rumination, and whether one reappraisal strategy – compassion-focused reappraisal or benefit-focused reappraisal – was better than the other in countering the effects of offence-related rumination.

The two positive reappraisal strategies differed in their focus. The compassion-focused reappraisal cultivated compassion for the offender by emphasizing his or her humanity, and by viewing the offence as evidence that this person needed to experience positive change or healing. The benefit-focused reappraisal emphasized the offence as an opportunity to grow, learn, or become stronger, and it identified ways in which one developed self-understanding, demonstrated strengths, or noticed relational improvements. Whereas compassion-focused reappraisal emphasized giving; benefit-focused reappraisal accentuated receiving. Compassion-focused reappraisal was oriented toward the other; benefit-focused reappraisal emphasized the self.

Despite their distinct emphases, both reappraisal strategies had many similar effects. Because they focused on the real-life offender and offence, both reappraisals stimulated more aroused and angry ratings as well as more cost-oriented language in comparison to a relaxation period. However, compared to offence rumination, both ways to reappraise the transgression decreased aroused, angry, and cost-oriented measures. Similarly, both approaches significantly calmed tension at the brow (corrugator) muscle associated with negative emotion. In addition to lessening the negative responses associated with rumination, both compassion-focused reappraisal and benefit-focused reappraisal significantly increased control, happiness, and joy ratings and positive emotion language in the written narratives.

As expected, compassion-focused reappraisal prompted the highest empathy ratings and most forgiveness language. Benefit-focused reappraisal yielded the most benefit language and highest gratitude ratings and word counts. Showing a cross-over influence, compassion-focused reappraisal not only prompted forgiveness, but also recognition of benefits and increases in gratitude. Benefit-focused reappraisal not only stimulated writing about one's benefits and increased gratitude, but also forgiveness toward the offender. When bolstered by benefits – and experiencing the greatest joy – people reported greater forgiveness for the offender.

In the compassion-focused reappraisal, the participants cognitively reappraised the offender as a human being whose behaviour shows that person's need to experience a positive transformation or healing. The participants were instructed to try to genuinely give gifts of mercy and compassion and to give that person goodwill. Compassion-focused reappraisal uniquely increased social language in the written narratives, compared to rumination and to benefit-focused reappraisal (which prompted a decrease in social language). These findings are consistent with theorizing about forgiveness that has an altruistic approach.[15] Only compassion-focused reappraisal decreased tension under the eye (at the orbicularis oculi muscle) and calmed the cardiac cycle, corresponding to reduced affective arousal.

Benefit-focused reappraisal included the ability to appreciate and to be thankful for benefits recognized or gained in the face of – but not gratitude for – an interpersonal transgression. It significantly stimulated greater gratitude ratings and writing (as well as benefit language) than compassion-focused reappraisal did. Benefit-focused reappraisal stimulated the highest levels of joy and smiling (measured at the zygomatic muscle). Furthermore, benefit-focused reappraisal buffered the parasympathetic nervous system, countering the impairments in heart rate variability associated with rumination.

The linguistic data reflect the nature of the reappraisals in that benefit-focused reappraisal explicitly focused the participants on themselves and their own perceived benefits, whereas compassion-focused reappraisal was centred on compassionately and generously reappraising the offender in a way that stimulated the granting of forgiveness to that offender. Benefit-focused reappraisal is a less social and more self-focused coping approach, which may be a more accessible positive reappraisal for individuals who are not motivated or ready to engage in compassion-focused forgiveness. Despite its focus on receiving benefits for the self, however, benefit-focused reappraisal did stimulate forgiveness for one's offender. For people who struggle with genuinely offering forgiveness or compassion to their offenders in an altruistic way, choosing benefit-focused reappraisal may still facilitate forgiveness toward an offender.

5. Reflections on Altruistically Oriented Forgiveness, Truth-Telling and Transformation

Each of the series of three experiments presented here examined the implications of reliving interpersonal hurts in contrast to compassionate responding. Compassionate reappraisal of the offender involved remembering that the offender is a human being, that the offence is evidence of the offender's need to experience positive transformation, and that compassion can be given to the offender while maintaining boundaries which protect the forgiver. Each study included at least one other contrasting condition that illuminated aspects of altruistically oriented forgiveness.

A common thread throughout these studies and the broader literature is that empathy plays a vital role in forgiveness. Because we are concerned with both truth-telling and transformation, it is important to have viable compassion for the offender. Truth-telling requires that we see the injustice clearly and take it seriously while also refusing to dehumanize the offender. Within this volume, truth-telling themes run through Wigura's chapter,[16] and transformation themes are found in Arvanitakis's work.[17] The dual frame of truth-telling and transformation finds strong resonance in Richard Kyte's articulation of perspective and transformation,[18] Mucci's future-orientation that takes seriously the hurts visited upon future generations,[19] and Armstrong's reflections on restorative justice that demands multifaceted truth-telling and transformation to create the very conditions in which forgiveness can authentically emerge.[20] These themes also implicitly run through conceptualizations in Worthington et al.'s reference to relational spirituality and forgiveness,[21] Sandage's work on self-differentiation,[22] and Rye's work on implications for ex-spouses who forgive for the sake of their children.[23]

In this research, I advocate for a compassion focus that clearly sees the offence (e.g., lie, betrayal, failed promise, and relational breach) for what it is and the damage it has caused, while it widens the view to include more aspects of who and where the offence came from. Compassion sees the complexity of the offender as a human being with all his flaws and strengths, and the life circumstances that equipped and failed him. Compassion does not flatten out all of our offences as if their differences did not matter. And yet, compassion sees that, for all of our differences, we all are prone to transgress. We all hurt people out of our own hurts and vulnerabilities, the prior offences done to us, our cognitive or emotional limitations, psychopathologies, or undeveloped virtues.

This altruistic- oriented approach to forgiveness can be a tenable response to transform the negative affect and physiological reactivity aroused by hurtful offence memories or grudge-holding into a calmer, more positive response oriented to the other's need for gracious transformation. This compassionate response allows the victim to maintain a more complex identity as one who can both hurt and heal, one who can maintain safe boundaries and also extend grace. Embodying compassion allows one to pursue both forgiveness and justice, to have self-respect and humility, and to address past and present brokenness with eschatological hope.

Notes

[1] Steven J. Sandage and Peter J. Jankowski, 'Forgiveness, Differentiation of Self and Mental Health', in *A Journey through Forgiveness*, ed. Malika Rebai Maamri, Nehama Verbin, and Everett L. Worthington, Jr. (Oxford, England: Interdisciplinary Press, 2010), accessed April 13, 2011, http://www.inter-disciplinary.net/publishing/id-press/ebooks/a-journey-through-forgiveness/, 87.

[2] Mark S. Rye, 'Forgiveness as a Way of Coping Following Divorce', in Maamri, Verbin and Worthington, Jr., 119.

[3] Geraldine Neal, 'Alternative Dispute Resolution: Are Apology and Forgiveness Simply Two Sides of the One Coin?' in Maamri, Verbin and Worthington, Jr., eds., 167.

[4] Jac Armstrong, 'Restorative Justice as a Pathway for Forgiveness: How Could Forgiveness Operate within the Criminal Justice System?' in Maamri, Verbin and Worthington, Jr., eds., 179.

[5] Karolina Wigura, 'Forgiveness or Reconciliation after the Shoah? An Ecumenical Perspective', in Maamri, Verbin and Worthington, Jr., eds., 59.

[6] Clara Mucci, 'Healing and Forgiveness after Traumatic Events: The Case of Holocaust Survivors from the Fortunoff Archives', in Maamri, Verbin and Worthington, Jr., eds., 109.

[7] Malika Rebai Maamri, 'Algerian President's Peace Plan: Political and Psychological Perspectives of Forgiveness', in Maamri, Verbin and Worthington, Jr., eds., 141.

[8] James Arvantakis, 'On Forgiveness, Hope and Community: Or the Fine Line Step between Authentic and Fractured Communities', in Maamri, Verbin and Worthington, Jr., eds., 149.

[9] Elisabeth Gedge, 'Radical Forgiveness and Feminist Theology', in Maamri, Verbin and Worthington, Jr., eds., 69.

[10] Everett L. Worthington, Jr. et al., 'Forgiveness and Religion: Update and Current Status', in Maamri, Verbin and Worthington, Jr., eds., 50.

[11] Charlotte vanOyen Witvliet, Thomas E. Ludwig and Kelly L. Vander Laan, 'Granting Forgiveness or Harboring Grudges: Implications for Emotions, Physiology, and Health,' *Psychological Science* 12 (2001): 117-123.

[12] Charlotte vanOyen Witvliet, Nathaniel J. DeYoung, Alicia J. Hofelich, and Paul DeYoung, 'Compassionate Reappraisal and Emotion Suppression as Alternative to Offense-Focused Rumination: Implications for Forgiveness and Psycho-Physiological Well-Being', *The Journal of Positive Psychology* (in press).

[13] James J. Gross, *Handbook of Emotion-Regulation* (New York: Guilford Press, 2007), 3-614.

[14] Charlotte vanOyen Witvliet, Ross W. Knoll, Nova G. Hinman, and Paul DeYoung, 'Compassion-Focused Reappraisal, Benefit-Focused Reappraisal, and Rumination after an Interpersonal Offense: Emotion Regulation Implications for Subjective Emotion, Linguistic Responses, and Physiology', *The Journal of Positive Psychology* 5 (2010): 226-242.

[15] Charlotte vanOyen Witvliet and Michael E. McCullough, 'Forgiveness and Health: A Review and Theoretical Exploration of Emotion Pathways', in *Altruism and Health: Perspectives from Empirical Research*, ed. Stephen Post (New York: Oxford University Press, 2007), 258-276.

[16] Wigura, 'Forgiveness or Reconciliation', 59.

[17] Arvantakis, 'On Forgiveness, Hope and Community', 149.

[18] Richard Kyte, 'The Art of Forgiving: Conditions of Perspective and Transformation', in Maamri, Verbin and Worthington, Jr., eds., 79.

[19] Mucci, 'Healing and Forgiveness after Traumatic Events', 109.

[20] Armstrong, 'Restorative Justice as a Pathway for Forgiveness', 179.

[21] Worthington, 'Forgiveness and Religion', 54-55.

[22] Sandage, 'Forgiveness, Differentiation of Self and Mental Health', 87.

[23] Rye, 'Forgiveness as a Way of Coping Following Divorce', 119.

Bibliography

Aldao, Amelia, Susan Nolen-Hoeksema and Susanne Schweizer. 'Emotion-Regulation Strategies across Psychopathology: A Meta-Analytic Review'. *Clinical Psychology Review* 30.2 (2010): 217-237.

Armstrong, Jac. 'Restorative Justice as a Pathway for Forgiveness: How Could Forgiveness Operate within the Criminal Justice System?'. In *A Journey through Forgiveness*, edited by Malika Rebai Maamri, Nehama Verbin and Everett L. Worthington, Jr., 179-190. Oxford, England: Inter-Disciplinary Press (2010): Accessed April 13, 2011. Http://www.inter-disciplinary.net/publishing/id-press/ebooks/a-journey-through-forgiveness/.

Arvantakis, James. 'On Forgiveness, Hope and Community: Or the Fine Line Step between Authentic and Fractured Communities'. In *A Journey through Forgiveness*, edited by Malika Rebai Maamri, Nehama Verbin and Everett L. Worthington, Jr., 149-161. Oxford, England: Inter-Disciplinary Press (2010): Accessed April 13, 2011. Http://www.inter-disciplinary.net/publishing/id-press/ebooks/a-journey-through-forgiveness/.

Berry, Jack W., Everett L., Worthington, Jr., Nathaniel G. Wade, Charlotte Witvliet van Oyen and Rebecca P. Kiefer. 'Forgiveness, Moral Identity, and Perceived Justice in Crime Victims and their Supporters'. *Humboldt Journal of Social Relations* 29.2 (2005): 136-162.

Bono, Giacomo and Michael E. McCullough. 'Positive Responses to Benefit and Harm: Bringing Forgiveness and Gratitude Into Cognitive Psychotherapy'. *Journal of Cognitive Psychotherapy* 20.2 (2006): 147-158.

Bono, Giacomo, Michael E. McCullough and Lindsey M. Root. 'Forgiveness, Feeling Connected to Others, and Well-being: Two Longitudinal Studies'. *Personality and Social Psychology Bulletin* 34.2 (2008): 182-195.

Cassell, Eric J. 'Compassion'. In *Oxford Handbook of Positive Psychology (2nd ed.)*, 393-403. New York, NY US: Oxford University Press, 2009.

Emmons, Robert A. 'Gratitude, Subjective Well-Being, and the Brain'. In *The Science of Subjective Well-Being*, 469-489. New York, NY US: Guilford Press, 2008.

Emmons, Robert A. and Michael E. McCullough. 'Counting Blessings versus Burdens: An Experimental Investigation of Gratitude and Subjective Well-Being in Daily Life'. *Journal of Personality and Social Psychology* 84.2 (2003): 377-389.

Enright, Robert D. *Forgiveness is a Choice: A Step-By-Step Process for Resolving Anger and Restoring Hope.* Washington, DC US: American Psychological Association, 2001.

Enright, Robert D. and Richard P. Fitzgibbons. *Helping Clients Forgive: An Empirical Guide for Resolving Anger and Restoring Hope.* Washington, DC US: American Psychological Association, 2000.

Fredrickson, Barbara L. 'The Role of Positive Emotions in Positive Psychology: The Broaden-and-Build Theory of Positive Emotions'. *American Psychologist* 56. 3 (2001): 218-226.

Friedberg, Jennifer P., Sonia Suchday and Danielle V. Shelov. 'The Impact of Forgiveness on Cardiovascular Reactivity and Recovery'. *International Journal of Psychophysiology* 65.2 (2007): 87-94.

Gedge, Elisabeth, 'Radical Forgiveness and Feminist Theology'. In *A Journey through Forgiveness*, edited by Malika Rebai Maamri, Nehama Verbin and Everett L. Worthington, Jr., 69-76. Oxford, England: Inter-Disciplinary Press (2010): Accessed April 13, 2011. Http://www.inter-disciplinary.net/publishing/id-press/ebooks/a-journey-through-forgiveness/.

Gordon, Kristina Coop, Burton Shacunda and Laura Porter. 'Predicting the Intentions of Women in Domestic Violence Shelters to Return to Partners: Does Forgiveness Play a Role?' *Journal of Family Psychology* 18.2 (2004): 331-338.

Gross, James J., ed. *Handbook of Emotion Regulation.* New York, NY US: Guilford Press, 2007.

Hallich, Oliver. 'A Plea against Apologies'. In *A Journey through Forgiveness*, edited by Malika Rebai Maamri, Nehama Verbin and Everett L. Worthington, Jr., 19-25. Oxford, England: Inter-Disciplinary Press (2010): Accessed April 13, 2011. http://www.inter-disciplinary.net/publishing/id-press/ebooks/a-journey-through-forgiveness/.

Hargrave, Terry. *Forgiving the Devil: Coming to Terms with Damaged Relationships.* Phoenix, AZ: Zeig, Tucker, and Theisen, Inc US, 2001.

Helgeson, Vicki S., Kerry A. Reynolds and Patricia L. Tomich. 'A Meta-Analytic Review of Benefit Finding and Growth'. *Journal of Consulting and Clinical Psychology* 74.5 (2006): 797-816.

Kyte, Richard. 'The Art of Forgiving: Conditions of Perspective and Transformation'. In *A Journey through Forgiveness*, edited by Malika Rebai Maamri, Nehama Verbin and Everett L. Worthington, Jr., 79-86. Oxford, England: Inter-Disciplinary Press (2010): Accessed April 13, 2011. http://www.inter-disciplinary.net/publishing/id-press/ebooks/a-journey-through-forgiveness/.

Lawler-Row, Kathleen A. 'Forgiveness as a Mediator of the Religiosity: Health Relationship'. *Psychology of Religion and Spirituality* 2.1 (2010): 1-16.

Luchies, Laura B., Eli J. Finkel, James K. McNulty and Kumashiro Madoka. 'The Doormat Effect: When Forgiving Erodes Self-Respect and Self-Concept Clarity'. *Journal of Personality and Social Psychology* 98.5 (2010): 734-749.

Rebai Maamri, Malika. 'Algerian President's Peace Plan: Political and Psychological Perspectives of Forgiveness'. In *A Journey through Forgiveness*, edited by Malika Rebai Maamri, Nehama Verbin and Everett L. Worthington, Jr., 141-148. Oxford, England: Inter-Disciplinary Press (2010): Accessed April 13, 2011. http://www.inter-disciplinary.net/publishing/id-press/ebooks/a-journey-through-forgiveness/.

Maio, Gregory R., Geoff Thomas, Frank D. Fincham and Katherine B. Carnelley. 'Unravelling the Role of Forgiveness in Family Relationships'. *Journal of Personality and Social Psychology* 94.2 (2008): 307-319.

McCullough, Michael E., Lindsey M. Root and Adam D. Cohen. 'Writing about the Benefits of an Interpersonal Transgression Facilitates Forgiveness'. *Journal of Consulting and Clinical Psychology* 74.5 (2006): 887-897.

Mucci, Clara. 'Healing and Forgiveness after Traumatic Events: The Case of Holocaust Survivors from the Fortunoff Archives'. In *A Journey through Forgiveness*, edited by Malika Rebai Maamri, Nehama Verbin and Everett L. Worthington, Jr., 109-117. Oxford, England: Inter-Disciplinary Press (2010): Accessed April 13, 2011. http://www.inter-disciplinary.net/publishing/id-press/ebooks/a-journey-through-forgiveness/.

Neal, Geraldine. 'Alternative Dispute Resolution: Are Apology and Forgiveness Simply Two Sides of the One Coin?' In *A Journey through Forgiveness*, edited by Malika Rebai Maamri, Nehama Verbin and Everett L. Worthington, Jr., 167-177. Oxford, England: Inter-Disciplinary Press (2010): Accessed April 13, 2011. http://www.inter-disciplinary.net/publishing/id-press/ebooks/a-journey-through-forgiveness/.

Nolen-Hoeksema, Susan, Blair E. Wisco and Sonja Lyubomirsky. 'Rethinking Rumination'. *Perspectives on Psychological Science* 3.5 (2008): 400-424.

Rye, Mark S. 'Forgiveness as a Way of Coping Following Divorce'. In *A Journey through Forgiveness*, edited by Malika Rebai Maamri, Nehama Verbin and Everett L. Worthington, Jr., 119-130. Oxford, England: Inter-Disciplinary Press (2010): Accessed April 13, 2011. http://www.inter-disciplinary.net/publishing/id-press/ebooks/a-journey-through-forgiveness/.

Sandage, Steven J. and Peter J. Jankowski. 'Forgiveness, Differentiation of Self and Mental Health'. In *A Journey through Forgiveness*, edited by Malika Rebai Maamri, Nehama Verbin and Everett L. Worthington, Jr., 87-98. Oxford, England: Inter-Disciplinary Press (2010): Accessed April 13, 2011. Http://www.inter-disciplinary.net/publishing/id-press/ebooks/a-journey-through-forgiveness/.

Sandage, Steven J. and Everett L. Worthington, Jr. 'Comparison of Two Group Interventions to Promote Forgiveness: Empathy as a Mediator of Change'. *Journal of Mental Health Counseling* 32.1 (2010): 35-57.

Task Force of the European Society of Cardiology and the North American Society of Pacing and Electrophysiology, 'Heart Rate Variability: Standards of Measurement, Physiological Interpretation, and Clinical Use'. *European Heart Journal* 17 (1996): 354-381.

Tennen, Howard and Glenn Affleck. 'Benefit-Finding and Benefit-Reminding'. In *Handbook of Positive Psychology*, 584-597. New York, NY US: Oxford University Press, 2002.

Waltman, Martina A., Douglas C. Russell, Catherine T. Coyle, Robert D. Enright, Anthony C. Holter and Christopher M. Swoboda. 'The Effects of a Forgiveness Intervention on Patients with Coronary Artery Disease'. *Psychology & Health* 24.1 (2009): 11-27.

Wigura, Karolina. 'Forgiveness or Reconciliation after the Shoah? An Ecumenical Perspective'. In *A Journey through Forgiveness*, edited by Malika Rebai Maamri, Nehama Verbin and Everett L. Worthington, Jr., 59-67. Oxford, England: Inter-Disciplinary Press (2010): Accessed April 13, 2011. Http://www.inter-disciplinary.net/publishing/id-press/ebooks/a-journey-through-forgiveness/.

Witvliet, Charlotte vanOyen. 'Understanding and Approaching Forgiveness as Altruism: Relationships with Rumination, Self-Control and a Gratitude-Based Strategy'. In *A Journey through Forgiveness*, edited by Malika Rebai Maamri, Nehama Verbin and Everett L. Worthington, Jr., 99-107. Oxford, England: Inter-Disciplinary Press (2010): Accessed April 13, 2011. Http://www.inter-disciplinary.net/publishing/id-press/ebooks/a-journey-through-forgiveness/.

Witvliet, Charlotte vanOyen, Nathaniel J. DeYoung, Alicia J. Hofelich and Paul A. DeYoung. 'Compassionate Reappraisal and Emotion Suppression as Alternative to Offense-Focused Rumination: Implications for Forgiveness and Psychophysiological Well-Being'. *Journal of Positive Psychology*, in press.

Witvliet, Charlotte vanOyen, Ross W. Knoll, Nova G. Hinman and Paul A. DeYoung. 'Compassion-Focused Reappraisal, Benefit-Focused Reappraisal, and Rumination after an Interpersonal Offense: Emotion-Regulation Implications for Subjective Emotion, Linguistic Responses, and Physiology'. *The Journal of Positive Psychology* 5.3 (2010): 226-242.

Witvliet, Charlotte vanOyen, Thomas E. Ludwig, and Kelly L. Vander Laan. 'Granting Forgiveness or Harboring Grudges: Implications for Emotion, Physiology, and Health'. *Psychological Science* 12, no. 2 (2001): 117-123.

Witvliet, Charlotte V. O. and Michael E. McCullough. 'Forgiveness and Health: A Review and Theoretical Exploration of Emotion Pathways'. In *Altruism and Health: Perspectives from Empirical Research*, 259-276. New York, NY US: Oxford University Press, 2007.

Witvliet, Charlotte V. O., Everett L. Worthington, Jr., Lindsey M. Root, Amy F. Sato, Thomas E. Ludwig and Julie J. Exline. 'Retributive Justice, Restorative Justice, and Forgiveness: An Experimental Psychophysiology Analysis'. *Journal of Experimental Social Psychology* 44.1 (2008): 10-25.

Worthington, Everett. L., Jr. *A Just Forgiveness: Responsible Healing without Excusing Injustice*. Downers Grove, IL US: InterVarsity Press, 2009.

Worthington, Everett L., Jr., Don E. Davis, Joshua N. Hook, Daryl R. Van Tongeren, Aubrey L. Gartner, David J. Jennings II, Chelsea L. Greer and Todd W. Greer. 'Forgiveness and Religion: Update and Current Status'. In *A Journey through Forgiveness*, edited by Malika Rebai Maamri, Nehama Verbin and Everett L. Worthington, Jr., 49-57. Oxford, England: Inter-Disciplinary Press (2010): Accessed April 13, 2011. Http://www.inter-disciplinary.net/publishing/id-press/ebooks/a-journey-through-forgiveness/.

Charlotte vanOyen Witvliet is Professor of Psychology at Hope College, Holland, Michigan, USA. She gratefully acknowledges the Fetzer Institute and the Forgiveness Research Network for supporting this project, and notes that it also contributes to an interdisciplinary project on The Pursuit of Happiness established by the Centre for the Study of Law and Religion at Emory University and supported by a grant from the John Templeton Foundation.

Healing and Forgiveness after Traumatic Events: The Case of Holocaust Survivors from the Fortunoff Archives

Clara Mucci

Abstract
The first part of this chapter deals with the kind of forgiveness which, according to several psychoanalytic clinicians, comes as a sign that the working through and the reconstruction of trauma have been completed, the loss for the damaged self accomplished through a process of mourning – mourning of what cannot be retrieved or totally regained or even healed – and the relinquishing of any feelings of vengefulness and compensation for the traumatic fact has taken place. What is discussed here is therefore, trauma as caused by another human being, as happens in war, genocide, torture for political reasons, or in domestic family violence, including incest and psychological abuse, and not traumas provoked by an external cause or natural events such as an earth-quake. In the second part, the therapeutic process is likened to the process of testimony and a few examples of testimonies given by survivors from the Fortunoff Video Archives for Holocaust Testimonies, Yale University. Here the issue of forgiveness as compared to revenge towards the Nazi is touched upon. The case is made to demonstrate that forgiveness is necessary for the damaged individual as well as for the community in order for real healing to take place. Moreover, this kind of healing does not only concern the past, but it also involves future generations, putting an end to the death-repetition of the traumatic chain.

Key Words: Forgiveness, healing, trauma, survivors, holocaust, testimony, reconciliation, community.

*****

1. Forgiveness in Psychoanalysis

As psychoanalyst Salman Akhtar has recently noted,[1] it would seem as if psychoanalysis has had little to say about the topic of forgiveness, as if it were not a psychoanalytic concept to be dealt with in treatment, if we are to judge from the extremely rare occurrences of this word and concept in Freud's work. The word appears only five times in the entire corpus. By contrast, forgiveness has become a highly charged term in political and judiciary discourses, since several countries have extended public apologies to specific groups, for instance, South Africa towards the victims of the Apartheid, Britain towards the Maori people, Australia towards the stolen aboriginal children, the United States towards Native Americans, Japanese Americans and African Americans; and finally and most notably, Germany towards the victims of the Shoah and their children.

In a similar way, the topic has received a great deal of philosophical attention: after Paul Ricoeur's *Memory History and Forgetting*, there followed Vladimir Jankélévitch's *Forgiveness*, and Jacques Derrida's *To Forgive*. Julia Kristeva also contributed to the debate with her writings, stressing the fact, from her perspective as a psychoanalyst, linguist and philosopher, that forgiveness by its very nature outside the judiciary field, should be considered as limited to the private sphere of human interaction, or to the ethical realm only and should not be construed as extending to the political sphere *per se*. In Kristeva's view, the psychoanalytic process as cure is similar to the act of forgiveness in that it is achieved through interpretation, or through a different understanding of the traumatic event, and by giving meaning to what was originally devoid of it and therefore too painful.

In this regard, from my experience, forgiveness, though an ideal point of arrival for a successful treatment, does not equate automatically with understanding and giving meaning to what was meaningless even if the process of translating traumatic experience into words is a necessary preliminary step towards clear healing and, by implication, towards the final achievement of forgiveness

The question of meaning is evidently a very important one as James Arvanitakis has shown in his chapter, quoting Kelly Oliver, meaning is created in the very act or process of forgiveness. Meaning is also what is transformed or recreated through what Richard Kyte, following Edward Bullough in his contribution, terms 'psychical distance' or 'stepping out,' the first step, in his view, towards forgiveness, or the very condition of forgiving. For Kyte, this distance enables a kind of catharsis of negative emotions and a change in the way one reads the wrongdoer; the final step, the 'stepping in,' allows the 'resumption of love.' In a sense, the path towards forgiveness I am indicating here has some elements in common with Kyte's, but it is achieved through deep work on emotions and the recreation of the past reconstructed psychoanalytically. It is in fact a process closer to what Malika Rebai Maamri has defined as healing relational trauma through relational means, which in turn makes forgiveness the basis for a political process that happens within the ethical realm. In this way, I would say that the kind of 'reckoning with the past' that Maamri describes in her chapter is not too distant from the reconstruction of the past and the reconciliation that might stem from psychoanalytic work on trauma, which in turn becomes an ethical and political act.

I would say in fact that forgiveness comes as a final gift of analysis, to borrow Lacanian language, and it is not something we can strive for and aim at. It is, in a way like grace, if I may say so, a place we might arrive at or we might not, and which does not completely depend on our will. In other words, it is beyond our rational control, even when a 'successful' treatment is terminated. I am aware of striking chords that might sound spiritual in themselves, but I would like to stress that I do not consider traumatic forgiveness as a religious or even a spiritual concept at all, but as the basis for an achieved reconciliation between self and other, precisely the breach that had been made by the traumatic experience. And this is true both for the individual and the community, and therefore acquires a political value.

Outside the spiritual realm, after writing the first draft of this chapter, I have found the concept of forgiveness as grace only in Vladimir Jankélévitch. The French philosopher investigates the problem of how to respond to injustice and evil. He writes suggestively: 'The will can do all – except one thing: undo that which it has been done. The power of undoing is of another order: of the order of grace, if you will. It is a miracle.'[2] For Jankélévitch, forgiveness happens spontaneously and it alters the relationship between the victim and the wrongdoer. If, in a sense, forgiveness 'just happens,' in order for forgiveness to come about, some serious clinical work on trauma and the relationship with the perpetrator must be accomplished.

2. Phases in the Treatment of Trauma before Forgiveness

I would therefore envision three phases in the treatment of traumatized patients if forgiveness is to become possible at all: the first one has to do with the complete and thorough retrieval, not only of the events of the past, but also of the emotions and feelings involved with the occurrence of it. Without retrieval of the emotions connected to it, no abreaction of the trauma is possible and no overcoming of the trauma is accomplished.

In this regard the work done by psychoanalysts, such as Judith Herman, Ilde Grubrich-Simitis and Dori Laub in treating victims of traumas of the Shoah or incest survivors, is fundamental. As Dori Laub, a Holocaust survivor himself and a psychiatrist trained psychoanalytically to work with survivors and their children, writes:

> While the trauma uncannily returns in actual life, its reality continues to elude the subject who lives in its grips and unwittingly undergoes its ceaseless repetitious re-enactments. The traumatic event, although real, took place outside the parameters of 'normal' reality, such as causality, sequence, place and time. The trauma is thus an event that has no beginning, no ending, no before, no during and no after. This absence of categories that define it lends it a quality of 'otherness,' a salience, timelessness and a ubiquity that puts it outside the range of associatively linked experiences, outside the range of comprehension, of recounting and of mastery. Trauma survivors live not with memories of the past, but with an event that could not and did not proceed through to its completion, has no ending, attained no closure, and therefore, as far as its survivors are concerned, continues into the present and is current in every aspect. …

> In psychoanalytic work with survivors, indeed, historical reality
> has to be reconstructed and reaffirmed before any other work can
> start.[3]

I totally agree with the necessity to reconstruct the historical reality of the traumatic event 'before any other work can start,' and I would stress precisely how reality, or I should say that historical reality, is what psychoanalysis in the past has usually neglected or taken for granted in usual clinical discourse.

While traditional psychoanalysis has stressed the relevance of internal elements and of an intra-psychic dimension at the expense of real details and the external impact of trauma, a new direction seems to have been taken after what has come to be known as 'post-Shoah history.' The atrocities of twentieth-century wars and massive genocide have forced us to come to terms with the real events more than the fantasised issues related to them, a bias for which Freud himself seems to be responsible, when he shifted from what he called the 'seduction theory' to the fantasmatic reality of it.[4] For Freud, after a certain point in his theorization, in neuroses 'it is psychical reality which is the decisive kind.'[5]

In addition, events like September 11, 2001, touching our private lives in ways that even atrocious wars in distant countries like Rwanda or the former Yugoslavia might not have done, have enhanced a sensitivity to this kind of issues, which has made thinking of trauma in 'fantasised terms' impossible nowadays and even offensive to the victims. We live, as Van der Kolk and McFarlane argue, in a highly traumatized era.[6]

As psychotherapists, our first task therefore, is to make the details of the trauma come out of the silence and the dissociative states they are wrapped in. The timing, of the actual exploration of the details of the traumatic events and the reconstruction of it, has obviously to do with specific situations within the therapy and it has to be carefully evaluated by clinicians case by case. Nonetheless, the recuperation of the entire real event has to be achieved and established distinctively in order to proceed to the next steps. Grubrich-Simitis states this very clearly: 'It is only to the extent that the historical reality is ascertained that the patient will be able to approach his own inner and outer reality.'[7]

It is a moment in which truth is achieved, and it has a bearing not only on the internal psyche but also on the outside, real world. The fundamental value of re-discovering the truth and of proclaiming the truth within oneself and to the external world has been highlighted both in philosophical explorations and in psychoanalysis. As Charles Griswold states in the *Prologue* of his recent book on forgiveness,

> successful forgiveness and political apology depend on truth
> telling and that, more broadly, we are better off responding to
> wrong-doing with recognition of the truth rather than with

evasion. Truth telling is one of the ideals underpinning both forgiveness and apology... and reconciliation is furthered by truth telling and, as apposite, forgiveness or political apology (or both).[8]

Griswold subsequently stresses the relevance of the narrative in which the past is reconstructed, a very important step in psychoanalytic work as well.[9]

Judith Herman goes even further, saying that telling the truth together with remembering are prerequisites for the restoration of the social order.[10] This first moment, then, sees retrieval of memory, reconstructing the past and stating the truth as fundamental.

The second moment has to do, ideally, with a 'triple acknowledgment.' I would distinguish intra-psychic knowledge of the truth from public or interpersonal acknowledgment of the truth. This is what the French psychoanalyst, Michèle Bertrand, who works with refugees and survivors of various traumas, states: the victim asks for the social recognition of the harm done on her/him; she/he asks for a recognition on behalf of the culprit of the action performed on her/him; and finally the victim asks for the acknowledgement of the truth of her/his words. Bertrand stresses how reparation takes place symbolically and performatively through narrative and through the secondary processes at work in it, i.e. through a recuperation of a symbolic form of representation that was totally blocked before the 'putting into words'[11] process. Herman agrees in saying that 'the fundamental premise of the psychoanalytic work is a belief in the restorative power of truth-telling.'[12]

For that restorative-symbolic process to take place, though, (and here is Laub again) an empathic dyad has to be recreated, a relationship to be re-established, where trauma resulted in the disconnection of all relationships, a break of the empathic bond between human beings, and the total loneliness of the victim.

Judith Herman also testifies to this when she writes:

> The core experiences of psychological trauma are disempowerment and disconnection from others. Recovery, therefore, is based upon the empowerment of the survivor and the creation of new connections. Recovery can take place only within the context of relationships; it cannot occur in isolation. In her renewed connections with other people, the survivor re-creates the psychological faculties that were damaged or deformed by the traumatic experience. These faculties include the basic capacities for trust, autonomy, initiative, competence, identity and intimacy. Just as these capabilities are originally formed in relationships with other people, they must be reformed in such relationship.[13]

After this new kind of connection is rebuilt, mourning for what was lost of the self in the traumatic process can finally start to take place, and it might be a long, devastating place to be in, but it is the beginning of the final phase of the healing process. It is what Melanie Klein has termed the 'depressive phase'[14] that any treatment has to undergo if the cure is to be successful and which is usually followed by 'reparation' of the lost or damaged object within oneself. This is also the phase in which the patient has to 'give up' not only what was lost or damaged, but also ideal objects, what has never been there in the first place, as for instance, the idea of 'good parents,' in incest survivors or in severely abused children. As a strategy for survival, in fact, a battered child might prefer to cling to the idea that he or she is 'bad' but his/her mother or father is good, because what is really unbearable is the idea of not being loved at all, and love is necessary to survive. This idea will have to be given up and transformed if reality testing is to be achieved or strengthened. It is a process of grieving that might be long and painful, but it is an unavoidable step.

After this phase, what the patient needs to achieve is the overcoming of anger with the letting go of resentments and desire for retaliation. This moment is a necessary one towards possible forgiveness. As Herman underlines:

> During the process of mourning, the survivor must come to terms with the impossibility of getting even. As she vents her rage in safety, her helpless fury gradually changes into a more powerful and satisfying form of anger: righteous indignation. This transformation allows the survivor to free herself from the entrapment of the revenge fantasy and the anger linked to it in which she is alone with the perpetrator. It offers her a way to regain a sense of empowerment (Aktar speaks of a kind of 'sadism' that empowers the victim) without becoming a criminal herself, or resorting to evil-doing. Giving up the fantasy of revenge does not mean giving up the quest for justice; on the contrary, it begins the process of joining with others to hold the perpetrators accountable for his crimes.[15]

It is at this point, and at this point only, that forgiveness and I would say real gratitude for being alive or having been saved might occur. And it is precisely at this stage that it becomes more elusive and to my knowledge, none of the philosophers or psychoanalysts mentioned above has discussed it thoroughly. Herman speaks of 'restorative love'[16] and I am not satisfied with these words, since once again, we are in danger of substituting psychoanalytic concepts with spiritual or religious ones, which is not my point in this chapter.

I agree with Malika Rebai Maamri who states that forgiveness stops the vicious cycle of revenge and promotes a true sense of love. For Richard Kyte, as well, debilitating emotions need to be replaced eventually by love. Along with Judith Herman I do believe that,

> though the fantasy [of compensation] is about empowerment, in reality the struggle for compensation ties the patient's fate to that of the perpetrator and holds her recovery hostage to his whims. *Paradoxically, the patient may liberate herself from the perpetrator when she renounces the hope of getting any compensation from him.* As grieving progresses, the patient comes to envision a more social, general, and abstract process of restitution, which permits her to pursue her just claims without ceding any power over her present life to the perpetrator.[17]

And I would say that to remain in the grips of the perpetrator means quite often to remain ill as a way of making somebody pay for what has happened. It is way of making the illness itself a sort of accusation, to the expense sometimes of one's own life. I would not be surprised if Holocaust survivors (or sometimes victims of incest or other kind of abuse) who have committed suicide would be, in some ways, still desperately accusing/protesting against their perpetrators while destroying their own lives. It is what psychoanalysis terms after Anna Freud 'identification with the aggressor,' but here victim and aggressor are one and the same person. We have often heard about (and many have written upon) about the guilt of being alive that several survivors, especially from genocide or massive extermination, experience; life as an unbearable burden, when everybody else, friends, family, have died. The question is 'why me?': 'why me' for the traumatic events or sets of events, 'why me' for the survival. It is a fundamental question, and it might be a very destructive one, if it is not dealt with at length in therapy. This is a moment in which the patient/survivor has both to accept what has happened and to let go of any idea of retaliation or compensation or restoration from the outside.

I do not think that the relationship with the perpetrator needs necessarily to be changed in reality, with public acts of acknowledgement, nor is the wrongdoer's repentance necessary for forgiveness to be enacted. The kind of deep internal forgiveness I am describing here is issued from the intra-psychic mind towards parts of the self, and only as a secondary consequence might it be directed towards the perpetrator in real life, but this step is, to my mind, absolutely irrelevant for healing and forgiveness to take place. The 'letting go' of the traumatized patient has nothing to do with publicly granting forgiveness, and is not based on anything that the perpetrator might do after the event. It is an act of love, which has the self, the world, the other as object of love, without distinction. It is, as Kristeva says in 'Forgiveness: An Interview,' a rebirth, a new beginning, life born again (which always implies an act of love and trust). It is renaming and re-enabling the future to be.

3. Forgiveness, Reconciliation with the Other and the Necessity for a 'Testimonial Community'

It is only at this point, when mourning has been accomplished and basically the traumatic past retrieved in full detail and somehow accepted and resolved that forgiveness might step in, as an aftermath of the mourning process. It usually implies an acceptance of the irreparable nature of our specific past and the change in relationship with the other, any other, starting with the therapist and including possibly the perpetrator. It is this moment of acceptance that gives or might give way to reconciliation, and it is, I think, what makes even reconciliation as a political act possible, meaning that in order for social and political reconciliation to be enacted, individual acceptance of the past and some form of forgiveness between the two parts have taken place.

But reconciliation cannot be based on forgetting or putting aside and forgiving is not a way of forgetting or condoning, on the contrary, as I have mentioned earlier, it cannot but stem from the careful and painstaking retrieval of the truth of the past and the acknowledgment of the responsibilities of the wrongdoers, even if it might be extremely painful and excruciating. Forgiveness can exist only in remembering, it cannot exist in forgetting.

As Desmond Tutu has written (in a different context),

> In forgiving, people are not being asked to forget. On the contrary, it is important to remember, so that we should not let atrocities happen again. Forgiveness does not mean condoning what has been done. It means taking what happened seriously and not minimizing it; drawing out the sting of the memory that threatens to poison our entire existence. It involves trying to understand the perpetrators and so have empathy to try to stand in their shoes and appreciate the sort of pressures and influences that might have conditioned them... Forgiving is not being sentimental.[18]

At this point, memories of the past for the patient-victim become a form of testimony, which entails the presence of the third party, the analyst, who sits there as the guarantor of the recovered truth (my word, echoing Lacan).[19] Herman also notes that 'In the telling, the trauma story becomes a testimony; Inger Agger and Soren Jensen, in their work with refugee survivors of political persecution, point to the universality of testimony as a ritual of healing.'[20]

In this way, testimony becomes the basis for an act of reconciliation, and the foundation, I think, of both the ethical and the political dimension of it (in contrast with Kristeva's belief that in psychoanalysis, forgiveness is achieved through the process of interpretation and restoration of meaning but has no political dimension and has to be kept to the interpersonal sphere only, since the social is the sphere of the law and the judiciary rules, and only punishment can define the relationship between crime and perpetrator in that sphere).

In line with Herman, I do believe, on the contrary that testimony in this kind of therapy has both a private dimension, and a public aspect, which is political and juridical.[21] Working with survivors of various kinds, Laub argues that in giving testimony, a piece of individual and collective history has been retrieved and brought back for the self and to the community to enjoy: 'The testimony is, therefore, the process by which the narrator (the survivor) reclaims his position as a witness: reconstitutes the internal 'thou,' and thus the possibility of a witness or a listener inside himself.'[22]

But the process of testimony goes the other way round too: it is achieved both by the one who gives the testimony and by the one who receives it, the analyst or guarantor, and this is where the two-people process becomes a more collective and open process towards restoration of the historical and personal truth. When a testimony is rendered, there are not only two people there, but three subjects: the one who speaks, the one who listens, and what is recreated or liberated in the form of truth, which reverberates onto the community and are delivered to the community and to the people and to generations to come.

It is a very deep symbolic process that is not only interpersonal but political and social as well; one that has an impact on the community. It creates something new and true in the social sphere. It is a process similar to what Malika Rebai Maamri terms 'political forgiveness,' equating 'ethical thought,' following, in her turn, Donald Shiver and Emmanuel Levinas.

Dori Laub, who is one of the founders of the Fortunoff Video Archives for Holocaust Testimonies at Yale University and has video-taped and interviewed many of the survivors (the testimonies now number over 4000), has described in full detail the effects of the testimony on the listeners. Testimony is a process that does not spare the interviewer: 'Trauma – and its impact on the hearer – leaves indeed no hiding place intact. As one comes to know the survivors, one really comes to know oneself.' Laub adds:

> For the listeners who enter the contract of the testimony, a journey fraught with dangers lies ahead. There are hazards to the listening to trauma. Trauma – and its impact on the hearer – leaves indeed no hiding place intact. As one comes to know the survivor, one really comes to know oneself; and that is not a simple task. The survivor experience, or the Holocaust experience, is a very condensed version of what life is all about: it contains a great many existential, questions that we manage to

avoid in our daily living, often through preoccupation with trivia. The Holocaust experience is an inexorable and, henceforth, an unavoidable confrontation with those questions. The listener can no longer ignore the question of facing death; of facing time and its passage; of the meaning and purpose of living; of the limits of one's omnipotence; of losing the ones that are close to us; the great question of our ultimate aloneness; our otherness from any other; our responsibility to and for our destiny; the question of loving and its limits, of parents and children, an so on.[23]

But it is not only that, as extraordinary as this might be. It creates something which was not there before. It contributes to the process of restoration of truth in reality and history and leaves that as a legacy to the generations to come. It also adds to the communicative process, which is what is repressed in society in general as Kristeva noted in *La revolution du language poétique*. It is therefore healing both the individual and the community. In fact the survivor, before giving the testimony, does not totally know what he/she knows and what he/she is going to say, as Laub puts in an article in which he recounts how several highly traumatized survivors became psychotic and were interned in hospitals in Israel where they would not speak for thirty years without anybody even asking their story:

> To begin with, the testimony does not fully know what he/she knows. It is only as the testimony emerges that the survivor comes to know his or her full story and the impact it has had on his or her life. Even then, parts that are beyond the imaginable will remain left out or retained as frozen, encapsulated, and split-off foreign images. These are the parts of the story that have not been told... These parts of the survivor's story, and thus a piece of human history, are lost to silence. I have earlier searched for words for this muting or loss – and have come to call it an *erasure*.[24]

However, as some of these survivors started to speak again to Laub when he visited them, the latter concluded:

> What I realized was that the breaking of the silence, the lifting of muteness, that had begun with the arrival of a fully present and fully committed listener had, in fact, allowed memory, and with it, narrative, to flow again...*What is needed for healing is the creation of a testimonial community*.[25]

4. Testimonies from the Fortunoff Archives

In listening to some testimonies from the Fortunoff Archives at Yale University, I was surprised at the lack of anger and the absence of a desire for revenge in these people.

This is Edith P., deported to Auschwitz, who, among other things, speaks about the smell of the burned flesh, but says that she does not hate them (the Germans). She feels she would waste a lot of time. Sometimes, she wishes 'they would feel what we felt.' She cries that there is not even a grave to go to and mourn. She cries for all the destruction she still sees in the world and feels that the world has not learned the lesson. She feels guilty for the beautiful homes they have now and what pains her most is the fact that nobody seems to have learned anything from the past.[26]

Shifre Z., born in Poland in 1929, testifies about a slaughter in Vilna. She was twelve. She says that they mostly could not understand 'why all of the sudden they wanted to kill us.' She remembers a full moon with a red ring around it, 'as though the blood arrived at the sky.' She saw all the burned corpses in the ghetto, bodies of friends or people she knew, and could not understand. 'They were law-abiding people,' so she could not understand such cruelty. But she then says: 'I wanted so much to be alive, to be able to tell the stories, to teach them to the children,' and 'I believe in the goodness of man. Everyone has a right and responsibility to have one's life. There is a universal God. I blame no one. I speak to friends about this.'[27]

Paula J., born in Poland in 1921, says: 'we were like animals in Auschwitz, hungry animals.' She does not believe in God for 'if there were a God, he should not have permitted those things to happen.' She does not hate 'them' (the Germans) but does not want to have anything to do with them, although she is not bitter.[28]

Helen R., even if she feels guilty to have survived when the rest of the family died, says 'it is worth living.' 'Pain you have to forget, you can't live with pain. I remember the good things. The good childhood; you can't live with hate the rest of your life. I hate the people involved directly. If it is your decision to live, you have to make the best of it.' She remembers the holidays at childhood, the smell of food, her mother with the big apron, her smile. 'These are the things that sustained me, and I want to say this to the young generations. Thank you, young people,'[29] she says to the interviewer.

Helen R., Polish, born in 1923, always had great faith she would survive first in Plaszow, then in Auschwitz. She speaks about camaraderie. She was harshly beaten because she was sharing a piece of bread, but it felt good, 'they could not take away the human part.'[30] She always had faith.

Helen K. for her part notes: 'I still have nightmares about crematoriums. The world allowed this to happen.' 'Are you bitter?' 'No, very disappointed,' she says that she was very resentful at the end of the war, she was 21. There were pogroms after the war in Poland. She felt very hurt by this. After several years, she concluded that resentment and bitterness would have killed her (she has only one lung left); 'war has made beasts of some people, saints of others.' The Germans have offered money to her, but she did not want to see them. 'My husband... The man I married and the man he was after the war were not the same person. And I'm sure I was not the same person either...but somehow we had a need for each other because he knew who I was, he was the only person who knew...He knew who I was, and I knew who he was... And we're here; we're here to tell you the story.'[31]

Jolly Z. remembers days at Auschwitz, in lines for hours, whoever could not stand them or remained in the barracks would be put to death; food starvation, but she saw love, courage, fortitude among them, 'I saw friends stealing for each other and this made me realize that beasts or angels we have a choice... in the shadow of the gas chambers, I found my faith in the potential of man. We all have the potential for both extremes.' Once out of the camp, she saw some Jewish young men about to attack a young German woman with a baby; she screamed and tried to separate them, and an out-stander who knew her, asked her: 'how could you preserve so much love in you?' And she replied 'oh no, love preserved me!' Now she says: 'I'm allergic to hate. Hate is very self-destructive. The pain will always be there. I will never judge a nation, race, country, but will always judge one to one. Even the Germans made a choice, some helped them. For a long time, it was very difficult to have hope but continuing the hatred upset me very much. There is no life without pain...The world is engulfed again in hatred, society is passive.... It's important to share our experience. World choices will affect the future of mankind.[32]

5. Conclusion

Personally, I do not think that historical events like the Shoah or mass genocides can never or should ever be forgiven. Forgiveness, to my mind, cannot be attributed to an event or a social political act. But in order to be totally liberated from the past and from anger, the individual needs to reach in some way 'the place' of forgiveness, which nonetheless cannot be forced or decided, as has already been said. Individuals can be forgiven, not events. Besides, as Elie Wiesel rightly argues, we cannot forgive on behalf of those who are not here to forgive.[33] Forgiveness cannot be bestowed *in lieu* of another, it is a practice or a spontaneous performative act originating in the psyche and restoring a painful relationship from the past, which is achieved through painstaking clinical work. For me, the Shoah remains 'unforgivable' *par excellence* and yet, in line with Desmond Tutu, I do think that it is a sign of the resilience of a population to be able to forgive and go 'beyond trauma':

> True reconciliation is not cheap... Forgiving and being reconciled
> are not about pretending that things are other than they are. It is
> not patting one another on the back and turning a blind eye to the

wrong. True reconciliation exposes the awfulness, the abuse, the pain, the degradation, the truth ... In the act of forgiveness we are declaring our faith in the future of a relationship and in the capacity of the wrongdoer to make a new beginning on a course that will be different from the one that caused us the wrong. We are saying here is a chance to make a new beginning. It is an act of faith that the wrong-doer can change.[34]

I would conclude here, remembering Desmond Tutu's words that to choose to forgive rather than to demand retribution... It gives people resilience...'[35] And finally, along with Elie Wiesel, I would add that if we cannot forgive on behalf of those who are not here to forgive, nonetheless I do believe that

On the edge of the abyss, it is possible to dream of redemption. In the midst of darkness, it is possible to offer light and warmth to one's fellow human being. Even in prison one can be free. Though poisoned by the enemy, words must not be discarded. It depends on us whether they become spears or prayers, whether they carry compassion or curse, whether they provoked respect or disdain, whether they move us to despair or hope. I belong to a generation that has learned that whatever the question, despair is not the answer. Thank you.[36]

Notes

[1] Salman Akhtar, 'Forgiveness: Origins, Dynamics, Psychopathology, and Technical Relevance', *Psychoanalytic Quarterly* LXXI (2002): 175-212, 4-5.

[2] Vladimir Jankélévitch, *Une vie en toutes lettres. Correspondance* (Paris: Liana Levi, 1995), 195.

[3] Dori Laub, 'Bearing Witness, or the Vicissitudes of Listening', in *Testimony: Crises of Witnessing in Literature, Psychoanalysis and History*, ed. Shoshana Felman and Dori Laub (New York and London: Routledge, 1992), 57-74, 68-69.

[4] I discuss this in detail in the first chapter of *Il dolore estremo. Il trauma da Freud alla Shoah* (Roma: Borla, 2008).

[5] Sigmund Freud, *Introductory Lectures*, SE 1916-17, 356-398, 368.

[6] See Bessel A. van der Kolk and Alexander C. McFarlane, 'The Dark Hole of Trauma,' in *The Effects of Overwhelming Experience on Mind, Body, and Society*, ed. Bessel A. van der Kolk and Alexander C McFarlane (New York: The Guilford Press, 1996), 19-38.

[7] Ilse Grubrich-Simitis, 'Extreme Traumatization as Cumulative Trauma. Psychoanalytic Investigationn of the Effects of Concentration Camp Experiences

on Survivors and Their Children', *The Psychoanalytic Study of the Child* 36 (1981): 440.

[8] Charles L. Griswold, *Forgiveness: A Philosophical Exploration* (Cambridge and New York: Cambridge University Press, 2007), XXIV.

[9] See also Hunter Brown's references to Griswold and narrative in his article 'The Conditions of Forgiveness in Philosophical Thought', In *A Journey through Forgiveness*, ed. Malika Rebai Maamri, Nehama Verbin and Everett L. Worthington, Jr., (Oxford, England: Inter-Disciplinary Press, 2010), accessed April 13, 2011. Http://www.inter-disciplinary.net/publishing/id-press/ebooks/a-journey-through-forgiveness/.

[10] Judith Herman, *Trauma and Recovery: The Aftermath of Violence–from Domestic Abuse to Political Terror* (New York: Basic Books, 1992), 1.

[11] Michèle Bertrand, *Trois défis pour la psychanalyse. Clinique, théorie, psychothérapie* (Paris: Dunod, 2004), 51-52.

[12] Herman, *Trauma and Recovery*, 181.

[13] Ibid., 133.

[14] Melanie Klein, *Love, Guilt, and Reparation and Other Works* (New York: Free Press, 1975).

[15] Herman, *Trauma and Recovery*, 189.

[16] Ibid., 190.

[17] Ibid.

[18] Desmond Tutu, *No Future without Forgiveness* (New York: Random House, 1999) 271-272.

[19] See Jacques Lacan, *Ecrits* (Paris: Seuil, 1966).

[20] Herman, *Trauma and Recovery*, 181.

[21] Ibid.

[22] Dori Laub, 'An Event without a Witness: Truth, Testimony and Survival', in *Testimony*, Felman and Laub, ed., 75-92, 85.

[23] Laub, 'Bearing Witness', 72.

[24] Dori Laub, 'From Speechlessness to Narrative: The Cases of Holocaust Historians and of Psychiatrically Hospitalized Survivors', *Literature and Medicine* 24.2, (Fall 2005): 256.

[25] Ibid., 264. Emphasis mine.

[26] Fortunoff Video Archive for Holocaust Testimonies, Yale University, T 107.

[27] Fortunoff Video Archive, T 11.

[28] Fortunoff Video Archive, T 125.

[29] Fortunoff Video Archive, T 118.

[30] Fortunoff Video Archive, T 131.

[31] Fortunoff Video Archive, T 58.

[32] Fortunoff Video Archive, T 220.

[33] Elie Wiesel, *All Rivers Run to the Sea: Memoirs* (New York: Afred Knopf, 1995).
[34] Tutu, *No Future*, 273.
[35] Ibid., 31.
[36] Elie Wiesel, *Ethics and Memory.Ethik und Erinnerung* (Berlin and New York Walter de Gruyter, 1997).

Bibliography

Akhtar, Salman. 'Forgiveness: Origins, Dynamics, Psychopathology, and Technical Relevance'. *Psychoanalytic Quarterly* LXXI (2002): 175–212.

Bertrand, Michéle. *Trois défis pour la psychanalyse: Clinique, théorie, psychothérapie.* Paris: Dunod, 2004.

Derrida, Jacques. 'To Forgive: The Unforgivable and the Imprescriptible'. In *Questioning God*, edited by John D. Caputo, Mark Dooley and Michael J. Scanlon, 21–51. Bloomington: Indiana University Press, 2001.

Felman, Shoshana and Dori Laub. *Testimony: Crisis of Witnessing in Literature, Psychoanalysis and History.* New York and London: Routledge, 1992.

Freud, Sigmund. *Introductory Lectures on Psycho-Analysis*, III, SE 1916-1917. London: Hogarth Press, 1950.

Griswold, Charles L. *Forgiveness: A Philosophical Exploration.* Cambridge: Cambridge University Press, 2007.

Grubrich-Simitis, Ilde. 'Extreme Traumatization as Cumulative Trauma: Psychoanalytic Investigations of the Effects of Concentration Camp Experiences on Survivors and their Children'. *The Psychoanalytic Study of the Child* 36 (1981): 415-50.

Herman, Judith. *Trauma and Recovery: The Aftermath of Violence—From Domestic Abuse to Political Terror.* New York: Basic Books, 1992.

Jankélévitch, Vladimir. *Forgiveness.* Chicago: The University of Chicago Press, 2005.

Jankélévitch, Vladimir. *Une vie en toutes lettres: Correspondance*. Paris: Liana Levi, 1995.

Klein, Melanie. *Love, Guilt, and Reparation and Other Works*. New York: Free Press, 1975.

Kristeva, Julia. *Revolution in Poetic Language*. New York: Columbia University Press, 1984.

———. 'Forgiveness: An Interview'. PMLA 117.2 (2002): 278-80.

Lacan, Jacques. *Ecrits*. Paris: Seuil, 1966.

Laub, Dori. 'Bearing Witness, or the Vicissitudes of Listening'. In *Testimony: Crises of Witnessing in Literature, Psychoanalysis and History*, edited by Shoshana Felman and Dori Laub, 57-74. New York: Routledge, 1992.

Laub, Dori. 'An Event without a Witness: Truth, Testimony and Survival'. In *Testimony, Testimony: Crises of Witnessing in Literature, Psychoanalysis and History*, edited by Shoshana Felman and Dori Laub, 75-92. New York and London: Routledge 1992.

Laub, Dori. 'From Speechlessness to Narrative: The Cases of Holocaust Historians and of Hospitalized Survivors'. *Literature and Medicine* 24.2 (Fall 2005): 253-65.

Mucci, Clara. *Il dolore estremo. Il trauma da Freud alla Shoah*. Roma: Borla, 2008.

Ricoeur, Paul. *Memory, History and Forgetting*. Chicago: The University of Chicago Press, 2004.

Tutu, Desmond. *No Future without Forgiveness*. New York: Random House, 1999.

Van der Kolk, Bessel and Alexander C. McFarlane, 'The Dark Hole of Trauma'. In *The Effects of Overwhelming Experience on Mind, Body, and Society*, edited by Bessel A. van der Kolk and Alexander C. McFarlane, 19-38. New York: The Guilford Press, 1996.

Wiesel, Elie. *All Rivers Run to the Sea: Memoirs*. New York: Afred Knopf, 1995.

Wiesel, Elie. *Ethics and Memory: Ethic und Erinnerung*, Berlin: Walter de Gruyter, 1997.

Clara Mucci is Professor of English literature and psychoanalysis at the University of Chieti, Italy, where she teaches both within the Faculty of Humanities and the Faculties of Psychology, Clinical Section. She has written several books on Shakespeare and psychoanalysis and a book on trauma and the Shoah.

Part 2:

Does Religiosity Foster Forgivness?

Forgiveness and Religion: Update and Current Status

Daryl R. Van Tongeren, Everett L. Worthington, Jr.,
Don E. Davis, Joshua N. Hook, Aubrey L. Gartner,
David J. Jennings II, Chelsea L. Greer and Todd W. Greer

Abstract
We trace the history of the scientific study of forgiveness and religion within psychology. The early years were characterized by trying to answer the question of which religion produced the most forgiveness. Interest in that question waned with the realization that religions understand forgiveness differently. In 1999, McCullough and Worthington reviewed the empirical research on forgiveness and religion, and found out that the correlation between religion and trait forgivingness was about .4 whereas the correlation between religion and forgiveness of a particular transgression was only about .2. This discrepancy suggested that religious people might be acting hypocritically. In other words, religious individuals might say they are more forgiving because forgiveness is highly valued in religious communities, but in practice, they may not actually forgive more. Alternative reasons for this difference had been suggested. Recently, a meta-analysis has shown that the incongruity between trait and state forgiveness is only about .1 rather than .2, and it provided support for a methodological hypothesis that measures of religion and forgiveness were more strongly related if assessed at the same level of specificity (i.e., both traits or both states). We suggest that a model of relational spirituality and forgiveness can help future researchers measure the components of the relationship between forgiveness and religion. We briefly outline the main components of the model and pose research questions for future inquiry.

Key Words: Forgiveness, religion, spirituality, empirical research summary.

*****

Introduction

When science operates correctly, one set of interesting questions is answered, which reveals another set of questions, which in turn get resolved, and reveal yet another set. The psychological study of forgiveness and religion has been characterized by three questions. (1) Who wins the horserace of which religion forgives the most? (2) Are religious people hypocritical in reporting to be forgiving people but not really forgiving differently from non-religious people? (3) What are the basic elements of the relationship between religion and forgiveness?

To answer these questions, we (1) argue that the horserace question is outdated by demonstrating how various religions emphasize forgiveness differently, (2) we address the potential hypocrisy between religiosity and forgiveness by clarifying the methodological issues, such as imprecise measurement specificity, that may account for at least some of the apparent discrepancy, and (3) we review a recently proposed model of relational spirituality to advance scientific inquiry of forgiveness.

1. The Horserace: Which Religion is the most Forgiving?

Understanding forgiveness and religion in the past resembled a horse race. Spectators were heavily invested in which side won the race; that is, which religion was most forgiving. We believe, however, that the research stimulated by that horserace mindset is over. It will no longer draw the crowd. We offer explanations for this, but first define our basic terms.

A. What is Religion (and Spirituality)?

Religion has been defined in numerous ways, and involves a relationship with the Sacred (i.e., what an individual considers ultimate or divine) that occurs within the context of a community with consensually-validated beliefs and practices for relating to the Sacred. Furthermore, religions are typically practised in a community of like believers; thus, many of the practices are communal, not merely experienced individually. Religions often address issues central to morality (i.e., how should I live?) and meaning (i.e., what is the purpose of my life?). Spirituality, on the other hand, can be defined as feelings of closeness and connectedness to something an individual considers divine or sacred. Although many people experience their spirituality in the context of religion, not all incorporate religious beliefs into spiritual experiences. Furthermore, spirituality is fundamentally individual. We just defined spirituality as 'feelings of closeness and connectedness...' and feelings are individual, not communal. We propose that there are, at least, four types of spirituality: (1) *Religious spirituality* involves a sense of closeness and connection to God or a Higher Power that is often expressed through practising a specific religion; (2) *Humanistic spirituality* involves a sense of closeness and connection to humankind that is often evidenced by strong connections to particular people or groups, and adherents to this type of spirituality often espouse feelings of altruism, empathy, love, or reflection; (3) *Nature spirituality* involves a sense of closeness and connection to the environment or to nature that is experienced through emotions such as awe, elevation, or inspiration elicited by interactions with nature, such as enjoying a sunset on the beach, experiencing the natural wonder of the Grand Canyon, or feeling a general sense of connection with the natural environment; (4) *Transcendent spirituality* involves a sense of closeness and connection with the whole of creation or the natural order and might be experienced by meditating on the magnificence of the natural universe, contemplating the vastness of one's own existence, or looking into the sky on a clear night and having a sense of connection with all other natural objects. Moreover, transcendent spirituality may include addressing existential issues of human life. Humanistic, nature, and transcendental spiritualities can also be experienced within the context of religion. That is, one might believe that God created humans who experience awe, elevation, or inspiration at a powerful God who created marvelous beings who are able to connect with one another, enjoy nature, and ponder the fundamental qualities of existence. However, one might also experience those three spiritualities, and their concomitant emotions, apart from religion and without requiring reference to God or an ultimate being. For example, one's spiritual connection with other humans or with nature may not require belief in God to experience a feeling of closeness to something sacred.

We deem it important to include a discussion of the definition of spirituality because we foresee that the future of research on religion, especially as it pertains to forgiveness, will likely (we might even say, *should*) include a consideration of spirituality, which may or may not be directly associated with a particular religion. That is, spirituality is experienced independent of organised religion, yet research has heretofore left this domain unexplored. We encourage future researchers to more vigorously (relative to the past research) examine how spirituality is related to forgiveness, even outside the context of religion.

B. What is Forgiveness?

Forgiveness scholars in different fields have debated the best definition of forgiveness, including the variety of definitions evidenced in this book. In psychology, many of the definitional conflicts have been resolved, when psychologists struggled with agreement on definitions up until about 2005. Fields like religion, philosophy and literature, though they have written extensively about the topic of forgiveness, have not devoted so much effort to the systematic study of forgiveness as psychology has in recent years. As a consequence, psychological science, which has only focused on forgiveness since the mid-1980s, has concentrated on developing a concise definition of forgiveness. This has resulted in relative agreement.[1] The other disciplines, however, tend to seek rich and deep definitions of forgiveness and have formulated them over centuries of cultural and intellectual change. Hence, greater diversity of definition is seen in chapters arising from other disciplines. If we examine some psychologists' chapters such as Charlotte vanOyen Witvliet and Julie Exline's, for example, we find relative uniformity of definitions. But, comparing definitions by theologians, philosophers, and scholars of literature, we see much more variety and more nuanced distinctions.

We view forgiveness as two related but distinct processes. *Decisional forgiveness* is a behavioural intention statement in which the forgiver decides to act differently toward the offender by (1) treating him/her as a valued person and (2) eschewing vengeance. We note that a behavioural intention statement speaks only to how a person intends to act. The latter might actually not carry out his/her intentions due, for instance, to another offence or lack of opportunity to do so. In addition, decisional forgiveness does not consider motives. A victim could be motivated by a need to reconcile, to act benevolently, or even to get revenge or avoid the person, but still make a decision to behave forgivingly. In addition, the person might have unforgiving emotions toward the offender even though a sincere decision has been made to forgive. This suggests that a second type of forgiveness is needed. In *emotional forgiveness,* the victim replaces negative feelings towards the offender with positive ones.[2] Complete emotional forgiveness depends on the type of relationship the victim has with the offender. If the offender is a stranger or someone with whom the forgiver does not wish to continue a relationship, then complete forgiveness involves the elimination of negative unforgiving emotions, such as resentment, bitterness, hatred, anger, or anxiety. However, if the victim wishes to continue the relationship, then complete forgiveness replaces the negative emotions and goes on to build back a net positive emotional, affective stance. It is important to note that decisional and emotional forgiveness are two different phenomena, not two halves of the same phenomenon.

Reconciliation, which is the restoration of trust in a relationship, is generally thought to be distinct from forgiving.[3] It is interpersonal rather than intrapersonal. Likewise, communicating about transgressions must also be distinguished from forgiving. The need to make such distinctions is seen by imagining how one might forgive but not say so because by not saying 'I forgive you,' the silent forgiver can manipulate the offender with guilt. Dispositional *forgivingness,* one's tendency to be forgiving, is a somewhat stable tendency to forgive across time and situations.

C. The Value of Forgiveness in Religions

The psychological study of forgiveness and religion began by focusing on which religion was the most forgiving. Research has generally shown that religious people are more forgiving than non-religious ones. Additionally, Christians usually report being more forgiving than people who adhere to the other major religions.[4] Let us note, however, two points in qualification. (1) Although all major religions consider forgiveness a virtue, not all religions value forgiveness equally in their hierarchical ordering of virtues as has been described in one source in which various authors described forgiveness from their own religious points of view.[5] (2) Some people might believe that unilateral and unconditional forgiveness often allows harm and is not virtuous. Thus, rather than comparing which religions promote forgiveness rigidly across situations and relationships, it is more important to consider how religions may influence when and how a person forgives. Researchers have strived to define how the different religions understand forgiveness.[6] We offer a caveat about our generalizations to follow. Each religion has many ways of characterizing forgiveness, and we are merely drawing from prominent spokespeople to summarize some major positions.

In Christianity, forgiveness is encouraged and even required by the religion and should be undertaken unilaterally, regardless of the interpersonal context. It is informative to note that there are many different Christian theologies – just as there are many theologies within each of the major religions below. The Christian's response is supposed to be the same: a decision to forgive that one hopes will soon be followed by emotional forgiveness regardless of whether the offender apologizes, offers restitution, or makes an effort to repent.

Most Jewish theologians understand forgiveness as contextualized to relationships in which the offender repents or returns to the path of God (i.e., *tsheuvah*). Forgiveness is conditioned on the offender's *tsheuvah* and is required of a victim if the latter has been convinced of the offender's repentance. Note that the Jew may choose to forgive even without offender repentance, but is not obligated to do so.

Like Christianity and Judaism, Islam is characterized by a variety of interpretations of both Qur'an and Hadith. In Islam, forgiveness is a virtue, and God's character includes forgivingness. Thus, in most theological interpretations, forgiveness is seen as desirable though strict recompense for an injury is allowed. Forgiveness is seen, however, as a way to avoid unfair recompense remuneration for harm (which would exceed allowable recompense compensation, or justice). Thus, forgiveness is encouraged.

In Hinduism, many models for forgiveness exist. Forgiveness derives from a balance of *dharma* (i.e., sacred duty) and *karma* (i.e., immutable justice). If one pursues dharma diligently, one's karma will result in ultimate reward. If one fails at dharma, one's karma will result in ultimate degradation. Forgiveness is part of dharma. However, justice also cannot be simply put aside.

In Buddhism, there is no word for forgiveness. Two major strains of Buddhism exist. In one, compassion is one's ultimate duty, and being compassionate will inevitably lead to experiencing what in a different philosophical or religious system would be called forgiveness. In strains of Buddhism that favour detachment, forgiveness would be inherent in gaining an enlightened detachment. Thus, one would not respond to transgression with violence.

D. Summary

Although most religions value the virtue of forgiveness, they conceptualize it in nuanced ways that place differential emphasis on its importance. Accordingly, individuals may draw from their cherished religious beliefs to shape their understanding of and engagement in forgiveness. The horserace question of which religion is 'best' at promoting forgiveness has been settled; more exciting, and potentially enlightening, questions should be aimed at understanding how religious beliefs shape forgiveness experiences.

2. Hypocrisy: Are Religious People as Forgiving as They Describe Themselves?

A. A Research Review Ends the Horserace Question and Introduces Another

In 1999, McCullough and Worthington reviewed the empirical research on forgiveness and religion,[7] and concluded that religious people, particularly those who highly value forgiveness were more forgiving than were non-religious people. However, they focused on something curious. Religious people consistently described their personal stance as forgiving, which in psychology is called a trait. Yet when empirical studies measured individual transgressions, religious people who described themselves as highly trait-forgiving were sometimes not found to forgive individual transgressions, also called state forgiveness, significantly more than non-religious individuals low in trait-forgiveness.

The relationship between religion and trait forgivingness was consistently positive (about $r \sim .4$), whereas only some studies found a positive relationship between religion and state forgiveness (about $r \sim .2$).[8] This suggests that religious people might be hypocritical. They report that they are more forgiving, but they may not forgive actual transgressions much more than non-religious people do. In addition to this explanation, McCullough and Worthington suggested four other possible reasons for the discrepancy: small effect size hypothesis, social desirability hypothesis, level of specificity hypothesis, and the recall bias hypothesis.

A first reason why religion may be inconsistently related to state forgiveness is that, even in religious individuals, religion may not always be important in the causal chain of events leading to forgiveness. A variety of contextual factors such as apology, restitution, the victim's relationship with the offender, may overshadow or moderate any observed relationship between religion and state forgiveness. Social psychological research has long pointed toward the importance of situation factors in predicting behaviour. More salient contextual factors may reduce the relative importance of religion in affecting forgiveness experiences in certain circumstances, perhaps, in part, because of the small effect of religion on forgiveness.

Second, highly religious people tend to value forgiveness more than less religious people. Personal valuing of the virtue of forgiveness may influence self-reports of one's trait of forgivingness (i.e., over-reporting one's enduring disposition toward being forgiving) more than self-reports of state forgiveness (i.e., actual forgiveness toward a specific offence at a given moment in time). Thus, pressure to appear socially desirable may motivate religious individuals to report that they had more forgiving dispositions.

Third, as a general measurement principle, constructs tend to correlate more strongly when they are measured at the same level of specificity. Tsang et al. showed indirect evidence for this hypothesis.[9] In their first study, there was no relationship between trait religiosity and state forgiveness. However, in their second study, they used an aggregate of ratings from six transgressions to measure trait forgivingness. Thus both religiosity and forgiveness were measured as traits. In this case, they observed a correlation between trait religiosity and trait forgivingness ~ r = .20. Thus, imprecision in measurement approaches may account for the discrepancy.

Fourth, the method used to study forgiveness of actual offences may be prone to recall bias. Namely, participants are typically asked to recall a specific hurt or offence. Given the phrasing, 'hurt or offence,' participants may tend to think of unforgiven offences more frequently than forgiven offences. Thus, any actual differences in forgiveness between more religious people and less religious people may be obscured by recall bias. Tsang et al. also showed indirect support for the recall bias hypothesis. In their third study, they asked people to recall an offence which occurred within the last two months. They reasoned that restricting the time period of an offence would limit the influence of recall bias. As predicted, they found a moderate relationship between religiosity and state forgiveness, which was not found in their first study when they did not restrict recall.[10]

B. A Meta-Analysis of Forgiveness and Religion

Since 1999, numerous studies have investigated forgiveness and religion. A recent meta-analysis, a review of the literature that quantifies findings on a standardized metric, called *d*, conducted by Davis et al. addressed these hypotheses regarding the relationship between religion and forgiveness.[11]

A meta-analysis changes individuals' scores on religious or spiritual measures and on forgiveness or forgivingness measures to standard scores. A standard score tells how many standard deviations away from the mean is each person's score. Thus, studies can be analysed regardless of what specific measures were used for religion or spirituality or for forgiveness or forgivingness. This powerful tool allows many diverse studies to be analysed together, and variables such as the presence or absence of an apology or personality differences can be coded and analysed to see whether studies using different variables result in different outcomes.

C. Method

Davis et al. included studies in the meta-analysis if the study reported (a) a sample size and (b) the correlations between R/S and trait forgivingness, state forgiveness, or self-forgiveness. If the study did not report a correlation between R/S and forgiveness, these correlations were estimated through calculations of the *p* or *t* values that were reported. Alternatively, the study author was contacted to provide the correlation coefficients.

A large number of R/S measures have been developed. In their review, Davis et al. grouped R/S measures according to whether they assess trait constructs that tend to be fairly stable over time, such as religious commitment, God image, attachment to God, or according to whether they assess state constructs that might change time to time, such as a victim's appraisal that a transgression destroyed something sacred. Common measures of trait forgivingness, state forgiveness, and self-forgiveness were included.

Davis et al. searched data bases, examined reference pages of articles, and contacted authors of studies for file-draw studies and bibliographies. They found 54 independent samples on R/S and trait forgivingness, 47 independent samples on R/S and state forgivingness, and 19 independent samples on R/S and self-forgivingness that met inclusion criteria.

D. Results

As a result for studies examining the relationship between religion and trait forgivingness, the total number of participants from the 54 samples was 11,280. The overall effect size, denoted by *d*, was .30. The 95% confidence interval did not contain zero, indicating that the effect is reliable at the 95% confidence level.

For studies examining the relationship between religion and state forgiveness, the total number of participants from the 47 samples was 8,616. The overall *d* was .20 for forgiving an event (95% CI: .15 to .24). Note that the *d* with state forgiveness was slightly less than the *d* for trait forgivingness (.20 versus .30). State measures of R/S predicted forgiveness of a specific event (*d* = .37) better than did trait measures of R/S (*d* = .15), supporting the level of specificity hypothesis. On the other hand, in studies examining the relationship between R/S and self-forgiveness, the total number of participants from the 19 samples was 2,898. The overall *d* was .08, but the 95% confidence interval contained zero, indicating that there was no reliable connection between R/S and self-forgiveness.

In summary, McCullough and Worthington qualitatively reviewed a small number of studies relative to the 54 available to Davis et al. in 2010. McCullough and Worthington found a .20 difference in size of correlation between R/S and trait forgivingness (.4) and R/S and state forgiveness (.2). In Davis et al.'s meta-analysis, the difference was .1. Thus, the cause for concern over a hypocrisy effect was smaller than McCullough and Worthington estimated. Furthermore, there was some evidence that the level of specificity hypothesis might account for some of that discrepancy.

E. Summary

Because religions value forgiveness, albeit differently. One would expect a strong connection between religiousness and forgiveness. When an initial review of the research suggested potential hypocrisy among religious individuals (i.e., they reported being more forgiving in general but not when asked about actual offences), there was cause for concern. However, the more recent meta-analysis suggested that this apparent hypocrisy might merely be an artefact of methodological imprecision: the level of measurement specificity may have produced what looked like religious individuals over-reporting forgiveness tendencies and under-reporting actual forgiveness. As future researchers more finely tune their measurement approaches, they can turn toward perhaps the most pressing question in the relationship between forgiveness and religion yet proposed: how do religious beliefs shape the experience of forgiveness?

3. High-Energy Atom Smashers: The Need for More Detailed Analyses of the Relationships among Variables

After addressing the previous two questions, the field must turn its attention to new questions. The metaphor we suggest is the CERN particle accelerator. High-energy beams of particles are hurled at each other to try and uncover the basic particles that are the glue holding protons and neutrons together. Similarly, we suggest that within the study of forgiveness and religion, attention must now be turned to the relationships among the variables that hold these constructs together. What, then, are the new interesting questions about forgiveness and religion? We offer the following: (1) How do religion and spirituality specifically act to promote or inhibit forgiveness? (2) How can forgiveness among groups with different religious and spiritual identities promote more peace?

The answers to these questions, we believe, will almost certainly come about by understanding forgiveness in a relational context. We treat spirituality as a dynamic relationship with whatever one considers to be sacred. We explore how this *relational spirituality,* which we define as one's experience of relationship, closeness, intimacy, or connection with the Sacred, affects forgiveness.[12] Rather than making generalizations among different religious groups, we have begun to examine what kinds of spiritual experience, within people who are religious or spiritual, can help or hinder forgiveness.[13]

A. A Model of Relational Spirituality

Our model of relational spirituality and forgiveness describes three spiritual appraisals that a victim may make in the aftermath of a transgression. The model acknowledges that each offence has four main components: (a) the victim, (b) the offender, (c) the transgression, and (d) the Sacred. Both the victim's and the offender's perspective of the relationships among these features have important implications for forgiveness. We have developed measures of the individual and relationship variables that will facilitate the study of this model, such as viewing the offender as spiritually similar, the transgression as a desecration, or one's sense of connection with the Sacred.[14] Although we cover this topic in greater detail elsewhere, we provide a brief overview of the relationships entailed in the model below.[15]

B. The Victim

Several dispositional variables have been found to predict whether people will forgive, and many of these are highly associated with religion or spirituality. Let us consider some examples. Charlotte Witvliet, in this volume, discusses individual differences in self-control, rumination, gratitude, and altruism as personal characteristics that can affect forgiveness. Richard Rye for his part considers different coping strategies after a transgression as variables affecting forgiveness. Steven Sandage and Peter Jankowski examine how well a person is differentiated psychologically as a variable that influences forgiveness. We suggest that the victim's humility, which may be related to his/her religious beliefs, may affect whether he/she can forgive.[16] Furthermore, we suspect that differences among cultures may affect the victim's experience of forgiveness. For example, in individualistic Western societies such as the United States of America, forgiveness is positively related to self-esteem.[17] However, in collectivistic Eastern societies, such as the People's Republic of China, forgiveness and self-esteem are unrelated.[18] Thus, individual differences in the victim, even those which operate at a societal level, can alter how they perceive and experience forgiveness.

C. The Offender

The offender also affects the victim's level of forgiveness. Some offenders might be easier for the victim to forgive than others, for a number of reasons. For example, offenders who are contrite and humble may be more easily forgiven than those who are arrogant and narcissistic.[19] In our model of forgiveness and relational spirituality, we attend to the victim's perception of the offender, rather than the offender's self-construal. Thus, other event-related variables, such as the perceived culpability of the offender and the manner in which the offender was perceived to apologize and perhaps to ask for forgiveness can affect forgiveness. Other views consider apology or its lack as a condition related to forgiving. Finally, the perceptions of the offender's personality characteristics, can also affect the likelihood of victim experiencing forgiveness.

D. The Transgression

The specific aspects of the transgression exert considerable influence on whether or not the victim may forgive. For example, transgressions that are perceived by victims as avoidable, hurtful, intentional, severe, or resulting in long-lasting or permanent harm may be particularly difficult to forgive.[20] Moreover, if the transgression was similar to a wrongdoing that the victim has committed in the past, the victim is more likely to forgive his or her current transgressor.[21] This suggests that the transgression itself might affect forgiveness.

E. The Sacred

The inclusion of perceptions of the Sacred, as well as the relationship between the Sacred and the victim, offender, and transgression, is part of what makes this model unique. Considering an additional component in forgiveness processes allows for spiritual concepts to be incorporated into traditional frameworks of forgiveness models. Conceptualizations of the Sacred, which we describe as the object or being that is central to a person's experience of spirituality (i.e., God, ultimate truth), can also predict one's potential to offer forgiveness of offences, as well. Individual perceptions of the nature or character of the Sacred affect the experience and likelihood of forgiveness. Previous research revealed how people view the Sacred affects whether they feel anger towards the Sacred and eventually forgive the offender, an aspect Exline discusses at length in this volume.[22] Viewing the Sacred as active rather than passive may make the victim more likely to draw support from the Sacred. Moreover, the victim's religious beliefs about forgiveness affect events following an offence. For example, research has demonstrated that religious beliefs promoting unconditional forgiveness predict differences in forgiveness between Jews and Christians.[23] Thus, the victim's ideas about what the Sacred is like can certainly affect how he or she experiences forgiveness.

F. Exploring the Interrelations among these Features

Perhaps the most appealing and powerful feature of the model of relational spirituality is its consideration of the relationships among the four features: the victim, the offender, the transgression, and the Sacred. These relationships can be conceptualized from the point of view of either the victim or the offender. To illustrate each relationship, we focus on how the victim perceives these spiritual relationships. These relationships can also be perceived by the offender. The *Victim-Sacred relationship* refers to how the victim views his or her own relationship with the Sacred (e.g., sense of closeness, anger at God). The *Offender-Sacred relationship* refers to how the victim views the offender's relationship with the Sacred (e.g., viewing the offender as spiritually similar or different). The *Transgression-Sacred relationship* refers to how the victim imagines the Sacred's stance towards the transgression (e.g., viewing the transgression as evil or the defilement or desecration of something Sacred). Although these represent only a fraction of the possible relationships in the model, they readily demonstrate how flexible and useful this approach can be.

G. Looking Ahead: The Future Research on Religion and Forgiveness

We briefly explained how two questions that had previously dominated the field, such as which religion was 'best' at offering forgiveness and whether religious people are hypocritical when it comes to forgiveness, but these are no longer pressing questions among researchers and have largely been settled. We suggest, rather that future research examine the specific components of religion (and spirituality) and forgiveness in order to further advance the field of inquiry. Toward that end, we contend that the relational model of spirituality and forgiveness is a useful paradigm for catalyzing research. Accordingly, we propose several pressing questions for future research.

First, how does spirituality affect forgiveness? Earlier, we described four types of spirituality, suggesting that the study of religion in isolation, without examining other types of spirituality in parallel, will provide only a partial account of the relationship between the Sacred and forgiveness. Many people are spiritual but do not ascribe to a particular religion. Future research should explore how these different types of spirituality (including religious spirituality) affect forgiveness processes. In doing so, research would capture a fuller and more complete picture of the dynamic relationship between these types of beliefs and experiences and the process of forgiveness.

Second, what types of religious beliefs help or hinder forgiveness? Drawing on the model of relational spirituality, we posit that there are situations in which one's spirituality and religious beliefs may help forgiveness (e.g., viewing forgiveness as a religious mandate; superordinate prioritization of forgiveness as a chief virtue) and times when they may hinder forgiveness (e.g., viewing the offence as a desecration; holding a grudge against God). Further research should explore these interactions, rather than simply rely on 'main effect' (e.g., religion is always helpful) hypotheses. In addition, examining how religious beliefs may help or hinder forgiveness at a group or societal level has both theoretical and practical appeal, and it warrants effort by future researchers.

Third, how can forgiveness change religious beliefs? Most research has assumed a prescribed directionality between religion and forgiveness, presuming that the former causes (or, at least, predicts) the latter. But are there conditions in which one's forgiveness, or lack of forgiveness, might change their religious beliefs? What if a loved one withholds forgiveness and dies before amends are made? Might that change one's view of God or the Sacred? Similarly, might receiving forgiveness for an egregious wrong make people more likely to explore their own religious and spiritual beliefs? Future work should investigate the potential bi-directionality between forgiveness and religion.

H. Summary

Research on religion and forgiveness is becoming increasingly more complex, which is important for advancing this area of inquiry. Future research must turn attention toward understanding the central components of religious experiences and forgiveness processes. Adopting a model of relational spirituality is one fruitful approach. By understanding the dynamic relationship between the victim, offender, transgression, and the Sacred, research can more fully understand, predict, and promote forgiveness experiences. Moreover, future research must address spirituality (in addition to religion), explore the specific situational features of an event that are related to greater or less forgiveness, and work toward understanding the interactive nature of forgiveness and religion.

4. Conclusion

Science is advanced by incorporating diverse, yet complementary perspectives to fully describe the rich nature of a phenomenon. Our approach to forgiveness has been informed by, and hopefully informs, other approaches in this volume and the preceding e-book. By attending to the other authors, we see the possibilities that recent experimental work by a variety of psychologists, such as Witvliet, Rye, Sandage and Jankowski, Exline, and perhaps our own, might inform some of the definitional inquiries from disciplines like theology, philosophy, and literature. On the other hand, we appreciate the rich and nuanced studies through literature, philosophy, theology, and even less quantitatively oriented psychological approaches. These approaches highlight additional new and essential research questions for quantitative psychological researchers to consider.

In this chapter, we have suggested that the question of which religion or spirituality forgives the 'best,' which characterizes the horserace mentality, is dead. A more interesting question might be: how do religious groups fluidly shift their emphasis on forgiveness to adapt to their current social context? We also drew the conclusion that the question of whether religious people are hypocritical in their reporting of forgiveness is less of a problem than originally thought. Finally, we suggested that simply correlating measures of religion with measures of trait or event-specific forgiveness is also an exercise without much future, and similar to operations of an atom-smasher, we need to uncover the elemental features of how forgiveness and religion are related. We proposed that forgiveness needs to be studied in a more nuanced way, and suggested the study of relational spirituality and forgiveness as one way this might be done. We believe that the future of research on religion and forgiveness will be at this intersection.

Notes

[1] Everett L. Worthington, Jr., ed., *Handbook of Forgiveness* (New York: Brunner-Routledge, 2005), 4.

[2] Everett L. Worthington, Jr., *Forgiveness and Reconciliation: Theory and Application* (New York: Brunner-Routledge, 2006), 25.

[3] Ibid.

[4] Michael E. McCullough and Everett L. Worthington, Jr., 'Religion and the Forgiving Personality', *Journal of Personality* 67 (1999): 1145.

[5] Mark S. Rye, et al., 'Religious Perspectives on Forgiveness', in *Forgiveness: Research, Theory, and Practice*, ed. Michael E. McCullough, Kenneth I. Pargament and Carl E. Thoresen (New York: Guilford Press, 2000), 17.

[6] Ibid.

[7] McCullough and Worthington, 1999, 1151.

[8] Ibid.

[9] Jo-Ann Tsang, Michael E. McCullough and William T. Hoyt, 'Psychometric and Rationalization Accounts for the Religion-Forgiveness Discrepancy', *Journal of Social Issues* 61 (2005): 795.

[10] Ibid.

[11] Don E. Davis, Everett L. Worthington, Jr. and Joshua N. Hook, 'Meta-Analytic Review of Research on Forgiveness and Religion/Spirituality', Manuscript under editorial review, 2010.

[12] F. LeRon Shults and Steven J. Sandage, *Transforming Spirituality: Integrating Theology and Psychology* (Grand Rapids, MI: Baker Academic, 2006), 25.

[13] Everett L. Worthington, Jr., *A Just Forgiveness: Responsible Healing without Excusing Injustice* (Downers Grove, IL: InterVarsity Press, 2009), 73; Don E. Davis, Everett L. Worthington, Jr. and Joshua N. Hook, 'Relational Spirituality and Forgiveness: The Roles of Attachment to God, Religious Coping, and Viewing the Transgression as a Desecration', *Journal of Psychology and Christianity* 27 (2008): 293.

[14] Don E. Davis, Everett L. Worthington, Jr., Joshua N. Hook, Daryl R. Van Tongeren, Jeffery D. Green and David J. Jennings, II, 'Assessing a Victim's Understanding of an Offender's Spirituality: Development of the Spiritual View of the Offender Scale', *Psychology of Religion and Spirituality* 1 (2009): 249.

[15] Everett L. Worthington, Jr., et al., 'Religion, Spirituality and Forgiveness', in *Handbook of Religion and Spirituality*, 2nd ed., ed. Ray F. Paloutzian and Crystal L. Park (New York: Guilford Press: under review).

[16] Wade C. Rowatt, Christie Powers, Valerie Targhetta, Jessamy Comer, Stephanie Kennedy and Jordan Labouff, 'Development and Initial Validation of an Implicit Measure of Humility Relative to Arrogance', *Journal of Positive Psychology* 1 (2006): 198.

[17] Laura B. Luchies, Eli J. Finkel, James K. McNulty and Madoka Kumashiro, 'The Doormat Effect: When Forgiving Erodes Self-Respect and Self-Concept Clarity', *Journal of Personality and Social Psychology* 98 (2010): 735.

[18] Hong Fu, David Watkins and Eadaoin K.P. Hui, 'Personality Correlates of the Disposition towards Interpersonal Forgiveness: A Chinese Perspective', *International Journal of Psychology* 39 (2004): 312.

[19] Julie J. Exline, Roy F. Baumeister, Brad J. Bushman, W. Keith Campbell and Eli J. Finkel, 'Too Proud to Let Go: Narcissistic Entitlement as a Barrier to Forgiveness', *Journal of Personality and Social Psychology* 87 (2004): 909.

[20] Jeanne S. Zechmeister and Catherine Romero, 'Victim and Offender Accounts of Interpersonal Conflict: Autobiographical Narratives of Forgiveness and Unforgiveness,' *Journal of Personality and Social Psychology* 82 (2002): 680.

[21] Julie J. Exline, Roy F. Baumeister, Anne L. Zell, Amy J. Kraft and Charlotte V. O. Witvliet, 'Not So Innocent: Does Seeing One's Own Capability for Wrongdoing Predict Forgiveness?' *Journal of Personality and Social Psychology* 94 (2008): 506.

[22] Julie J. Exline, Crystal L. Park, Joshua M. Smyth and Michael P. Carey, 'Anger toward God: Five Foundational Studies Emphasizing Predictors, Doubts about God's Existence, and Adjustment to Bereavement and Cancer,' *Journal of Personality and Social Psychology* 100 (2011): 143.

[23] Adam B. Cohen, Ariel Malka, Paul Rozin and Lina Cherfas, 'Religion and Unforgivable Offences,' *Journal of Personality* 74 (2006): 89.

Bibliography

Cohen, Adam B., Ariel Malka, Paul Rozin and Lina Cherfas. 'Religion and Unforgivable Offences'. *Journal of Personality* 74 (2006): 85-117.

Davis, Don E., Everett L. Worthington, Jr. and Joshua N. Hook. 'Meta-Analytic Review of Research on Forgiveness and Religion/Spirituality'. Manuscript under editorial review (2010).

Davis, Don E., Everett L. Worthington, Jr. and Joshua N. Hook. 'Relational Spirituality and Forgiveness: The Roles of Attachment to God, Religious Coping, and Viewing the Transgression as a Desecration'. *Journal of Psychology and Christianity* 27 (2008): 293-301.

Davis, Don E., Everett L. Worthington, Jr., Joshua N. Hook, Daryl R. Van Tongeren, Jeffery D. Green and David J. Jennings, II. 'Assessing a Victim's Understanding of an Offender's Spirituality: Development of the Spiritual View of the Offender Scale'. *Psychology of Religion and Spirituality* 1 (2009): 249-262.

Exline, Julie J., Crystal L. Park, Joshua M. Smyth and Michael P. Carey. 'Anger toward God: Five Foundational Studies Emphasising Predictors, Doubts about God's Existence, and Adjustment to Bereavement and Cancer'. *Journal of Personality and Social Psychology* 100 (2011): 129-148.

Exline, Julie J., Roy F. Baumeister, Anne L. Zell, Amy J. Kraft and Charlotte V.O. Witvliet. 'Not So Innocent: Does Seeing One's Own Capability for Wrongdoing Predict Forgiveness?' *Journal of Personality and Social Psychology* 94 (2008): 495-515.

Exline, Julie J., Roy F. Baumeister, Brad J. Bushman, W. Keith Campbell and Eli J. Finkel. 'Too Proud to Let Go: Narcissistic Entitlement as a Barrier to Forgiveness'. *Journal of Personality and Social Psychology* 87 (2004): 894-912.

Fu, Hong, David Watkins and Eadaoin K.P. Hui. 'Personality Correlates of the Disposition towards Interpersonal Forgiveness: A Chinese Perspective'. *International Journal of Psychology* 39 (2004): 305-316.

Luchies, Laura B., Eli J. Finkel, James K. McNulty and Madoka Kumashiro. 'The Doormat Effect: When Forgiving Erodes Self-Respect and Self-Concept Clarity'. *Journal of Personality and Social Psychology* 98 (2010): 734-749.

McCullough, Michael E. and Everett L. Worthington, Jr. 'Religion and the Forgiving Personality'. *Journal of Personality* 67 (1999): 1141-1164.

Rowatt, Wade C., Christie Powers, Valerie Targhetta, Jessamy Comer, Stephanie Kennedy and Jordan Labouff. 'Development and Initial Validation of an Implicit Measure of Humility Relative to Arrogance'. *Journal of Positive Psychology* 1 (2006): 198-211.

Rye, Mark S., Kenneth I. Pargament, Ali M. Amir, Guy L. Beck, Elliot N. Dorff, Charles Hallisey, Narayanan V. Vashudha and James G. Williams. 'Religious Perspectives on Forgiveness'. In *Forgiveness: Research, Theory, and Practice*, edited by Michael E. McCullough, Kenneth I. Pargament and Carl E. Thoresen, 17-40, New York: Guilford Press, 2000.

Shults, F. LeRon and Steven J. Sandage. *Transforming Spirituality: Integrating Theology and Psychology*. Grand Rapids, MI: Baker Academic, 2006.

Tsang, Jo-Ann, Michael E. McCullough and William T. Hoyt. 'Psychometric and Rationalization Accounts for the Religion-Forgiveness Discrepancy'. *Journal of Social Issues* 61 (2005): 785-805.

Worthington, Jr., Everett L. ed. *Handbook of Forgiveness*. New York: Brunner-Routledge, 2005.

————. *A Just Forgiveness: Responsible Healing Without Excusing Injustice.* Downers Grove, IL: InterVarsity Press, 2009.

————. *Forgiveness and Reconciliation: Theory and Application.* New York: Brunner-Routledge, 2006.

Worthington, Everett L. Jr., Don E. Davis, Joshua N. Hook, Daryl R. Van Tongeren, Aubrey L. Gartner, David J. Jennings, II., Chelsea L. Greer and Yin Lin. 'Religion and Spirituality and Forgiveness'. In *Handbook of Religion and Spirituality*, 2nd ed., edited by Ray F. Paloutzian and Crystal L. Park, under review. New York: Guilford Press.

Zechmeister, Jeanne S. and Catherine Romero. 'Victim and Offender Accounts of Interpersonal Conflict: Autobiographical Narratives of Forgiveness and Unforgiveness'. *Journal of Personality and Social Psychology* 82 (2002): 675-686.

Daryl R. Van Tongeren is a doctoral candidate in Social Psychology in the Department of Psychology at Virginia Commonwealth University. He studies meaning in life, religion, relational humility, forgiveness and reconciliation, and positive psychology.

Everett L. Worthington, Jr. is Professor of Psychology at Virginia Commonwealth University. He studies forgiveness and reconciliation, virtues, marriage and couple enrichment, and religion/spirituality.

Don E. Davis is a doctoral candidate in Counselling Psychology in the Department of Psychology at Virginia Commonwealth University. He studies relational humility, forgiveness and reconciliation, and positive psychology.

Joshua N. Hook is Assistant Professor of Psychology at the University of North Texas. He studies forgiveness, humility, sexuality, couple counselling, and religion/spirituality.

Aubrey L. Gartner is a doctoral candidate in Counselling Psychology in the Department of Psychology at Virginia Commonwealth University. She studies mercy, accepting forgiveness, reconciliative processes, and virtues.

David J. Jennings II is a doctoral student in Counselling Psychology in the Department of Psychology at Virginia Commonwealth University. He studies communication processes around forgiveness, reconciliative processes, and virtues.

Chelsea L. Greer is a doctoral student in Counselling Psychology in the Department of Psychology at Virginia Commonwealth University. She studies forgiveness, religious groups, organisational psychology, and virtues.

Todd W. Greer is a doctoral student in the Organizational Leadership in the School of Global Studies and Entrepreneurship at Regent University. He studies organisational psychology, organisational virtues, and forgiveness and reconciliation in organisations.

Anger toward God: A New Frontier in the Study of Forgiveness

Julie J. Exline

Abstract
In situations involving suffering, people often experience anger focused on God or a Higher Power. Psychology research suggests that anger toward God has many parallels with interpersonal anger both in terms of predictors and links with other emotional states. As such, the resolution of anger toward God has some parallels with interpersonal forgiveness. Yet the idea of a relationship with God raises unique complexities based on the 'virtual' nature of a relationship with an unseen deity and the attributes commonly ascribed to God within monotheism (e.g., holiness, omnipotence). Assessment of anger toward God can be difficult because people often see such feelings as morally wrong and may be reluctant to acknowledge them. When people reveal to others that they are angry at God, those receiving supportive responses tend to report increased faith and approach tendencies toward God, whereas those receiving unsupportive responses are more likely to suppress their anger, remain angry, use drugs or alcohol to cope, and exit the relationship with God. Several studies have shown that some non-believers report anger around the idea of God, either as part of their own personal history or when prompted to focus on a hypothetical image of God; thus non-believers should not be automatically excluded from conversations about anger involving God. Although formal intervention research has not yet been conducted, preliminary work suggests several potentially helpful strategies for managing anger toward God: increased awareness of one's anger and its possible causes, inspection of one's images and attributions about God, and imagery exercises that focus on open and positive exchanges involving God (or one's image of God). Theologically-based ways to resolve anger toward God, though perhaps helpful for some, introduce risks if they suggest insensitivity to a person's belief system or if they are offered prematurely as 'quick fixes' to those in crisis.

Key Words: Anger, God, spirituality, religion, struggle, atheism, imagery, forgiveness, monotheism, prayer.

*****

1. Overview of Chapter

The aim of this chapter is to give a brief introduction to recent psychological work on the topic of anger toward God. Although the idea that people can experience anger toward God is certainly not new within literary and religious writings, it is relatively new within psychology. The chapter will begin by describing the concept of anger toward God and comparing it with interpersonal anger. Next will be a brief discussion of some challenging issues surrounding the assessment of anger toward God, followed by suggestions of techniques that may help people resolve this type of anger.

2. The Phenomenon of Anger toward God

On the surface, the idea of anger toward God might seem to make sense only in religious systems that believe in one God – especially a personal God who interacts directly with human beings and can have a two-way relationship with them. In other words, anger toward God might seem to fit only within systems that use a relational form of spirituality, as described by Worthington et al.[1]

Individuals do seem to have an easier time reflecting on the idea of anger toward God when they see God in personal, relational terms. Yet, it is important to note that the topic of anger toward God may be relevant for people in many faith traditions including those that do not use a relational model of spirituality. What if a person sees God as an impersonal energy force, for example? Recent research in psychology clarifies that people can experience anger toward impersonal forces such as tornadoes or cancer cells, suggesting the possibility of anger toward an impersonal divine force.[2] Or consider these non-Judeo-Christian possibilities: a pantheist might experience anger at the universe, whereas a polytheist could switch allegiances from one god to another. Thus, even though most of the new research described here focuses on Western, Judeo-Christian samples that hold a personal view of God, the possibility of anger toward God within other belief systems should not be automatically ruled out.

One premise of this work is that people often experience the same types of emotions toward God that they experience toward other people. On the bright side, a perceived relationship with God might help to meet needs for closeness and attachment.[3] People might also see God as a divine protector who will take care of them. Seeing oneself as being in relationship with a benevolent God might also inspire people to be more forgiving, as described in Worthington et al's chapter.[4] Yet perceived relationships with God also carry the possibility of negative emotions such as anger, which will be the focus here.

In our research, we have typically framed anger toward God as a response to negative life events, especially those related to suffering and unfairness. When something painful happens and a person views God as being at least partly responsible, negative emotions can arise that are centred on God. We will focus primarily on anger here for the sake of brevity; however, it is important to note that the constellation of associated negative emotions can be quite varied. For example, people who see God as responsible for causing harm might experience emotions ranging from annoyance to mistrust to rage. When people believe that God is failing to intervene in an important situation, their emotional experiences might take the form of impatience or frustration. Some might also feel abandoned or rejected by God, triggering responses related to shame and loss. One can easily see the parallel with interpersonal relationships here: When people experience hurts or offenses at the hands of others, they can experience a wide range of emotions in response. However, this volume focuses on forgiveness, which typically focuses on managing emotions related to anger; this chapter will therefore emphasize anger and closely related emotional states that are focused on God, or the idea of God.

Events that trigger anger toward God include some that do not seem to involve human action, such as deaths, natural disasters, and accidents. However, a much wider range of life events seem to be capable of triggering anger toward God, even those for which some blame might readily be assigned to human action, or inaction. For example, people may get angry at God for allowing interpersonal suffering, which could range from romantic breakups to parental abandonment to wartime atrocities. Here the triggering thought might be, 'Why didn't God intervene to stop this person (or this group of people)?' Other individuals might become embittered in response to prayers for divine healing or help that seem to go unanswered. People may also become angry at God when they experience personal failures and disappointments. For example, people might see God as partly responsible for their loss of employment, an injury that stopped participation in sports, or failure of an academic class.

Another possibility, one that we are just beginning to explore, is that people may become angry at God for making them (or others) in a certain way – a way that has made them vulnerable to a certain behaviour seen as morally wrong, personally destructive, or socially unacceptable. For instance, one man might blame God for his genetic predisposition toward alcoholism, while another might see God as responsible for his sexual attraction to other men or to children. Here the logic might look like this: 'It's not entirely my fault that I think or behave in this way. Perhaps it's also God's fault for giving me this genetic predisposition.'

In terms of its psychological predictors, anger toward God tends to parallel interpersonal anger. For example, anger toward God tends to be greater when harm is severe; when it is difficult to find any sense of meaning in a negative event; when God's intentions are seen as cruel, and when commitment to the relationship (in this case, framed as religious commitment) is low prior to the negative event.[5] These same factors tend to increase anger and grudge-holding between individuals.

Our research suggests that many people experience anger toward God at least occasionally.[6] For example, a 1988 national survey in the United States showed that sixty two per cent of respondents reported that they were sometimes angry at God. However, very frequent anger toward God was rare, being reported by only two and a half percent of respondents.[7] Studies of undergraduates reveal that anger toward God is often reported; yet the anger is usually at low levels of intensity, with positive emotion toward God clearly predominating.[8] Positive and negative emotions toward God typically show only moderate negative correlations,[9] indicating partial independence.[10] In other words, positive emotions such as love and respect toward God do not necessarily rule out the possibility of anger, nor does the presence of anger mean that positive emotions are erased. Again, consider the parallel with interpersonal relationships: individuals can become angry at family members or close friends even when they care deeply about them.

Initial studies suggest some demographic differences as well. Within our United States samples, older participants, Protestant, and/or African American reported less anger toward God on average than members of other groups.[11] Also, within these predominantly Christian samples, greater religiosity was associated with lower reports of anger toward God. Closer inspection revealed that religiosity was actually linked with greater odds of seeing God as responsible for negative events, due largely to an associated belief in divine intervention; yet religious people tended to frame God's role in a positive light, seeing God's intentions as kind and not cruel.[12] By making benevolent attributions about God's intent, highly religious people could see God as playing some role in causing or allowing suffering without getting angry at God.

3. How Might Anger toward God Differ from Interpersonal Anger?

Much of the emphasis here is on demonstrating ways that anger toward God is similar to interpersonal anger. However, some important caveats also warrant mention. One factor is that most people do not report having seen, heard, or otherwise experienced God directly using their physical senses. Thus, people may find themselves engaged in what seems to be a virtual relationship: They cannot see or hear their relational partner, and they may even have doubts about whether the partner exists. Other differences centre on people's beliefs about the nature of God. Many people view God as being holy – that is, perfectly righteous and incapable of wrongdoing. In addition, if people see God as all-powerful and all-knowing, they may believe that God has no limitations and does not make errors.

Because of these differences between human relationships and perceived relationships with God, many of the tools that can help people resolve interpersonal anger may not apply directly to anger toward God. For example, one cannot expect God to apologize or offer an explanation, and these types of conciliatory actions often facilitate forgiveness.[13] In addition, many forgiveness techniques focus on empathy, an attempt to take another person's point of view.[14] But how would empathy be remotely possible with God, especially if God is seen as all-knowing, all-powerful, and omnipresent. Other forgiveness techniques encourage people to focus on the idea that all human beings share personal flaws and moral limitations,[15] and this is another strategy that would not work when focusing on a holy and unlimited deity. Finally, because many people see God as being morally perfect, use of the term *forgiveness* may not be appropriate when referring to resolution of anger toward God. Most psychological definitions of forgiveness require that some wrongdoing has been committed,[16] and they often use the language of moral repair.[17] Accordingly, we have begun to refer to resolution of anger toward God, rather than using the language of forgiveness, in our own recent work.

4. Assessment Challenges

The study of anger toward God poses unique challenges from an assessment perspective. First, because God is often seen as the ultimate authority figure, one who dominates the universe and exercises supreme power, many people may be fearful of doing, admitting, or even feeling anything that would seem to indicate protest against God. Many people – particularly the devout – see protest toward God as morally wrong,[18] which raises the possibility that they might not be willing to admit negative feelings involving God. Not only may they be reluctant to report such feelings to others or to God, but they might also be unwilling to admit them to themselves.

Because of the problems likely to surround self-reports of anger toward God, it will be useful to supplement self-report measures with other indicators of anger that do not require introspection and self-disclosure. For example, psycho-physiological techniques, peer reports, or behavioural observations could help to gauge emotions that people would not readily disclose on self-report instruments. Also, in interviews or surveys that include self-reports, it may be useful to include assessment of mild negative emotions such as frustration, disappointment, or impatience rather than focusing exclusively on anger. For example, the Anger/Disappointment subscale of the Attitudes toward God Scale (ATGS-9) includes not only a direct question about anger toward God, but also items on seeing God as unkind, and feeling abandoned or let down by God. Such questions have the potential to tap negative emotions toward God that people might not label directly as anger. For example, if a person were to think, 'Well, I wasn't exactly angry at God, but I did feel a little frustrated or disappointed,' it is useful to have self-report items that can capture such nuances.

5. Anger toward God and Nonbelief

Another challenging issue is that the idea of anger involving God may be relevant for some people who currently report non-belief in God. One of our early studies yielded a counterintuitive finding, suggesting that some non-believers reported difficulty forgiving God.[19] Several more recent studies have offered parallel findings, suggesting that some (though by no means all) non-believers do report anger around the idea of God.[20] For example, some non-believers report that they experienced anger toward God as part of their past history (i.e., at a time in their lives when they did hold some belief in God).[21] Other findings indicate that some non-believers report anger when prompted to focus on a hypothetical image of God.[22] Also, in a study of bereaved individuals, some non-believers reported negative feelings toward God as part of their present experience.[23] Such findings are probably most accurately interpreted in terms of anger around the idea of God rather than as actual anger toward God, since by definition these individuals do not believe in God at present. But regardless of the exact nature and cause of their feelings, the fact that some non-believers report anger around the idea of God suggests that atheists, agnostics, and others who identify as non-believers should not be automatically excluded from conversations about anger involving God. What role might anger play in a decision to stop believing in God? There are several possible explanations, all of which wait systematic empirical testing. One possibility is that anger is merely one facet of a broader set of responses characterized by intellectual questioning, doubt, and confusion. In such cases a person might think, 'I simply can't reconcile the idea of a loving or powerful God with the suffering (or evil) that was allowed on this situation,' or 'It just doesn't make logical sense to believe in a God that would allow such a terrible thing to happen.' In such cases the anger would not be a direct cause of the subsequent decrease in belief; instead, both the anger and the nonbelief would be a byproduct of an analytical process of questioning previously held beliefs.

Another possibility, captured by the construct of *emotional atheism*,[24] assigns a much more central role to anger. Here the notion is that some people may respond to strong feelings of anger toward God by deciding that God does not exist. In other words, they might cope with their anger by essentially exiting the relationship, an avoidance-based technique often used in response to interpersonal anger and conflict.[25] In cases in which anger toward God is intense, a decision to stop believing might be a way of symbolically cutting off the relationship, perhaps in a very deliberate way (e.g., 'I'll show you...I'll just stop believing that you exist!' or 'I'm going to pretend as though you don't even exist.')

Alternatively, a person might want to avoid facing feelings of anger toward God or other painful emotions that might coexist with anger, such as humiliation, hurt, loss, or abandonment. In such cases a person might turn to nonbelief as a means of avoiding or resolving angry feelings without having to examine them closely. Here the thinking might be along these lines: 'Rather than getting mad, I can just put the whole thing to rest by deciding that there is no God after all.'

6. Intervention Ideas

How might a person resolve anger toward God? Before offering some suggestions, it is important to note that there have not been, to my knowledge, any formal, empirically based intervention studies focusing specifically on this topic. The suggestions made here are derived from descriptive studies,[26] brief exercises from prior studies,[27] and interpersonal forgiveness interventions that have received some empirical validation.[28]

Is anger toward God problematic in terms of mental health? Anger toward God does tend to co-occur with other types of emotional distress (depression, anxiety) and spiritual struggles such as feeling punished by God or difficulties with members of one's religious group.[29] Yet the direction of causality is not clear: although it is possible that anger (including anger toward God) could prompt other forms of distress, it is equally plausible that emotional distress (such as a depressive episode) could lead to anger of many types, including anger toward

God. A one-year recent longitudinal study of cancer survivors suggested that in terms of mental health, anger toward God showed the clearest links with emotional distress when it was recurrent or prolonged.[30] Here again, there is a clear parallel to interpersonal processes: although a passing flash of anger may not suggest problems for mental or physical health, prolonged grudge-holding may be different.

Even when people are clearly distressed by feelings of anger toward God, care should be taken to evaluate whether the timing is right to launch an in-depth assessment or intervention focused on these feelings. When people have experienced trauma or are in the throes of serious mental health symptoms, the safest strategy would likely be to address these issues first. It is possible that once the mental health symptoms remit, anger toward God may also subside. More importantly, it may be ethically remiss to raise difficult spiritual or theological issues for people who are experiencing major life crises or fragile emotional states. Even if ethically permissible, such a strategy may not be effective if people are experiencing very high levels of negative emotion. In addition, some people might simply not be comfortable directly facing feelings of anger, especially if they have had frightening or shaming experiences in the past, mostly focused on the expression of anger.

Assume for the moment that a person is experiencing anger toward God and is seeking help in managing or resolving these feelings. As with interventions to facilitate interpersonal forgiveness,[31] a crucial first step may be to take a closer look at the incident that triggered the angry feelings, without any pressure to reduce the anger. For example, a woman might reflect on her brother's untimely death: How did she see God's role in that event? What seemed unfair, if anything? What other thoughts and feelings does she feel as she recalls the event? Through a process of thoughtful self-analysis, many people should be able to clarify their feelings and identify some of the events and thoughts that may have given rise to their feelings. At the same time, it is important to note that people differ in their levels of self-awareness and the degree to which they are comfortable with introspection. Furthermore, some people are more skilled than others in verbally identifying their emotional states. Thus, whereas some individuals may find it helpful to identify personal thoughts and feelings on their own (perhaps through an exercise such as journaling), others might benefit from the presence of someone who can ask evocative questions and listen carefully, reflecting back and helping to clarify the person's thoughts and emotions.

Recent research suggests that simply providing a safe place for a person to share negative feelings regarding God could be therapeutic. As described earlier, many people see anger toward God as morally wrong.[32] In a recent study of American adults,[33] seeing anger toward God as morally unacceptable was associated with less readiness to disclose such anger to others. Among those who did tell someone else about their anger toward God, there were several important psychological correlates of the types of responses they received. For instance, to the degree that participants reported supportive responses from others, they were more likely to report that they had approached God with their feelings and that the experience had strengthened their relationship with God. In contrast, unsupportive responses to anger disclosures were associated with attempts to suppress anger, greater substance use, non-resolution of anger, and exit behaviour ranging from rebellion and ignoring God to doubting God's existence.

Along these lines, it is worth mentioning a finding that has been replicated in several studies.[34] As might be expected, close, positive relationships with God were linked with seeing it as unacceptable to rebel against God or exit the relationship. Importantly, once this idea of not exiting the relationship was statistically controlled, perceptions of closer and more resilient relationships with God were positively linked with tolerance for anger, complaint, and questioning. As in interpersonal relationships, then, the healthiest relationships may be those in which some degree of dissent and negative emotion can be tolerated without a threat of losing or damaging the relationship. It is important to note, however, that these studies were carried out with college students in the United States, most of whom were from a Christian background. More research is needed to determine whether these conclusions can be generalized to members of other faith traditions or demographic groups.

People often need to go through a long process before willing and being ready to attempt behavioural change, as shown in studies of substance abuse and smoking.[35] Thus, it is probably prudent to assume that many people are *not* willing or ready to release their anger toward God, even if presented with techniques that might help them to do so. Some people might feel empowered by their angry feelings, for example. They may find that being angry gives them a sense of control or motivation in a situation where they might otherwise feel helpless or vulnerable. Others might hold on to anger for principled reasons if they see God as an unjust authority figure.[36]

To determine whether anger toward God is a worthwhile target for intervention, individuals may benefit by reflecting on their anger: What costs and benefits do they see with staying angry? Are they aware of the potential costs of prolonged anger for mental and physical health? How could their anger be channelled in positive directions? Others might earnestly desire to reduce their anger but feel overwhelmed by their emotions, perhaps seeing themselves as unable to resolve or manage them on their own.

As described above, studies have just begun to examine possible techniques for reducing anger toward God. Thus, the suggestions given here are speculative and should not be interpreted as empirically validated tools for treatment. In addition, some of these techniques pose ethical risks because they involve asking people to reflect on (and perhaps challenge) core beliefs. Such techniques should only be attempted in an atmosphere of respect for individuals, their emotional and spiritual needs, and their rights to their own beliefs. For example, in a faith-based context, scriptures or other readings that emphasize particular theological angles (e.g., God's goodness or justice) might be assigned. However, care should be taken to assess whether the person experiencing anger toward God agrees with the theological premises that are being presented.

Perhaps the riskiest techniques, in ethical terms, would be those that involve directly challenging theological beliefs. For example, given that people tend to become angrier when they clearly see God as responsible for negative events,[37] some might suggest that God should not be held responsible: The suffering was the fault of the devil, or human error, or natural events not directly caused by God. Some might resolve anger by concluding that God does not exist, as described earlier. In another vein, given that people become angrier when they see God's intentions as cruel, some people might try to challenge this belief by suggesting that God had good intentions: to help people grow stronger, for example, or to give them more compassion for others. The idea that God will eventually bring justice (perhaps in the afterlife) and will restore what has been lost may be a comfort for some believers. Others might find it helpful to consider the mystery and awesomeness of God and the humbling idea that the ways of God cannot be understood by mere mortals. Still others might take comfort in the thought that regardless of the cause of suffering, God is present with them in their suffering.

Although any of the above ideas are likely to be helpful for some people, it seems highly unlikely that a single theological solution will be identified that will prove helpful for everyone. Granted, it is possible that challenges to existing beliefs could have dramatic positive effects in some cases; yet there is the risk that some people might see such challenges as disrespectful or disaffirming – particularly if the person encouraging the belief change is someone from outside one's faith tradition. If people self-generate their own alternative thoughts, rather than being steered to them by another person, they may show a greater sense of ownership and greater commitment to the process.

Another, perhaps less intrusive set of techniques would centre on facilitating insight, with the hope that such insight might help to resolve negative emotions. For example, people could reflect on their images of God and the sources of those images, including the possibility that relationships with one's parents could have shaped one's perceived relationship with God.[38] People might also reflect on past times when they felt positive or negative emotions toward God, looking for patterns. Or they might reflect on the anger-triggering event with the aim of seeing whether they can find any benefits or lessons learned from the experience.

Another option, which has received some empirical support,[39] would be to encourage believers to openly express their concerns to God, followed by an imagery exercise in which they envision God granting unconditional love and acceptance. This exercise could take several forms, ranging from letter-writing to artistic expression to attempting to have a conversation with God. Note however that such techniques are unlikely to work for everyone. Problems might arise if people feel uncomfortable with imagery, have a harsh or distant God image, have major doubts about God's existence, or do not see God as having a personal form.

Notes

[1] Everett L. Worthington, Jr. et al., 'Forgiveness and Religion: Update and Current Status', in *A Journey through Forgiveness*, eds. Malika Rebai Maamri, Nehama Verbin and Everett L. Worthington, Jr. (Oxford, England: Interdisciplinary Press), accessed April 13, 2011, http://www.inter-disciplinary.net/publishing/id-press/ebooks/a-journey-through-forgiveness/, 54.
[2] Laura Y. Thompson et al., 'Dispositional Forgiveness of Self, Others, and Situations', *Journal of Personality* 73 (2005): 329.
[3] Lee A. Kirkpatrick, *Attachment, Evolution, and the Psychology of Religion* (New York: Guilford Press, 2004), 52.
[4] Worthington et al., 'Forgiveness and Religion', 54.
[5] Julie J. Exline et al., 'Anger toward God: Five Foundational Studies Emphasizing Predictors, Doubts about God's Existence, and Adjustment to Bereavement and Cancer', *Journal of Personality and Social Psychology* 100 (2011): 136.
[6] Ibid., 129.
[7] Ibid., 132.
[8] Ibid., 135, 136.
[9] Ibid.
[10] Benjamin T. Wood, et al., 'Development, Refinement, and Psychometric Properties of the Attitudes toward God Scale (ATGS-9)', *Psychology of Religion and Spirituality* 2 (2010), 154.
[11] Exline et al., 'Anger toward God,' 133.
[12] Ibid., 136, 137.
[13] Michael E. McCullough, et al., 'Interpersonal Forgiving in Close Relationships II: Theoretical Elaboration and Measurement', *Journal of Personality and Social Psychology* 75 (1998), 1596.
[14] Everett L. Worthington, Jr., 'The Pyramid Model of Forgiveness: Some Interdisciplinary Speculations about Unforgiveness and the Promotion of Forgiveness', in *Dimensions of Forgiveness*, ed. Everett L. Worthington, Jr. (Philadelphia: Templeton, 1998), 118.
[15] Michael J. Wohl and Nyla R. Branscombe, 'Forgiveness and Collective Guilt Assignment to Historical Perpetrator Groups Depend on Level of Social Category Inclusiveness', *Journal of Personality and Social Psychology* 88 (2005): 297.
[16] Robert D. Enright, et al., 'Interpersonal Forgiveness within the Helping Professions: An Attempt to Resolve Differences of Opinion', *Counselling and Values* 36 (1992): 84.

[17] Elisabeth Gedge, 'Radical Forgiveness and Feminist Theology,' in *A Journey through Forgiveness*, eds. Malika Rebai Maamri, Nehama Verbin and Everett L. Worthington, Jr. (Oxford, England: Interdisciplinary Press), accessed April 13, 2011, http://www.inter-disciplinary.net/publishing/id-press/ebooks/a-journey-throu gh-forgiveness/, 70.

[18] Julie J. Exline and Kalman Kaplan, 'Anger, Exit, Questioning, and Complaint: Do People See Protest toward God as Morally Acceptable?' (unpublished manuscript submitted for publication, May 26, 2010), 2.

[19] Julie J. Exline, Ann M. Yali and Marci Lobel, 'When God Disappoints: Difficulty Forgiving God and its Role in Negative Emotion', *Journal of Health Psychology* 4 (1999): 369.

[20] Exline et al., 'Anger toward God', 133.

[21] Ibid.

[22] Ibid.

[23] Ibid.

[24] Michele Novotni and Randy Petersen, *Angry with God* (Colorado Springs, CO: Piñon, 2001), 38.

[25] Michael E. McCullough and William T. Hoyt, 'Transgression-Related Motivational Dispositions: Personality Substrates of Forgiveness and their Links to the Big Five', *Personality and Social Psychology Bulletin* 28 (2004): 1561.

[26] Julie J. Exline and Alyce M. Martin, 'Anger toward God: A New Frontier in Forgiveness Research', in *Handbook of Forgiveness*, ed. Everett L. Worthington, Jr. (New York: Routledge, 2005), 73.

[27] Julie J. Exline, 'Imagery Exercises and Anger toward God: Two Experiments' (Presentation at the Annual Meeting of the American Psychological Association, Toronto, Ontario, CA, August 6, 2009).

[28] Worthington, 'Pyramid Model of Forgiveness', 109.

[29] Kenneth I. Pargament, Harold G. Koenig and Lisa M. Perez, 'The Many Methods of Religious Coping: Development and Initial Validation of the RCOPE', *Journal of Clinical Psychology* 56 (2000): 522.

[30] Exline et al., 'Anger toward God', 142.

[31] Worthington, 'Pyramid Model of Forgiveness', 113.

[32] Exline and Kaplan, 'Anger, Exit, Questioning, and Complaint', 2.

[33] Julie J. Exline and Joshua Grubbs, '"If I Tell Others about My Anger toward God, How Will They Respond?" Predictors, Associated Behaviors, and Outcomes in an Adult Sample' (March 1, 2011), 2.

[34] Exline and Kaplan, 'Anger, Exit, Questioning, and Complaint', 2.

[35] James O. Prochaska and Carlo C. DiClemente, 'The Transtheoretical Approach', in *Handbook of Psychotherapy Integration*, 2nd ed., eds. John C. Norcross and Marvin R. Goldfried (New York: Oxford University Press, 2005), 147.

[36] Exline and Kaplan, 'Anger, Exit, Questioning, and Complaint', 42.
[37] Exline, et al., 'Anger toward God,' 139.
[38] Todd W. Hall and Keith J. Edwards, 'The Spiritual Assessment Inventory: A Theistic Model and Measure for Assessing Spiritual Development', *Journal for the Scientific Study of Religion* 41 (2004): 341.
[39] Exline, 'Imagery Exercises'.

Bibliography

Enright, Robert D., David L Eastin, Sandra Golden, Issidoros Sarinopoulos and Susan Freedman. 'Interpersonal Forgiveness within the Helping Professions: An Attempt to Resolve Differences of Opinion'. *Counselling and Values* 36.2 (1992): 84-103.

Exline, Julie J. 'Imagery Exercises and Anger toward God: Two Experiments'. Presentation at the Annual Meeting of the American Psychological Association, Toronto, Ontario, CA, August 6, 2009.

Exline, Julie J. and Joshua Grubbs. '"If I Tell Others about My Anger toward God, How Will They Respond?" Predictors, Associated Behaviors, and Outcomes in an Adult Sample'. Unpublished manuscript, submitted for publication on March 1, 2011. Microsoft Word file.

Exline, Julie J. and Kalman Kaplan. 'Anger, Exit, Questioning, and Complaint: Do People See Protest toward God as Morally Acceptable?' Unpublished manuscript, submitted for publication on May 26, 2010. Microsoft Word file.

Exline, Julie J. and Alyce M. Martin. 'Anger toward God: A New Frontier in Forgiveness Research'. In *Handbook of Forgiveness*, edited by Everett L. Worthington, Jr. 73-88. New York: Routledge, 2005.

Exline, Julie J., Crystal L. Park, Joshua M. Smyth and Michael P. Carey. 'Anger toward God: Five Foundational Studies Emphasizing Predictors, Doubts about God's Existence, and Adjustment to Bereavement and Cancer'. *Journal of Personality and Social Psychology* 100 (2011): 129-148.

Exline, Julie J., Ann M. Yali and Marci Lobel. 'When God Disappoints: Difficulty Forgiving God and its Role in Negative Emotion'. *Journal of Health Psychology* 4 (1999): 365-379.

Gedge, Elisabeth. 'Radical Forgiveness and Feminist Theology'. In *A Journey through Forgiveness*, edited by Malika Rebai Maamri, Nehama Verbin, and Everett L. Worthington, Jr. Oxford, England: Inter-Disciplinary Press. Accessed April 13, 2011. http://www.inter-disciplinary.net/publishing/id-press/ebooks/a-Journey-through-Forgiveness/.

Hall, Todd W. and Keith J. Edwards. 'The Spiritual Assessment Inventory: A Theistic Model and Measure for Assessing Spiritual Development'. *Journal for the Scientific Study of Religion* 41 (2004): 341-357.

Kirkpatrick, Lee A. *Attachment, Evolution, and the Psychology of Religion.* New York: Guilford Press, 2004.

McCullough, Michael E. and William T. Hoyt. 'Transgression-Related Motivational Dispositions: Personality Substrates of Forgiveness and their Links to the Big Five.' *Personality and Social Psychology Bulletin* 28 (2004): 1556-1573.

McCullough, Michael E., Kenneth C. Rachal, Steven J. Sandage, Everett L. Worthington, Jr., Susan W. Brown and Terry L. Hight. 'Interpersonal Forgiving in Close Relationships II: Theoretical Elaboration and Measurement'. *Journal of Personality and Social Psychology* 75 (1998): 1586-1603.

Novotni, Michele and Randy Petersen. *Angry with God.* Colorado Springs, CO: Piñon, 2001.

Pargament, Ken I., Harold G. Koenig and Lisa M. Perez. 'The Many Methods of Religious Coping: Development and Initial Validation of the RCOPE.' *Journal of Clinical Psychology* 56 (2000): 519-543.

Prochaska, James O., and Carlo DiClemente, 'The Transtheoretical Approach'. In *Handbook of Psychotherapy Integration*, 2nd edn, edited by John C. Norcross and Marvin R. Goldfried, 147-171. New York: Oxford University Press, 2005.

Thompson, Laura Y., C. R. Snyder, Lesa Hoffman, Scott T. Michael, Heather N. Rasmussen, Laura S. Billings, Laura Heinze, Jason E. Neufeld, Hal S. Shorey, Jessica C. Roberts and Danae J. Roberts. 'Dispositional Forgiveness of Self, Others, and Situations'. *Journal of Personality* 73 (2005): 313-359.

Wohl, Michael J. and Nyla R. Branscombe. 'Forgiveness and Collective Guilt Assignment to Historical Perpetrator Groups Depend on Level of Social Category Inclusiveness'. *Journal of Personality and Social Psychology* 88 (2005): 288-303.

Wood, Benjamin T., Everett L. Worthington, Jr., Julie J. Exline, Ann M. Yali, Jamie D. Aten and Mark R. McMinn. 'Development, Refinement, and Psychometric Properties of the Attitudes Toward God Scale (ATGS-9)'. *Psychology of Religion and Spirituality* 2 (2010): 148-167.

Worthington, Everett L., Jr., 'The Pyramid Model of Forgiveness: Some Interdisciplinary Speculations about Unforgiveness and the Promotion of Forgiveness'. In *Dimensions of Forgiveness,* edited by Everett L. Worthington, Jr., 107-137. Philadelphia, PA: Templeton, 1998.

Worthington, Everett L., Jr., Don E. Davis, Joshua N. Hook, Daryl R. Van Tongeren, Aubrey L. Gartner, David J. Jennings II, Chelsea L. Greer and Todd W. Greer. 'Forgiveness and Religion: Update and Current Status'. In *A Journey through Forgiveness,* edited by Malika Rebai Maamri, Nehama Verbin, and Everett L. Worthington, Jr. Oxford, England: Inter-Disciplinary Press. Accessed April 13, 2011. http://www.inter-disciplinary.net/publishing/id-press/ebooks/a-journey-through-forgiveness/.

Julie J. Exline is an Associate Professor of Psychology at Case Western Reserve University. Her primary research and clinical interests focus on forgiveness and spiritual struggles, and she is grateful for support from the Fetzer Institute for this project.

Radical Forgiveness and Feminist Theology

Elisabeth Gedge

Abstract

If Christian forgiveness is to model the forgiveness of God, as some commentators argue, then forgiving requires us to will that God also forgives those who have wronged us. That is, in forgiving we must desire the eschatological wiping away of another's guilt as well as forfeiting our own demand for satisfaction. While an inspiring ideal, this radical notion of forgiveness may be at odds with the psychological and moral requirements for successful forgiving. Margaret Urban Walker argues that forgiveness is a process of moral repair which requires confidence that relations of trust can be restored, that there can be a shared affirmation of values, and that there is a basis for hope that continued moral relations are worthwhile.[1] Are these conditions of forgiving consistent with radical forgiveness? Further, there is always a cost to forgiving, therefore acts of forgiving are at the same time acts of 'giving up the demand that a cost be paid by one who in justice deserves to pay it.'[2] The costs of wrongdoing are then disproportionately borne by the wronged who, if they are radical forgivers, may be denied ultimate vindication in Divine judgment. The problem of cost is exacerbated when feminist understandings of systemic injustice and the gendered expectations of self-abnegation are introduced into the analysis. In this chapter, I consider whether radical forgiveness can be defended as a morally decent, theologically sound, and libratory strategy. I critically explore the claim that the *Via Feminina*[3] offers a way to engage in radical forgiveness without compromising personal dignity, political solidarity, or hope in Divine vindication.

Key Words: Christian, forgiveness, feminism, repair, vindication, cost, mysticism.

*****

1. Introduction

For Christians, the duty to forgive those who have wronged us is unambiguous. But to what exactly are we committed? Jesus' saying that we must forgive our neighbour 'seventy times seven'[4] suggests a duty that is unconditional in scope and attribution. His instructions in 'the Lord's prayer'[5] and in the parable of the ungrateful servant[6] suggest that our practice of forgiveness should be modelled on God's forgiveness which we find, is radical, separating us from our sins 'as far as the East is from the West'[7] and washing us 'whiter than snow.'[8] Furthermore, as Wade and Kidwell argue, forgiveness is a theological requirement of Islam and Judaism, and a karmic recommendation in Buddhism and Hinduism.[9] The radical nature of Christian forgiving sets a standard for us to follow which, we might argue, requires us to will the erasure of the wrong done to us, not only here and now but eschatalogically. In forgiving as God forgives, we must engage in radical forgiveness, which entails willing that God also forgives those who have wronged us, forfeiting our demand for satisfaction, and so absorbing the costs of the wrongdoing ourselves.[10]

The idea of a duty of radical forgiveness raises many questions for feminist theorists. Is the duty to forgive consistent with the demand for social justice that is constitutive of libratory movements such as feminism? Can radical forgiveness be understood without importing and exacerbating gendered expectations of self-abnegation which threaten the integrity and dignity of women? Can the costs of forgiveness be turned into benefits so that radical forgiveness forms part of a restorative and transformative feminist politics? In this chapter, I consider whether Barbara Lanzetta's feminist mystical theology offers a model for reconciling radical forgiveness with such feminist aspirations.[11]

2. The Moral Structure of Forgiveness

According to the feminist philosopher Margaret Urban Walker, the occasion of forgiveness is a perceived wrong done which disturbs basic assumptions about life, values, and our moral world.[12] Forgiveness, as a moral phenomenon, aims at moral repair, a restructuring of moral relations. In forgiving, the one wronged moves from 'having a need and right to grieve and to reproach the wrongdoer' to a morally reparative decision to 'release himself or herself from the position of grievance and reproach, and to release the wrongdoer from open-ended…demands for satisfaction.'[13] According to Walker, there are three common facets of forgiveness, none of which is separately necessary, but each of which is characteristic of forgiving: overcoming resentment, restoring relationships, and setting a wrong *as a wrong* in the past. First, in forgiving we abandon expressions of anger, mistrust, reproach or punishment which are no longer appropriate after we have forgiven.[14] Second, in forgiving we commonly seek to restore relationships, but in doing so, we must make moral adjustments. As Walker says, '…simply being able to go on with a relation, function in it, is not forgiveness…In forgiving something is 'set right.'[15] This takes place through the affirmation of shared values, the renewed setting of boundaries and responsibilities. Forgiveness, says Walker, 'is reparative where it revives or stabilizes trust and hope in authoritative moral understandings, and in the viability of moral relations, for the one who forgives.'[16] Third, in forgiving we commonly seek to set a wrong as a wrong in the past. In relinquishing resentment we *let go* of a wrong, but setting it *as* a wrong is different: it involves *interpreting* the act as a wrong. This element has urgency, since identifying a wrong under the correct description 'precedes all questions of what practical and moral possibilities are open to repair it, whether by forgiveness or other means.'[17]

Several aspects of Walker's account might seem to be at odds with radical forgiveness. For instance, she maintains that despite the *personal* relinquishment of resentment, it may be appropriate for the forgiver to believe the offender should accept punishment, or may in fact require him to do so, as a condition of forgiveness. Is this consistent with radical forgiveness? If radical forgivers must will that God also forgives, are we precluded from relegating an offender to God's judgment, something that might well be a psychological condition of the possibility of forgiveness as well as a requirement of justice? Second, there is the problem of cost. As Walker notes, notwithstanding the commitment to a policy of forgiving, the forgiver may still struggle with persistent feelings of disappointment, anger, hurt or despondency, which demand 'remedial self-control'[18] if the adopted policy of forgiving is to be maintained. This self-control, which may be profound in the case of terrible wrongs, is a cost unjustly borne by the person wronged. Does the demand for radical forgiveness then become complicit in this further injustice? Can such forgiveness be morally decent?

Problems with radical forgiveness are further complicated when viewed from the perspective of feminist politics. The problem of unjust costs is exacerbated when feminist understandings of systemic injustice and the gendered expectations of self-abnegation are introduced into the analysis. Feminist social analysis maintains that women and members of other disadvantaged groups, as group members, are harmed by structural injustices wrought through institutions and practices which exclude, marginalize, or subordinate them. Further, by inferiorising them, such institutions and practices shape their identities and self-understandings in ways that damage agency, dignity and self-respect.[19] If we then require them to be radical forgivers, to bear the costs of forgiveness with no expectation of ultimate vindication, are we not repeating and reinforcing the pattern of subordination? Furthermore, to the extent that the injustices of group subordination are systemic rather than intentional, it is difficult to see how the harms suffered as a result of them *can* be forgiven as long as the underlying institutions, assumptions and practices are in place. If forgiveness is, in part, the resetting of moral relations through a shared affirmation of values and responsibilities and the restoration of trust and hope, as long as systemic injustices persist, forgiveness is stalled. Walker discusses various public fora, such as truth and reconciliation commissions, in which public acknowledgments and apologies can be occasions for forgiveness by groups, but in the absence of such acknowledgments, with their implicit recognition that the shared moral understandings and relations must change, it is difficult to see how in a context of systemic subordination, forgiveness as the restoration of moral relations can take place, or how it can be required.

We are thus left wondering whether the Christian call for radical forgiveness can be theologically sound, morally decent, and libratory from a feminist perspective. The theological issue is the significance of vindication by God of victims of wrongdoing, and the problem that demanding radical forgiveness might render God complicit in reinforcing damaging stereotypes and unreasonable moral demands of women and other subordinates. The problem of moral decency is that of expecting victims of wrongdoing to bear the costs of forgiveness and to forgive in the absence of reassurance of reformed moral relations. An additional problem, from a feminist political perspective, is that the call for radical forgiveness appears to run against a libratory spirit that would view with a hermeneutic of suspicion the call for radical forgiveness.[20]

3. Lanzetta's *Via Feminina*

A possible response to the problems posed for feminists by radical forgiveness is offered by feminist mystical theology. Beverly Lanzetta has recently proposed a *Via Feminina*, a mystical practice which may offer a way to endorse radical forgiveness without compromising personal dignity, political solidarity, or hope in Divine vindication. Though not a strictly philosophical resolution to the problem of forgiveness, the *Via Feminina* takes feminist philosophical insights as its starting point, and should therefore be of interest to those within as well as outside the mystical tradition.

Lanzetta argues that because all symbols, language and ideology, including those of religion, are implicated in the oppression of women, women seeking spiritual comfort and understanding must engage in *critical* spiritual practice. For Lanzetta, women's 'soul suffering'[21] is an unrecognized aspect of women's oppression, an internalization of dualistic hierarchies in which women are inferiorised, defined in terms of embodiment, where the latter is denigrated as being opposed to the spirit. In order for the resulting 'soul suffering' to be remedied, women's spiritual practice must be able to deconstruct their internalised gender identity in such a way as to affirm women's worth and address the denigration of embodiment. In proposing a *Via Feminina,* Lanzetta offers women the resources of 'unsaying,' apophasis, a mystical path that 'enters into and moves through a woman's 'nothingness' – that is, through what diminishes, injures, humiliates, or shames her – to a positive affirmation of her dignity and worth.'[22]

As in traditional Western accounts of mystical contemplation, the end point is encounter with the Divine, but in the case of the *Via Feminina,* the encounter is viewed as an intimate, interior union, the discovery of an inner core of embodied selfhood where one is united to a Divine source. This discovery simultaneously affirms the value of the mystic as an embodied bearer of the Divine life, and of the female body as the site of that union. It also gives rise to a 'contemplative ethic [that] …brings us into deep association with creation, tears down the walls of segregation and exclusion, opens our hearts to the mysterious patterning of life's wholeness, and teaches us not to turn away from suffering and pain.'[23] The mystical state of consciousness is aware that all suffering is one's own, and accepts, through graced infusion of Divine love, the responsibility of compassion, mercy and forgiveness. With its emphasis on the identification and 'unsaying' of subordinating meanings, and on the particulars of the mystic's historical embodiment, the contemplative ethic is also an ethic of feminist praxis.

Interestingly, Lanzetta's account of the *Via Feminina* has resonance with the experiences of religious people seeking to forgive, as documented by Wade and Kidwell. In their empirical research on forgiveness in the lives of religious people, Wade and Kidwell found that there were both religious and secular motivations for religious people to strive to forgive, and aiming to forgive was described as a 'long and intentional journey.'[24] A major motivator for the journey was a desire for closeness with God, and prayer and meditation were identified as key components of the journey. Becoming God-like was also identified as a calling which demanded forgiveness for wrongs done. The *Via Feminina*, indeed any mystical approach to the spiritual life, would be an appropriate vehicle for such a journey, thus Lanzetta's proposal reflects the priorities of religious believers.

Lanzetta's V*ia Feminina* begins to address the challenges noted earlier in the Christian call for radical forgiveness. First, the intimate union to which the *Via Feminina* leads encompasses a union of purpose so that the movement of the human will to forgiveness is already consciously in harmony with the Divine vision.[25] In some sense then, any forgiveness will be radical forgiveness, a joint willing of the erasure of guilt. Second, the need for vindication by God, which as we noted, might be a psychological as well as a moral requirement of human forgiveness, is an end point of the mystical path, while the exposure and unsaying of acts and structures which have demeaned the Self are intermediate points along the way. These are points of forgiveness in the sense of fixing a wrong *as* wrong. They also allegedly contribute to the resetting of moral relations, for in taking full account of women's historical embodiment and the causes of women's soul suffering, injustices are exposed, responsibility assigned, and renewed moral relations demanded. For this reason, the Divine call for radical forgiveness cannot be seen as in complicity with structural injustice. Insofar as radical forgiveness is part of a transformative process for the individual, it offers some compensation for structural injustice. And insofar as it operates as part of a contemplative ethic aimed at reducing segregation and exclusion, it also offers a remedy for structural injustice.

The second set of concerns over radical forgiveness arose because of a worry about the disproportionate costs of forgiving. In forgiving, radical or not, the emotional cost of containing or resolving the emotional aftermath of harm done and the attendant trauma of disrupted moral relations is unjustly borne by the forgiver. Two distinct factors would exacerbate this unfairness: the pointlessness of the costs, and the absence of a basis for hope in the restoration of moral relations. Regarding the latter, as Walker noted, for some people the action of God in the world is the basis for hope in resetting moral relations, and Lanzetta's vision of a contemplative ethic arising from Divine indwelling is an example of this. 'Contemplation,' she says, 'is always revolutionary, for it takes apart what is comfortable and convenient, asking us to see the world from God's perspective.'[26] What the intimate union confirms for the mystic is the sacredness and interconnectedness of all, and the need and possibilities for a reparative praxis. Thus, the costs of forgiving, which *are* unjust, can be weighed against renewed confidence in the moral character of the world. As for the question of whether suffering is pointless, we can say, cautiously, that the cost of suffering on the mystical path is viewed by *insiders* as bearable and even welcome when it is seen as transformative for the individual and for the world.[27] Radical forgiveness ought not to count the cost, but in the mystical vision the burden is light because it is shared with the Divine.

Again, Wade and Kidwell's research offers interesting insights into the challenges faced by the demand for forgiveness. Whereas the *Via Feminina* focuses on the acceptance of suffering as a transformative necessity, religious believers in Wade and Kidwell's study articulated the personal *benefits* of forgiveness, which may be seen as offsetting what otherwise appears to be an unjust burden. The research participants spoke of feelings of gratitude and appreciation for being able to forgive, and of the importance of achieving peace after forgiving. Spiritual growth was seen as a deeply important outcome, and the injuries endured a means to a more profound spiritual life. The researchers identified such comments as 'cognitive reframing,'[28] a process by which negative thoughts are replaced by positive ones. The example they gave is of attributing an injury to the wrongdoer's alcoholism rather than seeing it as a cruel action. Such reframing encourages forgiveness, but also empathy, which we might see as a dimension of the broadening of the Self in mystical union to encompass the suffering of all.

However, at this point we need to refer again to the feminist hermeneutic of suspicion which would cast doubt on the call for radical forgiveness. Mystics of every tradition have proclaimed the libratory benefits of detachment from resentment, but feminists and other sceptics have asked 'who benefits?' Is the *Via Feminina* really a way of honouring women as embodied bearers of the Divine spark, or another invitation to compliance with a disciplinary norm? As one feminist commentator points out, '...mystical theology becomes doubly suspicious because of its strong commitment to self-sacrifice, self-negation, passivity and effacement of the soul in the abyss of divinity.'[29] Does approval of the idea of cognitive reframing contribute to a mystification of wrongdoing, personal and structural, and erase wrongdoing *as* wrongdoing? While replacing bitterness with empathy may be a laudable transformative strategy of an individual, its moral decency is questionable when understood as a mechanism to, once again, require the injured party to 'make things right.'

The hermeneutic of suspicion is appropriate if we see the *Via Feminina* as obscuring or denying the personal and structural wrongs endured by subordinated groups, or requiring spiritual seekers to repress or 'reframe' justified feelings of anger, resentment, and affront. Feminist theorists have commented on the importance of legitimate anger as a signal of the presence of injustice, and as a source of empowerment for women.[30] If one must abandon righteous anger in order to walk the mystical path, the latter may well be at odds with the libratory strategies of feminist politics, and at odds with the psychological requirements of transcending injury. Julie Exline's work is pertinent in this connection.[31] Exline's study documents the phenomenon of anger toward God with some surprising results, for instance, that anger may be stronger among non-believers in God. Like Wade and Kidwell, Exline draws attention to the importance of weighing costs and benefits in the relationship with God, noting that exiting the relationship in an aggrieved state might not be the most beneficial response to an injury thought to be caused or tolerated by God. For our purposes, though, the most interesting observation is Exline's comment that a tolerance for anger, complaint and questioning correlates positively with better relationships with God. This is a welcome finding from the perspective of the feminist understanding of the role of righteous anger mentioned above. If our concern is over the moral decency of forgiveness, we might trace the role of anger in the *Via Feminina* as a testament to wrongdoing, and even incorporate into our understanding of the spiritual path instances of Divine anger, such as Jesus' cleansing of the Temple,[32] if our conception of the Divine offers such parallels.

A further and more challenging feminist critique of Lanzetta's proposal arises from disquiet over the *individualising, universalising* and *essentialising* tendencies in her account. As we have seen above, forgiveness, at least on Walker's account, takes place in a relational setting, and is in some sense a public phenomenon. Forgiveness aims to set a wrong *as* a wrong, invites and requires uptake from members of the moral community, especially in cases where the offender refuses to acknowledge the wrong. Questions can be asked about whether the intensely private intimate union Lanzetta described can do justice to the public dimension of forgiveness, relying, as it does, on what Exline calls a 'virtual' relationship, that is, a relationship with an unseen God.[33] Granted, in the process of 'unsaying' an identity damaged by structural and personal oppression, the wrongs are identified and the worth of the Self affirmed. But is this private process sufficiently robust to meet the ethical demand for setting and remedying the wrong within the moral understanding of moral peers? And is the uptake of an unseen God sufficient for resetting moral relations concretely rather than simply aspirationally?

The implicit individualism of the *Via Feminina* (somewhat paradoxically) parallels a tendency to essentialise and universalise women's experience. Lanzetta speaks of *the* way of intimacy, *the* unity of mystical consciousness, and the quest for 'women's original, non-separated being.'[34] While this articulation in Lanzetta's work sends a strong message about the importance of dismantling dualistic understandings of personhood and of revering embodiment, it suggests a commonality of experience unwelcome to contemporary feminist critics. Claims to common experience, whether the experience of oppression or of intimate union with the Divine, are at odds with the preponderance of current feminist theorising about difference. As Sigridur Gudsmarsdottir points out:

> If a feminist mystical theology is to be authentic for a contemporary feminist discussion, it needs to be capable of difference... it must be able to express concerns for the different bodies and lives of women in their different power, racial, sexual, cultural, geographical locations.[35]

Lanzetta sees her insistence on the historicity of particular bodies, combined with the body's role as the vehicle for union with the Divine, as accommodating difference; yet this is surely, as the critics say, in tension with the assertion of an original unified female being. Nevertheless, Gudsmarsdottir sees the emphasis on embodiment as offering some distinctiveness to a feminist mystical path which avoids the pitfalls of essentialism and universalism. As she says,

> I read Lanzetta's *Via feminina* as an authentic and radical apophatic gesture of 'within-ness'. Her insistence of unsaying, her 'ungrounding ground' and 'the dark night of the feminine' resonate powerfully with some of the main symbols of mystical theology. This mystical symbolism is channelled into apophatic unsaying, *insofar as such symbols keep on moving, unsaying each other, ungrounding, and filtrating light with darkness.*[36]

Gudmarsdottir's solution to Lanzetta's problem of essentialising and universalising is thus to make the method of unsaying recursive, an ongoing interrogation of labels, whether they name the supposed end state of the mystical journey, the integrated woman, or the Divine Self. If unsaying were to culminate in mere receptivity, or in the appropriation of an essential female identity of unconditional forgiving, suspicions about whether the mystical path is truly libratory would be well founded. However, situating radical forgiveness in a practice of repeated 'unsaying' and in a contemplative ethic structured around the dismantling of oppressive meanings, practices and acts offers an appropriate corrective, and balances the risks of radical forgiving against the transformative benefits of taking the *Via Feminina*.

A more radical line of criticism, linking doubts about the degree to which the *Via Feminina* meets the demands of justice with worries about its individualism, comes from those who question the accepted view of mysticism within the history of religious thought. The late feminist critic Grace Jantzen, for instance, has argued against a fetishizing of the mystic, and maintained that the mystical tradition itself must be seen in a historical context of gender oppression and the struggle for authority over religious knowledge.[37] What may be salvaged from such a 'deconstruction' of mysticism remains to be seen, and is beyond the limits of this discussion. However, a critical 'unsaying' of the tradition itself is surely consistent with Lanzetta's goal of exposing the sources of women's 'soul sickness' and affirming women's embodied worth.

4. Conclusion

The concept of radical forgiveness is problematic theologically, morally, and from the perspective of feminist politics. Forgiving is reparative, but it has costs and is surrounded by conditions. Radical forgiveness seems to discount the costs and abandon the conditions. I have suggested that some of the problematic features of radical forgiveness can be addressed if the Christian call to radical forgiveness is positioned within a feminist mystical practice. In the process of mystical 'unsaying,' radical forgiveness can be seen as transformative and libratory, as a gesture of human/Divine generosity that is not at odds with seeking justice. Radical forgiveness is an element in the healing of individual 'soul suffering,' and can exemplify the image of the Divine when exercised freely. And as part of a contemplative ethics, it can have a transformative force in challenging and resetting moral relations. As Lanzetta says, 'There is no liberation for one without liberation for all,'[38] and radical forgiveness can be an integral part of that liberation.

Notes

[1] Margaret Walker, *Moral Repair: Reconstructing Moral Relations after Wrongdoing* (Cambridge: Cambridge University Press, 2006).
[2] Ibid., 182.
[3] Beverly Lanzetta, *Radical Wisdom: A Feminist Mystical Theology* (Minneapolis: Fortress Press, 2005).
[4] Matthew 18: 21-22.
[5] Matthew 6: 12
[6] Matthew 18: 23-35. Also Colossians 3:13.
[7] Psalm 103
[8] Isaiah 1:18; Psalm 15: 7.
[9] Nathaniel Wade and Julia Kidwell, 'Understanding Forgiveness in the Lives of Religious People: The Role of Sacred and Secular Elements', in *A Journey Through Forgiveness* (Oxford: Inter-Disciplinary Press, 2011), 39, accessed May 21, 2011, http://www.inter-disciplinary.net/publishing/id-press/ebooks/a-journey-through-forgiveness/.
[10] This is a contested view. There is debate both over the question of modelling (does the as in the 'Lord's prayer' mean we model our forgiving on God's or does

God forgive us according to our willingness to forgive?) and over whether Christian forgiveness ought to be unconditional.

[11] Lanzetta, *Radical Wisdom*, 174.

[12] Walker, *Moral Repair*, 162.

[13] Ibid., 153.

[14] Ibid., 157.

[15] Ibid., 161.

[16] Ibid., 164.

[17] Ibid., 171.

[18] Ibid., 157.

[19] See Misha Strauss, 'The Role of Recognition in the Formation of Self-Understanding', *Recognition, Responsibility and Rights: Feminist Ethics and Social Theory*, eds. Robin Fiore and Hilde Lindemann Nelson (Lanham, MD: Rowman and Littlefield, 2003), 37; and Paul Benson, 'Feeling Crazy: Self-Worth and the Social Character of Responsibility', eds. Catriona Mackenzie and Natalie Stoljar, *Relational Autonomy: Feminist Perspectives on Autonomy, Agency, and the Social Self* (Oxford: Oxford University Press, 2000), 72.

[20] The 'hermeneutic of suspicion' is associated with feminist theologian, Elisabeth Schussler Fiorenza's admonition to denaturalise and deconstruct biblical texts so as to expose linguistic practices of domination. See *In Memory of Her: A Feminist Theological Reconstruction of Christian Origins* (New York: Crossroads, 1992).

[21] Lanzetta, *Radical Wisdom*, 9.

[22] Ibid., 22.

[23] Ibid., 201.

[24] Wade and Kidwell, 'Understanding Forgiveness', 42.

[25] Lanzetta's notion of 'within-ness' or 'indwelling' and the idea of a harmony of wills reflect the mystical theology of the Johannine gospel, especially as found in the farewell discourses.

[26] Lanzetta, *Radical Wisdom*, 66.

[27] Lanzetta comments extensively on the role of suffering in the apophatic path. She notes that medieval women mystics, in particular Teresa of Avila and Julian of Norwich, see their suffering as integral to their openness to the Divine presence, and to the growth of compassion.

[28] Wade and Kidwell, 'Understanding Forgiveness', 43.

[29] Sigridur Gudmarsdottir, 'Feminist Apophasis: Beverly J. Lanzetta and Trinh T. Minh-ha in Dialog', *Feminist Theology* 16.2 (2008): 163.

[30] See for example Lynne McFall, 'What's Wrong with Bitterness?' in *Feminist Ethics*, ed. Claudia Card (Lawrence, Kansas: University of Kansas Press, 1991), 146-167.

[31] Julie Exline, 'Anger toward God: A New Frontier in the Study of Forgiveness', *A Journey Through Forgiveness* (Oxford: Inter-Disciplinary Press, 2011), 29-37, accessed May 21, 2011, http://www.inter-disciplinary.net/publishing/id-press/ebooks/a-journey-through-forgiveness/.
[32] Mark 11, 15-19; Matthew 21, 12-17; Luke 19, 45-48; John 2, 13-22.
[33] Exline, 'A New Frontier,' 29.
[34] Lanzetta, *Radical Wisdom*, 135.
[35] Gudmarsdottir, 'Feminist Apophasis', 161.
[36] Ibid., 166. Italics mine.
[37] Grace Jantzen, *Power, Gender and Christian Mysticism* (Cambridge: Cambridge University Press, 1995).
[38] Ibid., 201.

Bibliography

Benson, Paul. 'Feeling Crazy: Self-Worth and the Social Character of Responsibility', In *Relational Autonomy: Feminist Perspectives on Autonomy, Agency, and the Social Self*, edited by Catriona Mackenzie and Natalie Stoljar, 72-93. Oxford: Oxford University Press, 2000.

Exline, Julie. 'Anger toward God: A New Frontier in the Study of Forgiveness', In *A Journey Through Forgiveness*, edited by Malika Rebai Maamri, Nehama Verbin, and Everett Worthington Jr., 29-37. Oxford: Inter-Disciplinary Press, 2010, accessed May 21, 2011, http://www.inter-disciplinary.net/publishing/id-press/ebooks/a-journey-through-forgiveness/.

Fiorenza, Elisabeth. *In Memory of Her: A Feminist Theological Reconstruction of Christian Origins*. New York: Crossroads, 1992.

Gudmarsdottir, Sigridur. 'Feminist Apophasis: Beverely J. Lanzetta and Trinh T. Minh-ha in Dialog'. *Feminist Theology* 16.2 (2008): 157-168.

Jantzen, Grace. *Power, Gender and Christian Mysticism*. Cambridge: Cambridge University Press, 1995.

Lanzetta, Beverly. *Radical Wisdom: A Feminist Mystical Theology*. Minneapolis: Fortress Press, 2005.

McFall, Lynne. 'What's Wrong with Bitterness?' In *Feminist Ethics*, edited by Claudia Card, 146-160. Kansas: University of Kansas Press, 1991.

Muers, Rachel. 'Feminist Theology as Practice of the Future'. *Feminist Theology* 16.1 (2007): 110-127.

Strauss, Misha. 'The Role of Recognition in the Formation of Self-Understanding'. In *Recognition, Responsibility and Rights: Feminist Ethics and Social Theory*, edited by Robin Fiore and Hilde Lindemann Nelson, 37-52. Lanham, MD: Rowman and Littlefield, 2003.

Wade, Nathaniel and Julia Kidwell. 'Understanding Forgiveness in the Lives of Religious People: The Role of Sacred and Secular Elements'. In *A Journey Through Forgiveness*, edited by Malika Rebai Maamri, Nehama Verbin and Everett Worthington Jr., 39-48. Oxford: Inter-Disciplinary Press, 2010, accessed May 21, 2011, http://www.inter-disciplinary.net/publishing/id-press/ebooks/a-journey-through-forgiveness/.

Walker, Margaret. *Moral Repair: Reconstructing Moral Relations after Wrongdoing*. Cambridge: Cambridge University Press, 2006.

Elisabeth Gedge is Associate Professor of Philosophy at McMaster University in Hamilton, Ontario, Canada. Her research interests are feminist ethics, feminist philosophy of religion, and feminist jurisprudence.

Part 3:

The Practice of Peace and Reconciliation

Memorials as Sites of National Conscience

Cayo Gamber

Abstract
In my chapter, I interrogate how national memorials – that commemorate those who died for their nation in World War I, those whose nations marked them for death in World War II, and those who died for their nation during the Vietnam War – have become sites of national conscience. Kollwitz's Mourning the Fallen, Duszenko and Haupt's Stones of Treblinka, Hoheisel's Aschrott's Fountain, Eisenman's Monument to the Murdered Jews, and Lin's Vietnam Veterans Memorial mark a site of historical rupture, a rupture that provokes visitors to contemplate the way the people of a nation think about its citizens and its identity as a nation-state. Memorials, such as these, function as sites of memory; to that end, they preserve places and commemorate people and events deemed important in the nation's history. It is at these sites that a nation talks about itself and its history. In this chapter, I ask: what is the dialogue that is initiated at national sites of memory? In addition, I contemplate how these memorials ask us to consider the means by which forgiveness and remembrance are negotiated at sites where a nation consciously mourns its history and its dead.

Key Words: Duszenko, Eisenman, Haupt, Hoheisel, Holocaust, Kollwitz, Lin, memorial, monument, nation.

*****

1. Wiesenthal's Painful Epiphany

In *The Sunflower: on the Possibilities and Limits of Forgiveness*, Simon Wiesenthal recounts a personal story of his experience as a camp prisoner brought face-to-face with a member of the SS, dying in the hospital, who sought a Jew to forgive him so that he might die in peace. The German soldier had been implicated in an atrocity that involved rounding up over one-hundred-and-fifty Jewish men, women, and children, confining them to a house, setting the house on fire while throwing in hand grenades and shooting at anyone who tried to escape. Haunted by the memory of this crime, the soldier seeks to make a deathbed confession, explaining to Wiesenthal, 'In the long nights while I have been waiting for death, time and time again I have longed to talk about it to a Jew and beg forgiveness from him.'[1] As the title of the book indicates, in recounting this encounter, Wiesenthal first asked his 'bunkmates' in the concentration camp and later the readers of this story what constitute 'the possibilities and limits of forgiveness.' As a result of the question he asks: what would you have done in his place? The focus of his fellow prisoners and, years later, of many readers is on whether or not Wiesenthal should have or could have forgiven a member of the SS for the atrocities the German soldier participated in. In fact, in the more recent editions of the story, fifty-three responses have been offered from distinguished writers and political figures worldwide, all of whom attempt to answer what she or he would have done in Wiesenthal's place.

On the day when he went on the forced work detail that made possible that chance encounter with the SS officer, Wiesenthal saw sunflowers that marked the graves of the German soldiers who recently had died. It is those sunflowers that are referenced in the title of the story. However, when he tells his fellow camp prisoners about being brought to the bedside of the dying SS officer, Wiesenthal refrains from telling them about his sighting of the sunflowers and his ruminations on those flowers that so captured his attention. It is intriguing that he remains silent about the flowers when he first tells Josek and Arthur his story. In fact, it is not until he recounts the story in written form that he signals the importance of the sunflowers – in particular, by entitling the written account, *The Sunflower*. He tells his readers he coveted the tall flowers that marked the graves of the dead German soldiers. Wiesenthal remarks:

> [s]uddenly I envied the dead soldiers. Each had a sunflower to connect him with the living world, and butterflies to visit his grave. For me there would be no sunflower. I would be buried in a mass grave, where corpses would be piled on top of me. No sunflower would ever bring light into my darkness, and no butterflies would dance above my dreadful tomb.[2]

In fact, in the end, even the nameless mass grave that Wiesenthal envisions would have been denied him. In the nine-and-a-half hour acclaimed film, *Shoah*, Claude Lanzmann obsessively follows what happened to the corpses of the murdered Jews. From Motke Zaidl and Itzhak Dugin, Lanzmann learns that those bodies buried in mass graves were dug up in the later years of the war. Following is the exchange between Lanzmann, the two survivors, and the woman who translates Lanzmann's questions and Zaidl's and Dugin's responses:

> So it was they who dug up and burned all the Jews of Vilna?

> Yes. In early January 1944 we began digging up the bodies. When the last mass grave was opened, I recognized my whole family.

> Which members of his family did he recognize?

> Mom and my sisters. Three sisters with their kids. They were all in there.

How could he recognize them?

They'd been in the earth four months, and it was winter. They were very well preserved. So I recognized their faces, their clothes too....

The Nazi plan was for them to open the graves, starting with the oldest?

Yes. The last graves were the newest, and we started with the oldest, those of the first ghetto. In the first grave there were twenty-four thousand bodies.

The deeper you dug, the flatter the bodies were. Each was almost a flat slab. When you tried to grasp a body, it crumbled; it was impossible to pick up. We had to open the graves, but without tools. They said: 'Get used to working with your hands.' ...

The head of the Vilna Gestapo told us: 'There are ninety thousand people lying there, and absolutely no trace must be left of them.'[3]

In the course of following what happened to the bodies of the murdered Jews, Lanzmann learns that everyone was to be reduced to smoke, ash, and a fine powdered bone that consciously was dispersed so that no trace would remain.

Wiesenthal's and Lanzmann's attention to the bodies of the German war dead and those of the murdered Jews offers a study in contrast. On the one hand, the bodies of the German soldiers were to be buried with national honour and marked with a sunflower. On the other hand, the bodies of Europe's Jews were violated as Jewish religious practice forbids the cremation of the body. And the corpses themselves were disappeared so that their very bones would not remain in order to testify to the existence of the Jewish people who once lived throughout Europe. Wiesenthal's attention to the sunflowers invites us to consider how the dead will be remembered, how the dead are (or are not) connected to the living through burial rites and commemorative practices. He imagines a dreadful tomb in an unmarked mass grave. And as the historical record indicates, even those dreaded tombs were unearthed so that there would be no resting place, no memory space, for the murdered Jewish people.

In her preface to *The Sunflower*, Bonny Fetterman asks what will happen once 'the killing has stopped;' in particular:

> how can a people make peace with another who moments before
> were their mortal enemies? What are the limits of forgiveness,
> and is repentance – religious or secular – enough? Is it possible
> to forgive and not forget?[4]

In his longing to have a sunflower of his own, Wiesenthal also focuses on how the dead will be remembered and how that remembrance is potentially tied to notions of forgiveness. Wiesenthal asks us to consider, in the aftermath of the Shoah: what markers have been offered to the Jewish people? What role do these markers play? How do these markers gesture (or not) toward a nation's accountability in perpetrating a genocide against a group of its citizens?

In order to right the historic wrong perpetrated against the Jewish people, various memorial sites throughout Europe have become the Jewish people's sunflowers and cenotaphs, paradoxically, marking both their existence and disappearance. In marking a void, the absence of what once was, these devastating spaces call into question the role of forgiveness. As the fifty-three responses appended to *The Sunflower* indicate, how we understand forgiveness is culturally and religiously inflected. For some, forgiveness may only be achieved through repentance and active contrition. For some, forgiveness requires that she who seeks forgiveness demonstrates she will not repeat the action again. For others, forgiveness requires a negotiation with God or is an act of volition that can only be achieved if the one who seeks forgiveness can make that supplication to the individual or individuals he has wronged. For many, forgiveness involves a combination of the aforementioned. These understandings of forgiveness are further complicated when they are applied to or enacted upon a national level. How might repentance, contrition, a promise never to repeat the crime again, or forgiveness itself be achieved by a nation? For as Karolina Wigura argues in 'Forgiveness or Reconciliation after the Shoah? An Ecumenical Perspective,'

> Nations and religious groups are not individuals; one cannot
> automatically shift forgiveness or reconciliation from the
> individual to the collective level without deep reflection on
> the difference between them.[5]

What follows here is a discussion of how addressing forgiveness on the collective and national level requires deep reflection on the forms forgiveness may or may not take and on the reasons why forgiveness may be forestalled.

In some cases, forgiveness may be precluded. Memorials to the Shoah reveal that the loss of the Jewish people can neither be forgiven nor redeemed. This revelation, for example, was made a stipulation in the design competition for the new Jewish museum of Berlin. In their brief for the design competition, Rolf Bothe and Vera Bendt, respectively directors of the Berlin Museum and the Jewish

Museum Department of the Berlin Museum, noted that no one who entered the competition should falsely believe that his or her work could-redeem the loss of Berlin's or Europe's Jews:

> a fate whose terrible significance should not be lost through any form of atonement or even through the otherwise effective healing power of time. Nothing in Berlin's history ever changed the city more than the persecution, expulsion, and murder of its own Jewish citizens. This change worked inwardly, affecting the very heart of the city.[6]

In his evaluation of Bothe and Bendt's proviso, James Young argues that such a provision suggests that the successful designer should recognize how the very character of the nation's capitol was changed by the annihilation of its former inhabitants. As Young explains,

> [i]n thus suggesting that the murder of Berlin's Jews was the single greatest influence on the shape of this city, the planners also seem to imply that the new Jewish extension of the Berlin Museum may even constitute the hidden center of Berlin's own civic culture, a focal point for Berlin's historical self-understanding.[7]

It is this question of historical self-understanding that I will explore more fully. National memorials and monuments function as sites of memory. To that end, they preserve places and commemorate people and events deemed important in a nation's history. In this chapter, I ask: what is the dialogue that is initiated at national sites of memory.

2. Memorials to the Shoah

In his work, James Young repeatedly refers to the rupture that occurred and void that remained when the Jews of Europe were persecuted and systematically murdered. For example, in 'Germany's Holocaust Memorial Problem – and Mine,' he concludes that Berlin's design competition for the Memorial to the Murdered Jews of Europe solidified the fact that this nationally-imposed place of rupture and void would, in part, define Germany:

> For whether Germans like it or not, in addition to their nation's greatest accomplishments over the last several centuries, they will also always be indentified as that nation which launched the deadliest genocide in human history, which started a world war that eventually killed some 50 million human beings, and which

used this war to screen its deliberate mass murder of some 6 million European Jews. It is not a proud memory. But neither has any other nation attempted to make such a crime perpetrated in its name part of its national identity. For this space will always remind Germany and the world at large of the self-inflicted void at the heart of German culture and consciousness – a void that at once defines national identity, even as it threatens such identity with its own implosion.[8]

Memorials to the Shoah differ from other efforts to commemorate those who died in times of warfare because the sites of/to the Shoah do not allow for the void left behind – by the murder of six million and the suffering of many more Jewish citizens – to be lessened through exoneration. In recognizing this void, one of the projects of the Post-Holocaust memorialist, then, is to point to an inability on the part of the nation as a whole, to be forgiven for the systematic murder of its former citizens.

In addition, Post-Holocaust memorialists are conscious that their commemorative spaces could lose their memorial function with the passage of time; thus, the memorial sites themselves reveal the artists' concern with forgetting, repressing, or rewriting history. These memorial sites therefore are often created as physically startling negative spaces, spaces that haunt us with a sense of absence or inversion. In evoking absence, these sites remind us of all those who were murdered and all their individual promise that never came to be. To evoke a sense of inversion, the sites often symbolically enact a volte-face by reversing what is expected (e.g., rather than rising above ground, a fountain is inverted below ground). In addition, these sites annul our complacent belief that civilisation always improves itself as it moves forward. That is to say, confidence in the 'progress' of civilisation consistently bettering itself was negated with the Holocaust, with the execution of the Nazi plan that came to be understood as a crime against humanity. Moreover, these negative memorial spaces may be constructed for the perpetrators or for the victims. In his dissertation, *Das Mahnmal als in Auftrag gegebene Bewaltigungsarbeit: eine Untersuchung des sogenannten Holocaustmahnmals am Wiener Judenplatz*, Klaus Mosettig distinguishes between two types of memorials.[9] A *denkmal*, he contends, is constructed for the victims as it focuses on those who were persecuted and calls for visitors to bear witness for them. A *mahnmal*, on the other hand, is constructed for the perpetrators; it seeks reconciliation, ascribes blame, comments on the role of remembering, or gestures toward atonement.

In 'Healing and Forgiveness after Traumatic Events: The Case of Holocaust Survivors from the Fortunoff Archives,' Clara Mucci argues forgiving is not a way of forgetting or condoning, on the contrary, it cannot but stem from the careful and painstaking retrieval of the truth of the past and the acknowledgment of the responsibilities of the wrong-doers, as painful and atrocious as that might be.[10]

This effort, as Mucci clarifies, requires the presence of a 'fully committed, fully present listener.'[11] Mucci is speaking here about the way a testimonial alliance is forged between the survivor who offers testimony and the individual who collects her oral history. The listener actively affirms the survivor. In this case, *denkmals* and *mahnmals* are mute presences that offer a testimonial presence; however, they are not able to assert the agency necessary to forge an alliance. That alliance, as will be noted later in this chapter, is developed when individuals actively personalize the commemorative 'work' of a given memorial site.

3. The Memorial to the Fallen, Vladslo, Belgium (1932)

Image 1: 'Kathe Kollwitz, *Die Eltern* (The Parents).' Courtesy of the Australian Government's Department of Veterans' Affairs.

While memorials to the Holocaust insist upon the impossibility of clemency, there are some national memorials that call for forgiveness. For example, Kathe Kollwitz's sculptural memorial of the two grieving parents ('Memorial to the Fallen,' 'The Parents,' *'Die Eltern'*) at the Vladslo cemetery, administered by the German War Graves Commission, calls for the remembrance of those German soldiers who died in Belgium during World War I. The remains of more than 25,644 German soldiers are buried here. In fact, when these soldiers were first interred, this site may well have been planted with the sunflowers that Wiesenthal so coveted. Not only does this military cemetery honour those who died in battle, as a result of the inclusion of Kollwitz's sculpture, this memorial space also potentially asks the dead to forgive their nation for sending them into battle and to their deaths. The monument's two grieving parents are modelled on Kollwitz and her husband. Each life-size granite figure, hunched over in pain, is alone in his/her grief, yet they stand sentry together, looking out at all of the war dead.[12] Kathe and Karl's son's grave is just in front of the statues. These parents grieve their child, for all the other parents who lost children, and for all those soldiers who once were children. In using herself and her husband as models, Kollwitz intimately and visibly personalizes her grief and her husband's. It is through such personalization that she makes forgiveness possible. Bowed over, before her son, she offers him, and all the other sons of Germany buried there, her sense of sorrow and guilt over their deaths.

Kollwitz's anguish is also intensified by the fact that she believed her son had been sacrificed by his nation and, thus, she seeks forgiveness on two levels: for the elders of her nation who sent their children to die and, personally, for not believing in the war effort, since when Peter went off to war, he believed he was fighting for a noble cause. Twenty-two days before Peter's death, Kollwitz confided in her diary,

> there is war, and one cannot hold on to any illusions any more. Nothing is real but the frightfulness of this state, which we almost grow used to. In such times it seems so stupid that the boys must go to war. The whole thing is so ghastly and insane.[13]

Her sense of bewilderment over the terrible toll of warfare is evidenced in her 11th October 1916 entry in which she observes:

> I shall never fully understand it all. But is clear that our boys, our Peter, went into the war two years ago with pure hearts, and they were ready to die for Germany. They died – almost all of them.... Is it a breach of faith with you, Peter, if I can now see only madness in the war? Peter, you died believing. Was that also true of Erich, Walter, Meier, Gottfried, Richard Noll? Or had they come to their senses and were they nevertheless forced to leap into the abyss? Was forced involved? Or did they want to? Were they forced to?[14]

Kathe and Karl's figures are forever huddled and longing; their eternal sorrow and the violent deaths of so many German youths are conjoined. In creating these kneeling sentries before the 'pure-hearted' dead of Germany, Kollwitz initiates a place and time for forgiveness and healing. It should also be noted that in this piece, Kollwitz politicized her grief. In expressing their sorrow rather than a sense of pride, these mourning parents question the waging of war on behalf of one's fatherland/motherland. When Hitler came to power, he ensured that Kollwitz and her anti-war message would be silenced. Consequently as early as 1933, Kollwitz was forced to resign her position as head of the Master Class for the Graphic Arts at the Prussian Academy of Arts. And by 1938, her works had been removed from public display and she was prohibited from exhibiting altogether.

4. The Memorial Stones of Treblinka, Treblinka, Poland (1964)

Image 2: '17,000 stones set in concrete in a circle form a symbolic cemetery.' Courtesy of Scrapbookpages.com, Photographer: Gen Baugher.

Initially, the full nature of the Holocaust was not understood. As Edward Linenthal argues in *Preserving Memory: The Struggle to Create America's Holocaust Museum,*

> what came to be known as 'the Holocaust' was often indistinguishable, in the immediate postwar years, from the millions of noncombatant casualties due to terror bombing of civilian populations, epidemic illness, or starvation. It was considered by most as simply part of the horror of war.[15]

While the remains of the concentration camps and death camps 'provided material evidence of the murderous work of the Nazis,'[16] they were not immediately recognized as places of national memory, in particular as ones that referenced Jewish victims. In fact, initially, many of the camps unequivocally recognized the plight of political prisoners while obscuring any mention of Jewish victims who suffered and/or died in the camps. It was not until the 1961 Eichmann Trial that the testimony of Jewish victims was sought. Moreover, it was during this period that victims became known, collectively, as *survivors*. Survivor testimony was collected not only for the purposes of the Trial, but also in order to establish a historical record of the persecution of the Jewish people of Europe.

Once the true nature of the 'final solution of the Jewish question' – the systematic extermination of a people – was recognized, efforts were made to memorialize their loss. In these endeavours, the memorialists actively chose a particular perspective from which to see the tragedy, focusing either on the victims (and thereby creating a *denkmal*) or on the perpetrators (thereby creating a *mahnmal*). The Memorial Stones of Treblinka, for example, testify to and for the Jews murdered in the death camp that once operated in this space. The monument symbolically evokes how the Jewish people were systematically murdered. During *peak* times, one thousand people could be gassed in one hour. The 17,000 stones here stand for the largest number of Jewish people to be gassed in one day. In addition to standing for the many who were murdered, individual stones are engraved with the names of different locales where the Jews lived prior to their forced deportation.

These commemorative stones are all that remain of the camp; they are all that gesture at those who once arrived there. Treblinka was divided into two camps: Treblinka I, a forced-labour camp, and Treblinka II, a killing centre. Prior to the Soviet liberators' arrival, Treblinka had been 'liquidated' by the Germans. All traces of the camp were obliterated: the members of the last group of prisoners killed; the area ploughed over; trees planted; and the camp turned into a farm. Moreover, since Treblinka II was designed as an extermination camp, there were no individual records kept of the thousands murdered there. The approximate number of those who died in the gas chambers has been determined, in large part, by looking at transit records which indicate the number of people transported in the trains, but not necessarily their individual names or whether or not they survived the transport and still were alive upon arrival at Treblinka II. The stones, then, stand as a haunting testimonial for all of the unnamed victims, a *denkmal*, that allows for the innocent victims and their witnesses to remember the many individuals who perished here.

Designed by sculptor Franciszek Duszenko and architect Adam Haupt, these many stones, set in a circle, become the silent spectres of those who perished. In addition, these stones silently witness for one another. They stand as synecdoches for the innocent victims who perished at Treblinka. Joined in their circle, they await those visitors who will witness with and for them.

5. The Memorial to the Murdered Jews of Europe, Berlin, Germany (2005)

While the Memorial to the Murdered Jews of Europe is referred to by both terms – *denkmal* and *mahnmal* – in news stories, scholarship, and tourist pamphlets, this memorial, I would argue, is a *mahnmal* in that it primarily evokes the void in the heart of the nation's capitol, one that recognizes the role of the perpetrators as well as the plight of the victims. This memorial site covers almost

five acres – one entire city block – in the centre of Berlin. The field of 2,711 stelae
(pillars) gestures toward no numerical meaning. In the original design, there were
to have been 4,200 stelae; however, the number was reduced for financial reasons
and 'by exigency, such as the addition of saplings, among them linden, and
capacious, hospitable sidewalks.'[17] The stelae are not marked in any way. The
number of dead is not mentioned. There are no names of the towns the dead once
inhabited or names of the victims themselves. There are also no names of the
transit, labour, concentration, or death camps where the Reich's victims were sent.

Image 3: 'The Memorial to the Murdered Jews of Europe, (*Denkmal für die
ermordeten Juden Europas*).' Courtesy of Clark B. May.

In addition, no effort is made to plot out how you should approach and journey
through the stelae. There is no marked entrance or exit to the field of pillars. You
may enter or exit at will. However, while walking through the maze of pillars, you
become aware of other visitors. You might see one person only once and then,
he/she disappears from view. Others you will see again and again. They pass by in
your periphery and become companions in your journey. In his analysis of the
memorial, Gunter Schlusche explains,

> [t]he field of stelae, without any words, strengthens at the same
> time the memorial's dialogue with its visitor, because it demands
> a certain 'shaping of memory that pulls the visitor inside.'[18]

'Everyone must find his own way,' Schlusche says, adding that many visitors will
not make it to the centre of the Monument, to its darkest passages, for '[m]any will
stay at the edge.'[19] Such negotiations are central to the artistic mediation of the
piece, a mediation that emphasizes 'experiencing the past (through artistic media),
instead of 'merely' learning about the past (the priority of history), [as] a
commemorative priority.'[20]

The memorial's architect, Peter Eisenman,[21] purposefully ensured that the Monument would call for an artistic mediation. In addition, he is unperturbed by how others may inscribe meaning to the memorial. For example, from its inception, there were concerns expressed by some that the stelae might be prey to graffitists:

> Although Berlin is one of the most tag-ridden cities in the world, the inevitable prospect of graffiti doesn't worry Eisenman. 'That's an expression of the people,' *he says, with a shrug*. The stones [stelae], however, have been given a graffiti-proof coating; and this in itself raised spectres from the past. In a stranger-than-fiction twist, the firm supplying the proofing was Degussa - co-owner of the company that made the Zyklon B gas used in concentration camps. By way of atonement, the company donated their product for free.[22]

As the gesture, which accompanies the quotation he offers above, is meant to convey, Eisenman's shrug indicates he is comfortable with the day-to-day negotiations that will take place in this space – young people playing on top of or among the stelae or people picnicking at the site – for these are 'an expression of the people.' It is in their expressive negotiations with this vast monument that individuals will develop, first, a civic *consciousness*, and, subsequently, a civic *conscience*. The fact that Eisenmen 'shrugs' at the various concerns that have been expressed about the way in which visitors will interact with the memorial, in my view, highlights this structure's role as a *Mahnmal*, a memorial that invokes the active role of remembering on the part of perpetrators and subsequent generations. As a result, when each visitor embarks on his singular journey through the field of stelae, he undertakes the civic negotiations that are inspired by the vast, imposing site itself. It is here, then, in the heart of the city, that ongoing personal and civic negotiations are enacted as visitors and Berliners remember the murdered, the murderers, and their numerous bystanders.

6. Aschrott's Fountain, Kassel, Germany (1987)
  While Eisenman's memorial demands a confrontation with the darkness at the heart of Berlin, Hoheisel's memorial to a-fountain-that-once-was, employs inversion and absence in order to create a murmuring *mahnmal* that movingly speaks to the people of Kassel. In 1908, in the centre of Kassel a prominent Jew, Sigmund Aschrott, had endowed the city with a fountain in the square in front of City Hall. The design of the fountain – an obelisk of sandstone – harmonized with its impressive civic location. In the late 1930s, however, the fountain was condemned as the Jews' fountain and in 1939, Nazi activists tore it down. In 1941 the first transports of Jews were rounded up in Kassel and sent on rail cars to their

deaths in the camps. In 1943, the Nazis filled in the basin where the fountain once had stood and planted the area with flowers, contemptuously renaming the site: 'Aschrott's Grave.' Twenty years later, another fountain had been erected on the site. Given that a number of years had passed, the townspeople no longer were sure of the earlier history of the site and 'when asked what had happened to the original fountain, they replied that, to the best of their recollection, it had been destroyed by English bombers during the war.'[23] In response to such (convenient) layers of forgetting, in 1984, the Society for the Rescue of Historical Monuments proposed that the fountain should be restored in such a way that its previous history would be honoured.[24]

Image 4: 'Aschrott's Fountain (*Aschrott-Brunnen*).' Courtesy of James E. Young.

Horst Hoheisel created the monument that stands on the site today. What Hoheisel chose to do was to create a counter-monument that would invert what once had been. Rather than create a towering fountain above the ground, he inverted the design and the obelisk became a funnel burrowing into the earth. Those who walk across the square see – and also hear – the water that cascades downward through channels. Glass blocks cover the upturned base of the structure, allowing visitors to see how the inverted fountain extends into the earth. Thus, one can look down to see the water funnelling downward and can hear the sound of water cascading. An encounter with Aschrott's Fountain immediately confounds one with a not-always-fully-understood sense of reversal and absence: 'what is going on here?; what is the sound I hear?; why is the fountain inverted?' A bronze plaque explains what once was above and why the fountain has been inverted below.

Those who visit this landscape are changed by it – they whisper as they listen to history murmuring. In marking the void that exists and making palpable the historical shame of the murder of its people in the name of the nation, memorial sites such as the *Aschrott-Brunnen* do not forgive. Memorials such as these ones ask us to be aware of the presence of absence, the void throughout Europe, the historical rupture that will never be healed.

7. The Vietnam Veterans Memorial (the Wall), Washington, D.C. (1982)

Image 5: 'Memento Left at the Vietnam Veterans Memorial'.
Courtesy of Patsy Lieberman.

Unlike Germany, the United States has not deliberately and visibly made crimes 'perpetrated in its name part of its national identity.'[25] For example, the singular effort to document the American use of nuclear weapons in time of warfare – the proposed exhibit, entitled: 'The Crossroads: The End of World War II, the Atomic Bomb, and the Origins of the Cold War' (1994-1995) – at the Smithsonian, was never brought to fruition, despite the fact that multiple drafts had been written to meet the demands of various critics of the proposed exhibition. The latter would have called for visitors to confront the choice of using atomic bombs and the consequences of having done so. Rather than presenting a purely laudatory version of American history, museum-goers would have been asked to think about what it meant that America used these weapons and what it means that America is the only country to have used nuclear weapons in time of war. As a result of the vociferous objections raised by the American Legion, members of Congress, and World War II veterans, the exhibit was quelled.[26]

In my view thus, while the United States Holocaust Memorial Museum (1993) makes a noteworthy contribution to the representation and study of the Holocaust, there is something unsettling about the fact that Americans are so willing to represent the crimes of the Third Reich while being so reluctant to question their own actions, in the same war, against Japanese people. In a similar fashion, questions have been raised about how well the crimes against Native Americans or against African Americans have been represented at sites of national conscience, such as the National Museum of African American History and Culture (2003) and the National Museum of the American Indian (2004).

There is a great deal that can be learned from Germany's effort to confront its history, to separate out combatant and non-combatant casualties of war from those the nation had marked for annihilation. Not all national history is praiseworthy. A multitude of atrocities have been committed in the name of a nation. A multitude of mistakes have been committed in the name of a nation. Acknowledging both, and potentially forgiving the mistakes if not the atrocities, should be integrated into the nation's identity. Memorial sites offer us a compelling way to initiate the conversations necessary to address the times and places of an anguished and/or shameful history.

The efforts made to commemorate what became the unpopular 'war' – the conflict in Vietnam – speak to the endeavour James Young identifies in Germany, the hard work that is needed in order for a nation to interrogate what many now regard as a bad war and a time of national deception and shame. Maya Lin's memorial is similar to Kollwitz's memorial in that the primary ethos of the memorial is to mark the number of youth who had been asked to die for their nation. Kollwitz's elders contemplate the rows of crosses that mark each soldier's grave site. In a similar way, visitors to the Wall contemplate the names of the missing and the dead. The names are listed on the seventy-panels that form the two intersecting walls. There is no 'right-hand' justification and thus the visitor reads each panel, as if reading a poem or the page of the book, the uneven right-hand edges propel his eyes down to the next line. No ranks are offered for those who are named on the Wall; as a result, all those believed to be Missing-in-Action or Killed-in-Action-are made equal in death.

Lin's memorial also calls for an artistic mediation. This mediation, similar to Eisenman's, asks the visitor to experience the space itself. Instead of confronting stelae, at the Wall visitors confront the black-granite panels of names. Lin's memorial enacts a purposeful journey in engaging with the names of the dead and those presumed dead. In its essential design, the memorial did not explicitly seek to invoke forgiveness; however, Lin always imagined that those who visited the memorial would be implicated in it – visually, physically, and emotionally – and in the process of creating this bond between memorial and visitors, the latter have augmented and magnified the Wall's meaning/s. To that end, visitors see themselves reflected in 'mirror' of black granite of the Wall. They are invited to touch the names, to make pencil rubbings of individual names, and to leave objects as offerings. As a result, the Wall has become a place of *descanso* – a resting place where highly personal offerings such as hand-written letters, packs of cigarettes, combat boots, flowers, even a brand-new Harley Davidson motorcycle – are brought in order for individual visitors to engage with and mourn the dead.

Traditionally, in Hispanic culture, the mourners in a funeral procession would erect *descansos*, or memorials, at the places where they paused to rest on the journey between the church and the cemetery. The pallbearers would often leave a cross at the site that would remain there indefinitely. Today *descansos* mark many roadways in America. They commemorate the place of fatal accidents where someone's life-journey was interrupted suddenly, violently, unexpectedly. Thus, they mark where a life ended, rather than where the dead lie buried. Often, the *descansos* are handmade. Hand-hewn crosses, plaques, wreaths, flowers, and inscriptions mark these sites as intensely personal places of grief. Time and again, the name of the dead is inscribed in the space. Frequently, mementos are left at the site —ones that would have personal meaning to the dead such as a teddy bear, baseball cap, letter, or poem. Some sites appear to be visited often by the bereaved; there is evidence that the offerings have been refreshed and any seasonal damage to the memorial has been repaired. While intensely private, these roadside memorials and shrines are also markedly public. They serve as warnings that the road conditions may be dangerous and thus remind passersby how quickly and randomly one's life-journey can be ended while also encouraging them to drive safely.

The Wall represents over 58,000 men and women who have been confirmed dead or who are now 'believed'[27] to be dead, and thus each name, etched in granite, marks the end of someone's life journey. It is to those names, those interrupted lives, that offerings are made. The practice of leaving mementos is due, in part, to the chronological arrangement of the names. While the Wall does not mark the site where the named individual was last seen alive, the Wall does mark the time of death, and, potentially, those along with whom she or he may have died. Moreover, given that it may never be known what happened to those who currently are classified as Missing in Action, the Wall may function as their only resting place given that, to date, their remains have not been recovered. Without any bodily remains, these dead can neither be confirmed Killed-in-Action nor can they be laid to rest in family cemeteries. As a result, similar to the pallbearers who rested on their journey from the church to the cemetery, the Wall marks the resting spot where these dead can be contemplated, many of whom may never reach a final resting space in a cemetery plot. The offerings that are made at this place of *descanso* become part of a larger dialogue with the Wall, a dialogue which allows the nation as a whole to bear witness, mourn, and acknowledge the cost of warfare, as measured in the loss of over 58,000 lives.

8. Summary

What each of these memorials indicates is that there is no cohesive entity known as either *the* national memory or *the* national narrative. However, these national sites of remembrance point to the ongoing, and changing role that both nation and memory play. Each site asserts something about what the nation should remember; in turn, over time, the citizens of a given nation assert what they are willing to remember. It was not known how well the public would receive any of these memorials. It is however clear that all five sites of national conscience have become oft-visited places of remembrance and observance. For instance, in Berlin, according to Uwe Neumarker, Director of the Memorial to the Murdered Jews of Europe,

> If you say to a taxi driver in the German capital 'Take me to the Memorial', he knows what you mean without asking – and in most cases he takes you, accompanied by an appropriate commentary, to the stelae field near the Brandenburg Gate. Since its opening in May 2005, the Memorial to the Murdered Jews of Europe has become one of Berlin's tourist attractions.[28]

In a similar fashion, the Vietnam Veterans Memorial – with at least 3 million visitors per year – easily is within the top-ten-most-visited sites in Washington, D.C.

War memorials bridge generations, connecting the dead to the living. One cannot encounter Kathe and Karl Kollwitz without experiencing their sense of pain and isolation. A visitor wants to stand in solidarity with them, in the hope that she can lessen their sense of anguish. A visit to the Vietnam Veterans Memorial also becomes a shared experience. While one makes his journey alone, he will be aware of others who made the journey as well. He will ponder over the significance of the various offerings made to a name or names on the Wall. These are memorials where the call to mourn personalizes a place of forgiveness – forgiving one's self, one's nation. It is here that a visitor and a nation may heal. Memorials to the Shoah, by contrast, respond to the chilling charge that the head of the Vilna Gestapo had made to Motke Zaidl and Itzhak Dugin who were forced to disinter the bodies of Jewish men, women, and children who had been buried in mass graves: 'Absolutely no trace must be left of them.'[29] These memorials offer trace evidence of past crimes. The stones of Treblinka speak, the stelae of Berlin silently haunt, and the *Aschrott-Brunnen* murmurs. These sites of memory unsettle visitors as they evoke places of rupture and absence, places that will not allow forgiveness. They refuse to erect sunflowers to light the darkness that was the Shoah. However, they may bring butterflies to dance – incongruously, innocently – among the eloquent stones, wordless stelae, and murmuring fountains of the Europe that might have been.[30]

All of these memorial sites ask us to self-consciously examine the ways we engage in acts or remembrance and to conscientiously analyse why we invite such remembrance. The commemorative impulse at each of these sites asks us to consider both the problems inherent in making war and the difficulties inherent in nation-making. In these sites of conscience, we not only mourn the dead, but we also contemplate why they died. These memorials, then, invite us to consider how forgiveness and remembrance are actively negotiated when a nation consciously confronts its history and its dead.

Notes

[1] Simon Wiesenthal, *The Sunflower: On the Possibilities and Limits of Forgiveness* (New York: Shocken Books, 1998), 54.

[2] Ibid., 14-15.

[3] Claude Lanzmann, *Shoah: The Complete Text of the Acclaimed Holocaust Film* (New York: Da Capo Press, 1995), 7-9.

[4] Bonny Fetterman, preface to *The Sunflower: On the Possibilities and Limits of Forgiveness*, xi-xx.

[5] Karolina Wigura, 'Forgiveness or Reconciliation after the Shoah? An Ecumenical Perspective,' in *A Journey through Forgiveness*, ed. Malika Rebai Maamri, et al. (Oxford, England: Inter-Disciplinary Press, 2010), accessed May 1, 2011, http://www.inter-disciplinary.net/publishing/id-press/ebooks/a-journey-through-forgiveness/, 64.

[6] Rolf Bothe and Vera Bendt, '*Ein eigenstandiges Judisches Museum als Abteilung des Berlin Museums*', in *Realisierungswettbewerb Erweiterung Berlin Museum mit Abteilung Judisches Museum* (Berlin, 1990), 12.

[7] James Young, 'David Libeskind's Jewish Museum in Berlin: The Uncanny Arts of Memorial Culture', *Jewish Social Studies* 6.2 (Winter 2000): 9.

[8] James Young, 'Germany's Holocaust Memorial Problem - and Mine', *The Public Historian* 24.4 (Autumn 2002): 80.

[9] Klaus Mossetig, *Das Mahnmal als in Auftrag gegebene Bewaltigungsarbeit: eine Untersuchung des sogenannten Holocaustmahnmals am Wiener Judenplatz.* (PhD diss., Dipl-Arbeit, Akademie der Bildenden Kilnste, Vienna, 2002).

[10] Clara Mucci, 'Healing and Forgiveness after Traumatic Events: The Case of Holocaust Survivors from the Fortunoff Archives', in *A Journey through Forgiveness*, ed. Malika Rebai Maamri, et al. (Oxford, England: Inter-Disciplinary Press, 2010), accessed May 1, 2011, http://www.inter-disciplinary.net/publishing/id-press/ebooks/a-journey-through-forgiveness/, 112.

[11] Ibid., 113.

[12] The memorial was first placed in the cemetery of Roggevelde (1932). Later, when Peter's grave was moved to the nearby Vladslo German war cemetery, the statues were also moved.

[13] Hans Kollwitz, ed., *The Diary and Letters of Kaethe Kollwitz* (Evanston, Illinois, Northwestern University Press, 1988), 62-3.

[14] Ibid., 74.
[15] Edward Linenthal, *Preserving Memory: The Struggle to Create America's Holocaust Museum* (New York: Penguin, 1995), 5.
[16] Ibid., 6.
[17] Johan Ahr, 'Memory and Mourning in Berlin: On Peter Eisenman's Holocaust-Mahnmal', *Modern Judaism: A Journal of Jewish Ideas and Experience*, 28 (October 2008), 288.
[18] Gunter Schlusche, 'A Memorial Is Built', in *Materials on the Memorial to the Murdered Jews of Europe* (Berlin: The Foundation for the Memorial to the Murdered Jews of Europe), 29.
[19] Michael Z. Wise, 'Berlin's Holocaust Memorial,' *Travel and Leisure* (March 2005), accessed 30 March 2011, http://www.travelandleisure.com/articles/concrete-memory.
[20] Abigail Gillman, 'Cultural Awakening and Historical Forgetting: The Architecture of Memory in the Jewish Museum of Vienna and in Rachel Whiteread's "Nameless Library"', *New German Critique* 93 (Autumn 2004): 151.
[21] Initially, architect Eisenman collaborated with sculptor Richard Serra in developing the memorial design; however, Serra pulled out of the project before the monument came to completion because he was uncomfortable with the modifications Chancellor Helmut Kohl had requested.
[22] Sarah Quigley, 'Holocaust Memorial: Architect Peter Eisenman, Berlin 2005', accessed 11 August 2010, http://www.war-memorial.net/Holocaust-Memorial--Architect-Peter-Eisenman,-Berlin-2005-2.66. Emphasis mine.
[23] James Young, *The Texture of Memory: Holocaust Memorials and Meaning* (New Haven: Yale University Press, 1993), 43.
[24] Hoheisel saw the proposal that won the original competition and was appalled by it. The winning proposal was 'to build another upright column on the site of the original fountain that would commemorate *all* the founders of the city together, the Nazis *and* Aschrott – the perpetrators and the victims – in a single monument.' If such a monument were built, Hoheisel feared that the layers of forgetting what happened to the fountain, and to the Jews would persist. Hoheisel was so adamant in his protest that the city finally gave him the right to create a monument where *Aschrott-Brunnen* (Aschrott's fountain) once stood. See Ellen Handler Spitz, 'Loss as Vanished Form: On the Anti-Memorial Sculptures of Horst Hoheisel', *American Virago* 62.4 (2006): 424.
[25] James Young, 'Germany's Holocaust Memorial Problem - and Mine', 80.
[26] The Air Force Association, for example, charged that the first draft for the exhibit expressed an unacceptable bias: Examination of the Smithsonian's own script, along with other factors we have reported, substantiate our belief that:

The exhibition as planned lacks balance and historical context; It is designed to play on emotions; It is part of a pattern in which the Smithsonian depicts US military airpower in a negative way. This stance was maintained in subsequent communications. For instance, in their response to the fifth script, the AFA asserted that, [o]ur written comments – supplemented by our extensive comments in the three-hour meeting with Smithsonian officials October 19 – about the military and strategic perspectives of the bombing campaign seem to have had little or no effect. The emphasis continues to be on death and destruction. See 'The Enola Gay and the Smithsonian Chronology of the Controversy, Including Key Documents (1993-1995)', Air Force Association, accessed 17 March 2011, http://www.afa.org/media/enolagay/chrono.asp.

[27] At one time there were many who held out hope that those who were Missing-in-Action (MIA) would return home. On the Wall, a plus sign follows the names of those believed to be MIA. Maya Lin also included a circle as a symbol for someone returning home alive. Thus, if someone returned home alive, the plus sign could be converted into a circle. A diamond sign follows the name of those confirmed as Killed-in-Action (KIA). When human remains are found and identified, the MIA plus sign also can be converted into a diamond. To date, the circle has not been used; however, with the ongoing effort to locate remains, some of the MIAs have been confirmed KIAs and the plus signs have been changed to diamonds.

[28] Uwe Neumaker, 'The Memorial to the Murdered Jews of Europe', accessed 11 March 2011, http://www.goethe.de/kue/arc/dos/dos/zdk/en3581894.htm.

[29] Claude Lanzmann, *Shoah: The Complete Text of the Acclaimed Holocaust Film* (New York: Da Capo Press, 1995), 9.

[30] There is more that can be said about Wiesenthal's reference to the incongruity of butterflies dancing in a place that once knew such cruelty and horror, of nature reasserting itself in places of such horror and destruction. Similarly, many of those who visit Auschwitz-Birkenau comment on the strangeness of encountering the carefully manicured lawns (lawns that primarily are meant to prevent erosion to the physical site) that flank so many of the buildings and so much of the property.

Bibliography

Ahr, Johan. 'Memory and Mourning in Berlin: On Peter Eisenman's Holocaust-Mahnmal'. *Modern Judaism: A Journal of Jewish Ideas and Experience* 28.3 (October 2008): 283-305.

Bothe, Rolf and Vera Bendt. '*Ein eigenstandiges Judisches Museum als Abteilung des Berlin Museu.s*'. In *Realisierungswettbewerb Erweiterung Berlin Museum mit Abteilung Judisches Museum*, 12-13. Berlin: *Senatsverwaltung für Bau-und Wohnungswesen*, 1990.

'The Enola Gay and the Smithsonian Chronology of the Controversy, Including Key Documents (1993-1995)'. Air Force Association. Accessed 17 March 2011. http://www.afa.org/media/enolagay/chrono.asp.

Fetterman, Bonny, Preface to *The Sunflower: On the Possibilities and Limits of Forgiveness*, Simon Wiesenthal, ix-xii. New York: Schocken Books, 1998.

Gillman, Abigail. 'Cultural Awakening and Historical Forgetting: The Architecture of Memory in the Jewish Museum of Vienna and in Rachel Whiteread's "Nameless Library"'. *New German Critique* 93 (Autumn 2004): 145-173.

Kollwitz, Hans, ed. *The Diary and Letters of Kaethe Kollwitz*. Evanston, Illinois: Northwestern University Press, 1988.

Lanzmann, Claude. *Shoah: The Complete Text of the Acclaimed Holocaust Film.* New York: Da Capo Press, 1995.

Linenthal, Edward. *Preserving Memory: The Struggle to Create America's Holocaust Museum*. New York: Penguin, 1995.

Mosettig, Klaus. *Das Mahnmal als in Auftrag gegebene Bewaltigungsarbeit: eine Untersuchung des sogenannten Holocaustmahnmals am Wiener Judenplatz*. Diss. Dipl-Arbeit, Akademie der Bildenden Kilnste, Vienna, 2002.

Mucci, Clara. 'Healing and Forgiveness after Traumatic Events: The Case of Holocaust Survivors from the Fortunoff Archives'. In *A Journey through Forgiveness*, edited by Malika Rebai Maamri, Nehama Verbin and Everett L. Worthington, Jr. Oxford: Inter-Disciplinary Press, 2010. Accessed May 1, 2011. http://www.inter-disciplinary.net/publishing/id-press/ebooks/a-journey-through-forgiveness/, 109-117.

Neumaker, Uwe. 'The Memorial to the Murdered Jews of Europe'. Accessed 11 March 2011. http://www.goethe.de/kue/arc/dos/dos/zdk/en3581894.htm.

Quigley, Sarah. 'Holocaust Memorial: Architect Peter Eisenman, Berlin 2005'. Accessed 21 September 2005. http://www.war-memorial.net/Holocaust-Memorial--Architect-Peter-Eisenman,-Berlin-2005-2.66.

Schlusche, Gunter. 'A Memorial Is Built'. In *Materials on the Memorial to the Murdered Jews of Europe*, 14-29. Berlin: The Foundation for the Memorial to the Murdered Jews of Europe, 2005.

Spitz, Ellen Handler. 'Loss as Vanished Form: On the Anti-Memorial Sculptures of Horst Hoheisel'. *American Virago* 62.4 (2006): 419-33.

Wise, Michael Z. 'Berlin's Holocaust Memorial'. *Travel and Leisure* (March 2005). Accessed 30 March 2011. http://www.travelandleisure.com/articles/concrete-memory.

Wiesenthal, Simon. *The Sunflower: On the Possibilities and Limits of Forgiveness.* New York: Schocken Books, 1998.

Wigura, Karolina. 'Forgiveness or Reconciliation after the Shoah? An Ecumenical Perspective'. In *A Journey through Forgiveness*, edited by Malika Rebai Maamri, Nehama Verbin, and Everett L. Worthington, Jr., 59-67. Oxford: Inter-Disciplinary Press, 2010. Accessed May 1, 2011, http://www.inter-disciplinary.net/publish ing/id-press/ebooks/a-journey-through-forgiveness/

Young, James. 'David Libeskind's Jewish Museum in Berlin: The Uncanny Arts of Memorial Culture'. *Jewish Social Studies* 6. 2 (Winter 2000): 1-23.

―――. 'Germany's Holocaust Memorial Problem - and Mine'. *The Public Historian* 24.4 (Autumn 2002): 65-80.

―――. *The Texture of Memory: Holocaust Memorials and Meaning.* New Haven: Yale University Press, 1993.

Cayo Gamber is an Assistant Professor of Writing at the George Washington University, and teaches Legacies of the Holocaust, Introduction to Women's Studies, and From Barbie Dolls to Guerilla Girls: A Study of Women in/and Media. Her research interests include analysing how the Holocaust is memorialized at sites of the Shoah and the role of popular culture in creating Western notions of girlhood and womanhood.

Algerian President's Peace Plan: Political and Psychological Perspectives

Malika Rebai Maamri

Abstract
The fruits of the victory Algeria won after eight years of bloody and brave struggle against French colonialism had been rapidly snatched from the Algerians in the 1990s, the most wretched period of Algeria's post-war history. Following the first round of the parliamentary elections of 26 December 1991, the fundamentalists of the Islamic Salvation Front (FIS) threatened the very stability of the State. After the suspension of the electoral process in January 1992, Algeria sunk into a decade of bloody terrorist Civil War which left the government with the staggering tasks of restoring order, and fostering reconciliation within Algerian society. Underlying that question was Algerian President, Abdelaziz Bouteflika's amnesty plan. Since his investiture in 1999, the Algerian President has been widely perceived as having brought not only peace and prosperity, but also a measure of national reconciliation to Algeria. One of his many challenges to reduce violence was his offer of forgiveness for repentant Islamist fighters. It was one of the first attempts at reconciliation after the tragedies of the black decade of terrorism in the 1990s in which Algeria lost thousands of people. As the title indicates, this chapter will shed some light, from an insider perspective, on the Algerian President's plan which he saw as one of the main guarantees of social order. However, the dynamics that emerged from his policies had been quite paradoxical. Given the level of fragmentation, both politically and socially, it became questionable whether such plan would succeed in building broad coalitions. The new strategy adopted sparked controversy and left many to speculate on the future of Algeria and its reconciliation policy. The greatest misconception about forgiveness has been the belief that forgiving the crimes committed meant condoning them. Among those who saw some legitimate use for the power to pardon in some cases, there were indeed those who saw it as being a profanation of the victims' tombs.

Key Words: Algeria, political Islam, terrorism, trauma, political forgiveness, reconciliation, ethics, social reconstruction.

*****

It seems right to begin this study of forgiveness in politics with this truth: most people feel like they know what forgiveness is. We think we are the most forgiving types, and we say that we would never hold a grudge. Sadly, what we learned about forgiveness as children often keeps us from forgiving. We find it so hard to make the first move to bring about forgiveness, especially when we consider we are the ones who have been wronged.

Those who have gone through hardship and suffering often experience lasting trauma from the event. Feelings of trauma generate feelings of frustration and revenge that can produce a cycle of violence. On this account, psychoanalyst Clara Mucci notes, in her 'Healing and Forgiveness after Traumatic events' chapter, that trauma results in the disruption of all relationships and the consequent aloofness of the victim.[1] Appallingly, through its effects on individuals, trauma has also a disastrous effect on communities. Wrongdoing isolates the offender both from the victims he has hurt and from the moral community he has upset by transgressing its established norms. When trauma becomes prevalent, society loses the sense of trust. Traumatic events fundamentally change not only the victims' way of life, but also their psychological outlook. This is equally true for natural disasters such as earthquakes and floods as it is for man-made catastrophes of terrorism and war. Man-made trauma, however, is often more difficult to deal with because frequently the perpetrators still live in close vicinity to victims, thereby providing constant reminders of the past. Given the irreversibility of the damages inflicted on the offended party, the urgent question is: how can post-violence communities learn to live side by side in peace?

If groups are to live together peacefully, reconciliation is necessary. By reconciliation is meant accepting one another, developing mutual trust, and looking for the possibility of a constructive relationship. And this requires forgiving. Forgiveness has often been portrayed as an interpersonal act involving individuals in the private sphere. Recently however, discourses of forgiveness have infiltrated the political field. Forgiveness, in a political context often has to begin, as it does between individuals, with the statement, 'I'm sorry.' But an act of apology without a corresponding act of forgiveness is really only half the story. If forgiveness is withheld, the apology is left hanging. Reconciliation opens the way for forgiveness and ultimately, the restoration of a moral community,[2] and politics is sustained by the recognition of community as depending upon the citizens' common action. What animates political reconciliation is the citizens' will to share a polity with their historical enemy or oppressor, to transform their relation to their neighbour into one of civic friendship. Political reconciliation, moreover, is both retrospective, in coming to terms with the past, and prospective in bringing about social harmony. Donald Shriver sees forgiveness as a practical necessity in the political arena[3] while Jacques Derrida argues that forgiveness plays an essential, yet paradoxical role in the fraught politics of reconciliation and in the legal, political and moral responses to crimes against humanity. Although Derrida admits that forgiveness leaves him torn[4] with reference to post-colonial violence in Algeria, to him, it is possible 'to forgive the unforgivable.'[5] However while Derrida opposes the symmetry between punishing and forgiving, Heinrich Heine seems to admit a possible combination between the two, stating that 'one must, it is true, forgive one's enemies – but not before they've been hanged.'[6] Where do you find this: in the Bible, the Koran, or in any other religion? I guess not. Does this claim, thus, not open the way for hopelessness and despair?

In order to lay the groundwork for discussion of the issues addressed above and during the third global conference on forgiveness, one should consider the atrocities committed in the name of racial superiority, the daily abuse and murder of children around the world, the anger that cries for revenge and retribution in the face of great evil. Within these examples lie real people for whom the pain of injury is so grave that the hope offered through forgiveness appears as only a pipe dream. There are however historical examples where the pitfalls of revenge had been successfully avoided. Recourse to reconciliation by Archbishop Tutu in South Africa serves as an example. Also memorable in this field is the Algerian President's call for national repentance for the evil committed during the dark decade of terrorism. Building on Shiver's and Derrida's profound insights into the nature of forgiveness in the political arena, and on the idea that reconciliation comes at the end of a process that forgiveness begins, Algerian President, Abdelaziz Bouteflika, came to see that political change requires not only new constitutions, but also a reckoning with the past, a reckoning that entails forgiveness. Only through forgiveness could the Algerians work together to achieve their goals.

This chapter, therefore, explores the Algerian case as an approach that embraces the process of forgiveness within the framework of social reconciliation, a collective attempt to rebuild a co-operative civil society. To this end, I will explore a variety of questions that have come to the forefront in post-genocide in Algeria. In particular, I am concerned with the prospects for peace in the aftermath of the gross abuses of human rights that occurred. But before embarking on the process of reconciliation, I deem it important to focus on the political ideology of fundamentalism in order to explain the breakout of violence following the repression of Islamist groups in some Muslim countries, and in Algeria in particular. I will then proceed to examine the nature of forgiveness proposed by Abdelaziz Bouteflika as an alternative road to peace and social reconstruction.

1. Political Islam in North Africa

The modern era has witnessed violence on an unprecedented scale in wars, genocides and massacres. And since the end of World War II, terrorism has become a major component of contemporary conflict. One of the indicators of contemporary crises is the pervasive recourse to religion, not primarily in its function as faith but as an ideology. The result is the political ideology of fundamentalism. Islamic political thought underwent a dramatic revival in the nineteenth century mainly because of the unprecedented incursion of the Muslim homeland by infidels. To try and cope with this invasion, the fundamentalists resorted to a return to the origins of Islam. And with the decolonisation of the Muslim world in the twentieth century, Islamic political thinkers went a step further. As a reaction to the nationalist, secularist or socialist policies of native Muslim rulers, they began to ask for an Islamicisation of the political system. As the most intensively colonised region of the Muslim world for the longest periods of time, North Africa offers an interesting laboratory for a study of political Islam.

In the words of James Ciment, 'discussions of political Islam [should] begin with a discussion of terms.'[7] I deem it thus worth clarifying certain terms because colonialism had devastated traditional culture so much that interpretations of Islam seemed to be up for grabs. A firm foundation for reasoning and judgment about Islam is to consider the historical usage of the term 'Islam.'

Islam is a religion that has existed for over fourteen centuries and in many different countries. This religion has been hard to understand because it is deemed complex and contradictory. Not surprisingly, it has lent to diverse interpretations. Western media and documents reflect violent and aggressive images of Islam, and academic literature is no less tinged with such stereotypes.[8] As a result, the Muslims have been viewed as the unbending enemies of the world and Western Christendom continues to view them as a threat, especially after the events of September 11th. It is therefore important to reveal the true nature of Islam, and distinguish the terms 'Islamist' and 'Islamism' from 'Muslim' and 'Islam.'

Etymologically, the word 'Islam' comes from *istislam,* which means surrender, that is, surrender to God's precepts. The word is also derived from the word *salam,* or peace, for if we follow God's laws, we will achieve peace in its broadest sense – peace of soul, peace between individuals as well as peace between nations. Islam moreover, propounds the idea of the entire human race as being one family of God. It therefore, transcends all those false impediments of race, ethnicity, status and wealth, and its tenets are those written down in *The Declaration of Human Rights.* Islam moreover presents a message of life and hope, and of a heavenly future, but this message has been distorted. There is a well-publicized Western assumption that Islamic religion and culture contradict the very precepts of peace-building and non-violence. Some *experts* see Islam as a brutal, backward, woman abusing, violent, intellectually narrow ideology that is out to annihilate civilisation.

The term 'Islamism,' coined in eighteenth-century France as a synonym for Islam, began to be displaced by the purely Arabic term 'Islam' by the turn of the twentieth century. As the term gained popularity, the concept 'Islamism' became controversial, not just because it posits a political role for Islam, but also because its advocates have interpreted it in an obscurantist way. Islamism has indeed become more specifically associated with political groups such as the Taliban, the Algerian Armed Islamic Group (FIS), the MIA and Armed Islamic Group (GIA), as well as with repression of free expression and individual rights, and above all with violence.

Over the decades, Islam has thus become a point of reference for a wide range of political activities and opposition movements. Samuel Huntington equates political, economic, and cultural differences with confrontation, and transformed

Islam into a mastermind of terrorism. But I would argue that terror has no religion, and crimes are committed in the name of all religions. We need thus to rethink this basic framework. Although a 'clash of civilizations' might be used to justify aggression, Huntington's most provocative articulation of a clash of civilisations between Islam and modern secular (or Judeo-Christian) democratic values and culture, or between Islamic civilisation and the West[9] is, in my view, founded on misconceptions about Islam and the Islamic world.

It is equally important to note that Islam divides the world into Muslims and unbelievers, or *kafirs*. A kafir is not only a non-Muslim, but also a person who falls under a different moral code from the Muslim, and 'Political Islam' is the doctrine that relates to the latter. More commonly known as Islamic fundamentalism, Political Islam is actually not interested in the religion which it invokes. It must be viewed as a response to the penetration of Western ideas and practices into Muslim societies, and North Africa, geographically closest to the European imperial powers, suffered the most penetration and exhibited the greatest variety of responses over the past century. Against expectations, so-called Westernized Muslim societies such as Egypt, Tunisia, Morocco and Algeria, emerged as centres of Islamic politics.

2. The Growth of Algerian Islamism

The Iranian revolution of 1979-1980 was a turning point in the growth of Algerian Islamism, and became a hotbed of religious activism. Algerian Islamists indeed saw Ayatollah Khomeini as an inspiring Muslim figure for proving that Islam could triumph over political systems.

In Algeria, the relationship between Islam and the state is highly complex and is crucial to an understanding of the country's political and social identities. The Islamist sociologist, François Burgat, argues that the growth of Islamism in Algeria corresponds to a 'third stage' in decolonisation. Islam, according to him, reflects the desire of a formerly colonised country to recapture its cultural past devastated by the French colonisers. Burgat's first stage is political independence and his second is economic independence.[10] This is clearly true. In Algeria where the question of identity is crucial, the Islamists viewed themselves as the purveyors of national authenticity. At independence, the Algerian government stressed the Muslim nature of Algeria and therefore a return to the basic values extolled in the Koran. 'Islam is my religion, Arabic my language, and Algeria my country' was its motto.

In the late 1980s and early 1990s, both economic failures and the euphoria accompanying the fall of the Soviet Union and liberation of Eastern Europe led to an opening of political systems. Islamist candidates in Egypt, Jordan, Tunisia and Algeria emerged as the opposition.

A. The Seeds of the Algerian Crisis

The post-independence Algerian state encountered many difficulties at the economic level, and these predicaments had been replicated at the political and social levels. In the late 1970s, hopelessness about the economy and the country's political future consumed the Algerian population and turned it to the streets. The first stirrings occurred in October 1988. The country's societal ills fed an Islamist opposition much as it did in a number of other Muslim countries. The fundamentalists used the unrest among the large urban population of unemployed people to impose both political change and an Islamic agenda on the National Liberation Front (FLN), the ruling party. Accusing the government of encouraging social division (*fitna*), small groups of armed revolutionists started to challenge the establishment in the name of Islam. Islamicised spaces began to sprout and became centres of radical indoctrination.

The fundamentalists saw the Algerian Islamicisation as a national, rather than pan-Islamic project. They also claimed that under the rule of a secularist and pro-Western FLN, the country has been 'westintoxicated,' a term the FIS borrowed from Iranian Islamists. For many fundamentalists, the main reason why the nation drifted from its cultural and social roots was the satellite. The fundamentalists further argued that the so-called westintoxication of Algerian society has turned Muslim women into objects of desire. They therefore called for the wearing of the veil to free them from that objectification, and a return of the Algerian women home under the firm grip of patriarchal husbands and fathers. The two trends in Algerian political Islam, the techno-Islamists led by Abassi Madani and the neo-fundamentalists led by Ali Belhadj, envisioned an Algerian society in full conformity with the *sharia,* or Muslim law hence, underscored ethical behaviour as the criterion for political leadership.

The Islamist movement became a major force in the 1980s after Algeria's second President, Houari Boumediène, died in 1978. The accession of Chadli Bendjedid to power occasioned a radical change in politics. His regime created a policy vacuum of which the Islamists took advantage. Complaints about the breakdown of Islamic values began to be voiced mainly against those who spoke the French language. The government then proceeded to liberalize the political system. It decided on constitutional reform, allowing the emergence of political parties, and freeing the Press. Several parties, therefore, began to claim national leadership, including the FLN, the Berber-dominated Front of Socialist Forces (FFS), and the FIS. Besides these groups, some independent civic organisations emerged such as those representing women,[11] intellectuals and human rights activists. Thus, when given the opportunity to express themselves politically for the first time in the 1990 and 1991 municipal and parliamentary elections, the vast majority voted for the FIS, a radical Islamist party. In the first round of national legislative elections in late 1991, although the FIS received one million fewer votes than in the municipal elections, it still garnered twice as many as the ruling FLN.

The Front of Socialist Forces, (FFS) the secularly oriented party with particular strength in Berber areas which took a smaller percentage of the vote, came in a distant third. The FLN suffered a disastrous setback at the polls. The FIS managed to secure 188 of 430 seats, though not an absolute majority. The Islamist party's crushing victory shocked the ruling elite, and pushed the government to alter its strategies because neither the Algerian military nor the current regime was ready to accept this verdict for changes in state and society. On January 4, 1992, a presidential decree suspended the National People's Assembly, and a week later under pressure from the military high command, the army forced President Bendjedid, who seemed willing to cohabit with the Islamists, to resign and a temporary five-member High State Committee (*Haut Comité d'Etat*, an institution not provided for by the Constitution) was installed. The Committee recalled Mohamed Boudiaf, a historic figure and founder of the FLN, from his twenty-eight-year exile in Morocco, at the head of the country. As the Islamists' armed attacks increased, the HCE decreed a state of emergency for one year,[12] cancelled the results of the December elections (since no party had won a majority in the first round), banned the FIS, and arrested the remainder of its leaders. Boudiaf then, launched a serious campaign against the Islamists and against corruption in the state and army hierarchies, but he was assassinated by one of his security guards on June 29, 1992.

B. The Islamist Challenge

After the military-backed authorities decided to cancel legislative elections the radical Islamic party was poised to win in 1991, Algeria plunged into chaos. From that period until 2002, the country went through the most egregious violence since colonial times. At the heart of the insurgency were four groups: the Armed Islamic Movement (Mouvement Islamique Armé, MIA), the Islamic Salvation Army (Armée Islamique du Salut, AIS, the armed wing of the FIS), the Armed Islamic Group (Groupe Islamique Armée, GIA), and the Salafist Group for Preaching and Combat (Groupe Salafiste pour la Prédication et le Combat, GSPC). The Islamist militants launched a campaign of terror against the government and anyone who refused to live by their prohibitions. To them, violence was justified by the end sought: the downfall of the existing regime. By mid-1997, Algeria passed the test of 'gross and systematic violations of human rights that offend every precept of our common humanity,' or the 'conscience-shocking'[13] threshold. Following the Rais massacre of 28-29 August 1997, an official with the Algerian Medical Union reported that '[e]ven the foetuses have been taken from their disembowelled mothers to be mutilated and massacred.'[14] A survivor of the Béni Messous massacre saw armed men take 'my aunt and slit her throat, after slashing open her stomach.'[15] Another witness recalled for *Agence France Press* that '[a] baby was beheaded and as its mother run away, her breast was slashed with a sword.'[16] François d'Alançon spoke to a survivor of the Bentalha massacre who had watched attackers hack his wife and daughter to death with axes, and then saw his son butchered.[17] Following one of the massacres in Relizane, a city in the west of the country, the Algerian daily *Liberté* reported that infants' heads had been smashed against walls to kill them. And this is but half the story of the horrors that occurred in Algeria.

This terror regime to which the Algerian population had been subjected recalled the genocide perpetrated by the Nazis in the death camps, in Auschwitz-Birkenau as reported by Karolina Wigura. Were the Islamists and the Nazis not actually killing the God himself? If as Wigura pointed out 'Auschwitz [was] the biggest challenge for contemporary Christian theology,'[18] the fundamentalists' challenge in Algeria and in other Muslim countries was the greatest slap to Islam, a religion deemed of peace and tolerance. The Shoah, according to Ratzinger, Wigura goes on, 'was not a crime committed by Germans (or other nations who helped) towards the Jews, but by Christians towards the Jews, and also ... the Shoah ... changed the Christian concept of God'[19] much as the fratricide in Algeria changed the Muslim concept of God. After such knowledge, one might ask: how can the perpetrators of such massacres be forgiven? How can ethics and politics be reconstructed in the aftermath of such violence, through forgiveness? 'What would reconciliation mean here?'[20] Is it still possible to continue to strive for both hope and forgiveness as James Arvanitakis claimed in his chapter on 'forgiveness, hope and community?'[21] Or can there be radical forgiveness for 'radical evil,'[22] as Elizabeth Gedge suggested in her chapter on radical forgiveness? These questions inaugurate Derrida's thought of ethics, the possible and the impossible. In line with Derrida, the Algerian President claims that the impossible is possible. The President believes that forgiveness is a virtue, and sees reconciliation not as a demagogic slogan, but as a precisely defined stage in the peace process, one that obeys well-grounded principles established on the basis of conflict resolution experiences.

3. 'The Muse of Forgiveness'[23]

Following the 1990s genocide, the Algerian government was left with the staggering tasks of restoring some measure of order, and fostering reconciliation within Algerian society. Therefore, from the outset of his campaign, the Algerian President enunciated a clear direction of intent. 'I solemnly pledge that I will change things in Algeria from top to bottom,'[24] he told reporters after he cast his ballot near the presidential palace. He also declared, 'I am determined to make peace, and I am prepared to die for it.'[25] Following his investiture in 1999, the Head of the Algerian State immediately turned his attention to the legal and political resolution of the domestic conflict. His agenda focused initially on restoring security and stability to the country. He, therefore, set as a key objective the promotion of national reconciliation in Algeria's profoundly divided society. But for reconciliation to be effective there must be forgiveness, and there is no readiness for forgiveness without repentance, he declared. One of the many challenges to steer the country out of the spiral of violence was the President's offer of forgiveness to repentant Islamist fighters. That was one of the first attempts at reconciliation after the tragedies of the black decade of terrorism. In July 1999, the Algerian President introduced in the National People's Assembly, the Civil Harmony Law[26] which aimed at granting conditional amnesty to insurgents willing to lay down their arms and re-integrate into civil society. Though much criticized by various human rights organisations and met with considerable animosity from genocide survivors and family victims, this Civil Concord policy was widely approved in a nationwide referendum in September 2000.

President Bouteflika saw his plan of forgiveness as a means of breaking the cycle of hatred, resentment, anger and pain; as one of the main guarantees for social order; and a good step for regenerating the country, but also as a means to restore faith not only in his people, but in life itself. He effectively transmitted to the Algerians the hope inherent in making a lifelong commitment to pursue forgiveness, and linked the essence of forgiveness within a religious perspective to the salvation offered by God. Contrary to Daryl R. Van Tongeren et al's discussion on 'The Horserace: Which Religion is most Forgiving?' in which they seem to give prominence to Christianity as being 'the best' in forgiving,[27] I would posit that all major religious traditions extol the value of forgiveness and teach us that we can rectify the damage we cause by our sins through the process of repentance. Also some religious doctrines place greater emphasis on the need for humans to find some sort of divine forgiveness for their own shortcomings. Playing on the notion of pardon as a transmitted gift in the French *par-don*, Elizabeth Gedge, very much like Paul Ricoeur, proposes a radical forgiveness of past crimes. But Gedge underlines the fact that though 'an inspiring ideal, this radical notion of forgiveness may be at odds with the psychological and moral requirements for successful forgiving.'[28] Given the self-denying nature of Christian love, as Hannah Arendt shows in her *Love and Saint Augustine*, there seems to be a paradox inherent in the ideal of radical forgiveness. Jesus Christ's sermon, articulated on the mount, that people should love their enemies[29] seems to contradict our mundane experience of love, points out Arendt who wonders how the individual could be 'at all interested in his neighbour,'[30] a point I fully agree with. Certainly radical forgiveness may initiate political reconciliation, but this ideal is unduly optimistic and seems at odds with our materialistic and atheist world. Some people indeed might not see God as a divine protector, taking care of them after experiencing hardships. Concurrently, they will feel some anger towards Him. Much of the emphasis in Julie Exline's chapter is indeed on Western, Judeo-Christian examples of negative emotions towards God.[31] But protest toward God is morally wrong in Islam.

Forgiveness is an attribute which has received due attention in Islam and is extensively discussed in the Holy Koran. Islam teaches that God is the most forgiving and is the original source of all forgiveness. Allah's mercy is unlimited and His love infinite. There are many names of Allah given in the Koran, some of which are related to His mercy and forgiveness. Let us just mention some of these names: the name, *Al-Ghafoor* or the most forgiving occurs more than seventy times in the Koran. *Al-Tawwab* or the Acceptor of repentance is another name of Allah. The word *tawwab* gives the sense of oft-returning, which means that Allah again and again accepts the repentance. *Al-Halim,* or the Clement; *Al-Rahman,* the most Merciful; *Al-Rahim,* or the most compassionate. Other names, such as *Al-Afuw,* have another aspect of forgiveness. Literally the word *afw* means to release, to heal and to restore. Thus, in relation to God, the act of forgiveness releases us from the burden of punishment due to our sins and restores our honour after we have dishonoured ourselves by committing those sins. President Bouteflika recalled the Algerians that Islam is a religion that offers humanity a life filled with the peace and that reconciliation between individuals is predicated upon a universal love that banishes all distinctions between people, including that between friend and enemy. There is however more than a theological reason for choosing to forgive.

There is nothing to compare with the therapeutic effect of forgiveness. Forgiveness liberates, to a certain extent, both the forgiver and the forgiven from the burden of irreversibility. It has been advocated for centuries as a balm for hurt and angry feelings and can lead to decreased anger, depression, anxiety, stress as well as enhanced well-being, including peace of mind. In her programmatic experiments on 'altruistic forgiveness,' Charlotte van Oyen Witvliet noticed that empathy and pro-social forgiveness remarkably lessened negative emotions such as rumination about the transgression and grudge-holding while at the same time enhancing positive emotion.[32]

Failing to reconcile unresolved anger and blame for past hurt or offence can seriously impair physical and emotional health. Therefore, one should find within the capacity for letting wrongs go, no matter how horrendous the grievance, and try to forgive in order to step towards a more positive future. Otherwise, the wronged individual risks suffering a threefold oppression: first, by the wrong itself; second, by the hatred of others that may consume him/her; and third, re-entering a political dimension, by the continuing social conflict that a lack of forgiveness helps to keep alive.

4. Healing Relational Trauma through Relational Means

It is therefore necessary to base human relations on forgiveness. The innumerable situations that call for forgiveness attest to its centrality for life as each of us is bound to co-habit with others. Without forgiveness there can be no change, no growth, and no real freedom. Lives are transformed as hope takes the place of guilt, anger, as relationships are restored. Consider now its political implications. Politics is concerned with men in their neighbourly relations to each other as friends and enemies. Following from this, reconciliation necessarily anticipates a future community. A more politically focused interpretation of forgiveness thus depicts forgiveness and hope as a means of launching a new beginning by rebuilding social, political and economic structures on a national level. It is important then, for those who care about lasting relationships to better understand the dynamics of forgiveness. President Bouteflika thus, drew attention to revenge and retaliation as potent forces that destroy human bonds. He insisted that increased forgiveness can be a path to greater peace and understanding that has also both psychosocial and physiological value. As he pointed out, forgiveness is a commitment to a process of change. But the President added that forgiveness certainly does not change the past. It is making peace with the past. What ever happened ... has happened ... it is done. But our feelings about the past can change. This notion of breaking with the past does not mean wiping everything from memory. Contrary to popular belief that links forgiving to forgetting, forgiveness begins with memory. The President espoused a tough-minded conception of forgiveness, one that avoids the moral blindness of simply condoning actions. As Clara Mucci pointed out, 'Memories of the past for the patient-victim become a form of testimony,'[33] and testimony as the basis for reconciliation, becomes 'the [very] foundation of both the ethical and the political dimension of it.' While undoubtedly a solid foundation, President Bouteflika takes reconciliation to mean also a process that leads to developing a normative interaction between ethnic and political opponents based on mutual acceptance as distinct but equal co-members of the same, larger community. The President believes that conflict can be ended satisfactorily only with the establishment of a society between former enemies. It is this sense of forgiveness that creates an authentic community as James Arvanitakis discusses in his chapter. Arvanitakis's dominant conceptualisation of community 'crosses all political divides'[34] and entails reciprocity. And only hope and forgiveness can promote reciprocity despite the differences of the individuals that constitute this community, he further argues. What these members of community share, according to him, is 'a reciprocal desire to establish and maintain community.' This background also informs the Algerian President's peace plan. The Head of the Algerian State identified the restoration of mutual respect as one of the goals of forgiveness. From the perspective of this imagined common future, the experience of the present is interpreted as a possible new beginning. And political reconciliation is prompted by the hope of setting such a fresh start.

Moreover, the President's policy of amnesty was never meant to diminish the trauma that families and individuals had to go through. He saw amnesty as 'a collective act of forgiveness,' to borrow Bennett Christopher's words in his 2003 article which bears the same title. It is powerful because it combines backward-looking accountability and forward-looking reconciliation. His concept of forgiveness as an optimistic release empowering the giver also challenges Nietzsche's claim that forgiveness is weakness. President Bouteflika rather sees forgiveness as a 'shift in thinking,'[35] which can only be achieved through a psychical distancing as Richard Kyte explains in his chapter on 'The Art of

Forgiving: Conditions of Perspective and Transformation.' Kyte believes that forgiveness is a 'form of catharsis: it is a cleansing or washing away of debilitating emotions... Forgiveness is the resumption of love,'[36] the ultimate goal of social strategies such as reconciliation in line with the Head of the Algerian State's plan. If the Algerian society is to fully confront and overcome past evils and injustices, it will have to come to grips with the anger, distrust, and hatred. The President also explained that the act of revenge is self-perpetuating and unending while forgiveness stops the vicious cycle and promotes a true sense of love. It can heal both the forgiver and the forgiven. Forgiveness, he insisted, is a courageous and powerful expression of unconditional acceptance and love that can be seen as an attempt to stop the transfer of hatred from one generation to the next. Only this kind of relationship keeps open the possibility of reconciliation and closes the door on revenge.

     In this chapter, I have attempted to discuss political forgiveness as a new realm of ethical thought growing exponentially with the need to end social conflicts and heal wounds. To this end, I have explored the nature and role of political forgiveness proposed by the Algerian President as a means of reckoning with past political violence and a way of facilitating the healing of political society and promoting the political reconstruction of a fractured political society. Political and social solutions to violence are sought through the experience of the individual because violence is used against individuals not as individuals, but *qua* members of a political group. To this end, it is no surprise that concepts such as forgiveness and reconciliation have gained such popular appeal in political usage. Reconciliation has indeed become an authoritative discourse governing political transition in countries emerging from bloody conflicts. Beneath the surface of these healing processes and acts of contrition lies a common theme, the need for social reconstruction. Social reconciliation opens the door to forgiveness and offers an escape from the self-perpetuating cycle of revenge by encompassing a broader and different interpretation of justice as reconciliation that restores individual rights rather than simply punishing those perceived to be members of a group of perpetrators. Algeria, a country torn apart by a decade of civil war in the 1990s, can be seen as an example of the overlapping of religious, political, and cultural processes on the road to reconciliation. The Algerian President adopted an ethico-political approach to political violence and forgiveness. However, while Desmond Tutu linked the hope for an ethical reconstruction of South Africa to a religious position on forgiveness, President Bouteflika, very much like Jacques Derrida, tried to develop an 'ethics beyond ethics,'[37] and certainly an ethics beyond religion, a politico-theological conceptualisation of forgiveness to sustain what Hannah Arendt terms 'the web of relationships.'[38] The Algerian President's conflict-resolution initiative affirms his commitment to a more peaceful and harmonious future for the sake of achieving a political community after its fracture. By promoting national reconciliation, fostering mutual trust and confidence, the

Head of the Algerian State sought to remove the vestiges of political vendetta and victimization. He advocated forgiveness as a vital process of human interchange, and a strategy for the social recovery of the victim with the purpose of reconstituting the national whole. It is only when the various sectors of society affected are brought back together that the country could advance toward national reconciliation. The Algerian President understood that not forgiving those who violated human rights would allow the history of trauma to dominate the political arena in ways that would perpetuate those internal divisions rather than minimize them, undermining thus the move toward development. The President's gift for reconciling marks him as a politician of great skill who knew how to keep his people focused on a goal to soften their animosities towards each other. Of course, given past violence as well as present rage and distrust, many Algerians remain sceptical about the possibility for citizens to learn to relate in healthier ways. And although the practical implementation of Algeria's amnesty project remains the most problematic for some families inextricably caught in the web of their tragic history, the desire to put an end to violence and build a new and better future egged the Algerians on moving forward with a sense of common purpose, accusing, but forgiving in the words of Léopold Sédar Senghor.[39]

Notes

[1] Clara Mucci, 'Healing and Forgiveness after Traumatic Events: The Case of Holocaust Survivors from the Fortunoff Archives', in *A Journey through Forgiveness,* edited by Malika Rebai Maamri, Nehama Verbin, and Everett L. Worthington, Jr. (Oxford: Inter-Disciplinary Press, 2010), accessed May 19, 2011, http://www.inter-disciplinary.net/publishing/id-press/ebooks/a-journey-through-forgiveness/, 111.

[2] See Christopher Bennett, 'The Varieties of Retributive Experience', *The Philosophical Quarterly* 52.207 (2002): 145-163, and his 'Is Amnesty a Collective Act of Forgiveness?' in *Contemporary Political Theory* 2.1 (2003): 67-76.

[3] Donald W. Jr. Shriver, *An Ethic for Enemies: Forgiveness in Politics* (Oxford: Oxford University Press, 1995), 58.

[4] Jacques Derrida, *On Cosmopolitanism and Forgiveness* (New York: Routledge, 2001), 39.

[5] Ibid.

[6] Patrice Vecchione (ed), *Revenge and Forgiveness: an Anthology of Poems* (New York: Henry Holt, 2004), 108.

[7] James Ciment, *Algeria: The Fundamentalist Challenge: Conflict and Crisis in the Post-Cold War World* (New York: Facts on File, 1997), 63.

[8] Paulinus Chappe's work laid down the foundations to a tradition of books portraying various aspects of Turkish culture together with their so-called atrocities

against Christians. The atrocities which were alleged to have been committed were highly spiced to suit the spirit of the time. Accounts of atrocities were used to inflame the minds of the Christians and incite them to take the Cross against the infidels. For the purpose of propaganda, much was also made of the so-called idolatry of Muslims. The belief that Prophet Mohamed was worshipped as a god became widespread and was fostered by accounts written by some participants. The song of Roland for instance, says: '*The Muslim loves not God, serve Mahound and worships Apollon.*'

[9] See Samuel P. Huntington, *The Clash of Civilizations and the Remaking of the World Order* (New York: Touchstone, Rockefeller Centre, 1996).

[10] François Burgat and William Dowell, *The Islamic Movement in North Africa* (Texas: Austin Centre for Middle East Studies at the University of Texas, 1993), 67.

[11] It should be noted that some of these organisations existed well before 1989. The organisation of working women, for instance, dates back to the 1970s.

[12] But it has actually been in effect until February 24th 2011.

[13] See Gareth Evans, 'The Responsibility to Protect: An Idea whose Time has Come . . . and Gone?' in *International Relations* 22.3 (2008): 283-289.

[14] *Houston Chronicle*, '"We cried . . . but no one came": Scores Await Burial as Survivors Describe Massacres in Algeria', 31 August, 1997, A32.

[15] Rachid Khiari, 'Three Years Later, Algeria's Civil War has Gone International', *Associated Press*, 31 December, 1994.

[16] Agence France Press, '63 Civilians Massacred in Algeria', 6 September, 1997b.

[17] François d'Alançon, 'Algérie. A trois jours des élections municipales, Bentalha continue de panser ses plaies', *La Croix* (21 October, 1997) : 10.

[18] Karolina Wigura, 'Forgiveness or Reconciliation after the Shoah? An Ecumenical Perspective', in *A Journey through Forgiveness*, edited by Malika Rebai Maamri, Nehama Verbin, and Everett L. Worthington, Jr. (Oxford: Inter Disciplinary Press, 2010), accessed May 19, 2011, http://www.interdisciplinary. net/publishing/id-press/ebooks/a-journey-through-forgiveness/, 61.

[19] Ibid.

[20] Ibid.

[21] James Arvantakis, 'On Forgiveness, Hope and Community: Or the Fine Line Step between Authentic and Fractured Communities', in *A Journey through Forgiveness*, edited by Malika Rebai Maamri, Nehama Verbin, and Everett L. Worthington, Jr. (Oxford: Inter Disciplinary Press, 2010), accessed May 19, 2011, http://www.interdisciplinary.net/publishing/id-press/ebooks/a-journey-through-forgiveness/, 149.

[22] The concept of 'radical evil' comes from a recent philosophical position that suggests that contrary to traditional Greek, Jewish, and Christian thought where

evil was denied any positivity, and seen only as the privation of being itself, the unprecedented evil of the twentieth century cannot be viewed as privative, but as the positive will toward destruction and the cold infliction of suffering. The annihilation of human life of the last century suggests that evil can be pursued for its own sake, that is, as an end in itself. Evil, therefore, would be a pure act of perversity without ground. The development of this theory goes back to the first use of the term by Immanuel Kant in his essay *Religion within the Bounds of Mere Reason*, through Schelling, to Heidegger.

[23] I am borrowing here Wole Soyinka's phrase.

[24] Howard Schneider, 'Algerians Approve Rebel Amnesty Plan', *Washington Post Foreign Service Friday*, September 17, 1999, A17.

[25] *Al-Ahram Weekly*, no. 4141, August 5, 1999.

[26] Law no 99-08 of July 13, 1999.

[27] Everett L. Worthington, Jr. et al., 'Forgiveness and Religion: Update and Current Status', in *A Journey through Forgiveness*, edited by Malika Rebai Maamri, Nehama Verbin, and Everett L. Worthington, Jr. (Oxford: Inter Disciplinary Press, 2010), accessed May 19, 2011, http://www.interdisciplinary.net/publishing/id-press/ebooks/a-journey-through-forgiveness/, 55.

[28] Elisabeth Gedge, 'Radical Forgiveness and Feminist Theology', in *A Journey through Forgiveness*, edited by Malika Rebai Maamri, Nehama Verbin, and Everett L. Worthington, Jr. (Oxford: Inter Disciplinary Press, 2010), accessed May 19, 2011, http://www.interdisciplinary.net/publishing/id-press/ebooks/a-journey-through-forgiveness/, 69.

[29] Luke 6, 31-37.

[30] Hannah Arendt, *Love and Saint Augustine,* eds. J. V. Scott and J. C. Stark (Chicago, London: University of Chicago Press, 1996), 7.

[31] See Julie Exline, 'Anger toward God: A New Frontier in the Study of Forgiveness', in *A Journey through Forgiveness*, edited by Malika Rebai Maamri, Nehama Verbin, and Everett L. Worthington, Jr. (Oxford: Inter Disciplinary Press, 2010), accessed May 19, 2011, http://www.interdisciplinary.net/publishing/id-press/ebooks/a-journey-through-forgiveness/, 29-37.

[32] Charlotte van Oyen Witvliet, 'Empirical Studies of Forgiveness as an Altruistic Response: Relationships with Rumination, Suppression of Negative Emotions, and Benefit-Focused Reappraisal', in *A Journey through Forgiveness*, edited by Malika Rebai Maamri, Nehama Verbin, and Everett L. Worthington, Jr. (Oxford: Inter Disciplinary Press, 2010), accessed May 19, 2011, http://www.interdisciplinary.net/publishing/id-press/ebooks/a-journey-through-forgiveness/, 99.

[33] Clara Mucci, 'Healing and Forgiveness after Traumatic Events: The Case of Holocaust Survivors from the Fortunoff Archives', 112.

[34] James Arvantakis, 'On Forgiveness, Hope and Community: Or the Fine Line Step between Authentic and Fractured Communities', 154.

[35] Sonja Lyubomirsky, *The How of Happiness: A Scientific Approach to Getting the Life You Want* (New York: The Penguin Press, 2008), 171.

[36] Richard Kyte, 'The Art of Forgiving: Conditions of Perspective and Transformation', in *A Journey through Forgiveness*, edited by Malika Rebai Maamri, Nehama Verbin, and Everett L. Worthington, Jr. (Oxford: Inter Disciplinary Press, 2010), accessed May 19, 2011, http://www.interdisciplinary. net/publishing/id-press/ebooks/a-journey-through-forgiveness/, 84.

[37] Jacques Derrida, *Adieu to Emmanuel Levinas*, trans. Pascale-Anne Brault and Michel Nas (Stanford: Stanford University Press, 1999), 4.

[38] Hannah Arendt, *Crisis of the Republic* (New York: The Penguin Press, 1959), 163.

[39] 'J'accuse, mais, je pardonne', cited in Wole Soyinka, *The Burden of Memory, The Muse of Forgiveness* (Oxford: Oxford University Press, 1999), 93.

Bibliography

Amstutz, Mark. *The Healing of Nations: The Promise and Limits of Political Forgiveness*. Chicago: University of Chicago Press, 2005.

Arendt, Hannah. *Crisis of the Republic*. New York: The Penguin Press, 1959.

————. *Love and Saint Augustine*, edited by J. V. Scott and J. C. Stark, 7. Chicago, London: University of Chicago Press, 1996.

Arvantakis, James. 'On Forgiveness, Hope and Community: Or the Fine Line Step between Authentic and Fractured Communities'. In in *A Journey through Forgiveness*, edited by Malika Rebai Maamri, Nehama Verbin, and Everett L. Worthington, Jr. (Oxford: Inter-Disciplinary Press, 2010), accessed May 19, 2011, http://www.interdisciplinary.net/publishing/id-press/ebooks/a-journey-through-forgiveness/.

Bennett, Christopher. 'The Varieties of Retributive Experience'. *The Philosophical Quarterly* 52 (2002): 207, 145-163.

————. 'Is Amnesty a Collective Act of Forgiveness?' *Contemporary Political Theory* 2 (2003): 67-76.

Burgat, François and William Dowell. *The Islamic Movement in North Africa.* Austin Centre for Middle East Studies at the University of Texas, 1993.

Ciment, James. *Algeria: The Fundamentalist Challenge: Conflict and Crisis in the Post-Cold War World.* New York: Facts on File, 1997.

Digeser, Peter. *Political Forgiveness.* New York: Cornell University Press, 2001.

Derrida, Jacques. *On Cosmopolitanism and Forgiveness.* New York: Routledge, 2001.

D'Alançon, François. 'Algérie : A trois jours des élections municipales, Bentalha continue de panser ses plaies'. *La Croix*, 21 October, 1997, 10.

Du Bois, François and Antje Du Bois-Pedani. *Justice and Reconciliation in Post-Apartheid South Africa.* Cambridge: Cambridge University Press, 2008.

Exline, Julie. 'Anger toward God: A New Frontier in the Study of Forgiveness'. In *A Journey through Forgiveness*, edited by Rebai Maamri, Malika, Verbin, Nehama and Worthington, Jr., Everett L. Oxford: Inter-Disciplinary Press, 2010. Accessed May 19, 2011. http://www.inter-disciplinary.net/publishing/id-press/ebooks/a-journey-through-forgiveness/.

Gedge, Elisabeth. 'Radical Forgiveness and Feminist Theology'. In *A Journey through Forgiveness,* edited by Rebai Maamri, Malika, Verbin, Nehama and Worthington, Jr., Everett L. Oxford: Inter-Disciplinary Press, 2010. Accessed May 19, 2011. http://www.inter-disciplinary.net/publishing/id-press/ebooks/a-journey-through-forgiveness/.

Herman, J., *Trauma and Recovery.* New York: Basic Books, 1992.

Humphrey, Michael. *The Politics of Atrocity and Reconciliation: From Terror to Trauma.* London, New York: Routledge, 2002.

Huntington, Samuel. *The Clash of Civilizations and the Remaking of the World Order.* New York: Touchstone, Rockefeller Centre, 1996.

Jankélévitch,Vladimir. *Forgiveness.* Translated by Andrew Kelley. Chicago: University of Chicago Press, 2005.

Khiari, Rachid. 'Three Years Later, Algeria's Civil War has Gone International'. *Associated Press*, 31 December, 1994.

Kyte, Richard. 'The Art of Forgiving: Conditions of Perspective and Transformation'. In *A Journey through Forgiveness,* edited by Rebai Maamri, Malika, Verbin, Nehama and Worthington, Jr., Everett L. Oxford: Inter-Disciplinary Press, 2010. Accessed May 19, 2011. http://www.inter-disciplinary.net/publishing/id-press/ebooks/a-journey-through-forgiveness/.

Lyubomirsky, Sonja. *The How of Happiness: A Scientific Approach to Getting the Life You Want.* New York: The Penguin Press, 2008.

Mucci, Clara. 'Healing and Forgiveness after Traumatic Events: The Case of Holocaust Survivors from the Fortunoff Archives'. In *A Journey through Forgiveness,* edited by Rebai Maamri, Malika, Nehama Verbin and Everett L. Worthington, Jr. Oxford: Inter-Disciplinary Press, 2010. Accessed May 19, 2011. http://www.inter-disciplinary.net/publishing/id-press/ebooks/a-journey-through-forgiveness/.

Potter, Nancy Nyquist. *Trauma, Truth and Reconciliation: Healing Damaged Relationships.* Oxford: Oxford University Press, 2006.

Ransley, Cynthia and Terri Spy. *Forgiveness and the Healing Process: A Central Therapeutic Concern.* Hove, East Sussex : Brunner-Routledge, 2004.

Ricoeur, Paul. *La mémoire, l'histoire, l'oubli.* Paris: Seuil, 2000.

Shriver, Donald W. Jr. *An Ethic for Enemies: Forgiveness in Politics.* Oxford: Oxford University Press, 1995.

Soyinka, Wole. *The Burden of Memory, the Muse of Forgiveness.* New York, Oxford: Oxford University Press, 1999.

Tavuchis, Nicholas. *Mea Culpa: A Sociology of Apology and Reconciliation.* Stanford: Stanford University Press, 1991.

Tutu, Desmond. *No Future without Forgiveness: A Personal Overview of South Africa's Truth and Reconciliation Commission.* London: Rider, 1999.

Vecchione, Patrice. *Revenge and Forgiveness: An Anthology of Poems*. New York: Henry Holt, 2004.

Volcan, Vamik. *Killing in the Name of Identity: A Study of Bloody Conflicts*. Charlottesville: Pitchstone Pub., 2006.

Wigura, Karolina. 'Forgiveness or Reconciliation after the Shoah? An Ecumenical Perspective'. In *A Journey through Forgiveness*, edited by Rebai Maamri, Malika, Verbin, Nehama and Worthington, Jr., Everett L. Oxford: Inter-Disciplinary Press, 2010. Accessed May 19, 2011. http://www.inter-disciplinary.net/publishing/id-press/ebooks/a-journey-through-forgiveness/.

Witvliet, Charlotte vanOyen. 'Empirical Studies of Forgiveness as an Altruistic Response: Relationships with Rumination, Suppression of Negative Emotions, and Benefit-Focused Reappraisal'. In *A Journey through Forgiveness*, edited by Rebai Maamri, Malika, Verbin, Nehama and Worthington, Jr., Everett L. Oxford: Inter-Disciplinary Press, 2010. Accessed May 19, 2011. http://www.inter-disciplinary.net/publishing/id-press/ebooks/a-journey-through-forgiveness/.

Worthington, Jr., Everett L., Daryl R. Van Tongeren, Don E. Davis, Joshua N. Hook, Aubrey L. Gartner, David J. Jennings II, Chelsea L. Greer and Todd W. Greer. 'Forgiveness and Religion: Update and Current Status'.

Malika Rebai Maamri is a Senior Lecturer at the National School of Higher Education in Political Science in Algiers, Algeria. Her research interests include literature with a focus on cultural contact, political community in Africa, Teaching and Education. She is currently writing a book entitled *Citizenship and Fractured National Identity in Algeria*.

Forgiveness and Hope: Re-Building Fractured Communities

James Arvanitakis

Abstract
This chapter draws on Kelly Oliver's notions of social forgiveness and 'heroic particularity' and a cross section of papers from this volume to look at the agency in forgiveness. I argue that forgiveness exists as meaning rather than referring to absolution or even exoneration. Concentrating on this creation of meaning, this chapter considers the role of forgiveness in bringing together fractured communities by looking at a particularly case study: the Civil War in Bougainville, Papua New Guinea. While forgiveness is fundamental in rebuilding such fractured communities, I also argue that this must be accompanied by a sense of hope – or a vision that a better world is possible. Like forgiveness, this is an active rather than a passive hope – achieved through actions and a sense of agency.

Key Words: Forgiveness, hope, post-conflict societies, Bougainville, reciprocity, community.

*****

1. Introduction

The history of our world is, unfortunately, often one of war, violence and conflict. Countless scholarship has been devoted to understanding the triggers to these conflicts: from aggressive acts of unprovoked attack to the folly of human decision-making and revenge for past injustices (both real and perceived), to the desire to expand one's empire and mark the emergence of modern nationhood. In many of these historical accounts, the path to war is made to feel almost inevitable, as the key points and sparks are identified, described and analysed.

What receives much less scholarly attention, however, are the triggers to peace. That is, while the path to any specific conflict is clearly marked by particular episodes, the events that lead the combatants towards peace, particularly following a protracted war where all sides have committed acts of violence, injustice and aggression, are given much less consideration.

If we look at an intra-community conflict, for example, the various political, social, environmental and economic events that led to the dispute are often the focus of much discussion. When peace finally breaks out, we celebrate the political 'peace makers' and often award them international prizes for their efforts – something that they richly deserve.

What is often missing in discussions, however, are the moments when 'ordinary' people decide to 'let go' of the conflict and instead, concentrate on peace. As such, the following question is rarely considered: when do neighbours who have become enemies in a conflict, decide to lay down their arms, release the built up hatreds, and begin to work towards building a post-conflict society?

It is this question that has perplexed me in the many years I spent working in societies that had been in conflict, and it is this question that I attempt to answer in this chapter. To achieve this, I draw on Kelly Oliver's work and her notions of social forgiveness and 'heroic particularity,' and attempt to fuse some of the key themes raised by a cross section of other authors from this very volume. In so doing, I argue that the act of forgiveness exists as meaning rather than referring to absolution or even exoneration. Concentrating on this creation of meaning, I argue that 'forgiving' is an active process that requires a sense of agency 'to forgive.'

Additionally, I put forward that a second dimension that needs to be added to the act of forgiveness to achieve peace: the process of establishing a sense of hope. As will be discussed below, this is also an active process of both believing that a better world is possible, *and* also taking actions to make this world materialize. That is, while forgiveness is fundamental in rebuilding such fractured communities, this must be accompanied by a sense of hope, or a vision that a better world is possible. This too is an active rather than a passive process.

Consequently, this chapter considers both the role of forgiveness and hope in bringing together fractured communities. To do this, I draw on a particularly case study, the Civil War in Bougainville, Papua New Guinea. This conflict is one that I personally witnessed as a volunteer in a post-conflict project. As I facilitated a workshop, I was confronted with a stark realization that before me was a group of ex-combatants from different sides of the conflict working together to re-build their society. These men and women had only months before been armed and involved in a bloody confrontation that had left tens of thousands dead.

It is important to note that much of the island of Bougainville remained in conflict while this work was happening. During my time in Bougainville, United Nations peacekeepers remained deployed throughout the Island while a significant section was identified as a 'no go zone.' I was there when the fragile peace that had been established was at a crossroad and many were not convinced it would hold. Despite this, the ex-combatants involved in the workshop showed no signs of hostility, but only cooperation.

It was during this workshop that I witnessed the agency inherent in both forgiveness and hope. This case study highlights how both these elements are essential in moving societies from a conflict to post-conflict situation. Before discussing this in greater detail, it is important to provide some detailed background regarding the conflict.

2. Background: An Unforgiving Landscape

In 2000, the province of Bougainville, Papua New Guinea (PNG) was slowly emerging from a ten-year Civil War, a war that had not only pitted the indigenous population against the PNG Defence Force (supported by both the PNG and

Australian governments) but also saw intra-community fighting. Neighbours and friends turned on each other as a once united community fractured.

The trigger that ignited the conflict was a dispute over the land associated with the Bougainville Copper Ltd (BCL) mine based at Panguna.[1] This dissension challenged the very core of Bougainville society as it resulted in a redistribution of communal ownership to a private property rights regime.

Historically, the people of Bougainville considered their lands to be communally owned (or 'commons') with the concept of individual land ownership alien.[2] The communal land is not only fundamental for material needs such as food and housing, but also for identity and relationships. Following a prospecting licence granted to the Australian based mining company CRA by the then Australian colonial government, the land was effectively seized and the commons were privatised and enclosed. Physical displacement followed along with a dislocation of the community bonds. By establishing this mine, the very fabric of the society was dramatically altered.

In the process of setting up the mine, CRA cleared and poisoned two hundred and twenty hectares of the forests surrounding Panguna.[3] As was standard practice, the remains from the clear felling were discarded directly into the local river network along with a billion tons of toxic waste. This left a trail of environmental devastation approximately thirty-five kilometres long. The river network became obstructed with tailings and eventually overflowed, turning once vibrant flat lands into contaminated swamps as fish and animal species disappeared. While I had read about the environmental devastation caused by the mine, it was only when I personally witnessed the wastelands that I understood the true extent of the damage done.

The consequences were not only environmental but also social. The first round of mining forcibly displaced some eight hundred people, with another one thousand and four hundred lost their fishing rights. A second wave of human displacement followed the environmental destruction.

The fracturing of the community happened in stages. Since the opening of the mine, the majority of the population had opposed its existence. The resistance grew as the extent of the environmental damage became increasingly evident. While the indigenous population attempted to negotiate directly with CRA and the PNG government, to make their voices heard, they also began to undertake various acts of non-violent direct action including protests and blockades. Acts of protests, which failed to achieve any improvement in the local conditions, escalated over a twenty-year period. At each step, internal tensions grew between the few who were benefiting from the mine operations and the majority involved in civil disobedience. In the late 1980s, this further intensified when a large proportion of the indigenous population forcibly closed the copper mine, which at that time was the world's most profitable.

The PNG government responded to the closure by establishing a local militia, sending in riot police, and eventually the military with the aim of re-opening the copper mine.[4] The local population reacted by forming different factions with the eventual emergence of the Bougainville Revolutionary Army (BRA) as the dominant armed militia and wrestled control of the island. As the conflict expanded, the BRA employed more militant tactics, focusing on secession from PNG while the national government moved aggressively to quell the revolt, even resorting to the deployment of mercenaries.[5]

The PNG government, with the support of Australia, adopted a military strategy with two broad aims: first to isolate Bougainville through a military blockade then re-capture control of the island. The blockade lasted over ten years and effectively sealed off Bougainville from the outside world, depriving the population of medicines, fuel and humanitarian aid. Descriptions of the conflict were harrowing and resulted in widespread deaths and increasingly brutal human rights abuses perpetrated by both sides.[6] The conflict claimed more than ten thousand lives with an estimated sixty thousand people being displaced.

I arrived at Bougainville in 2000 as part of a re-building project. The aim was to work with local communities to re-establish a financial system that had collapsed during the conflict with the long-term goal of encouraging economic development. While the project concentrated on the financial infrastructure, the implications of the work were much broader as it aimed to re-establish trust and cooperation. As part of the project, ex-combatants from the different sides of the conflict began to work together to rebuild their island-nation. This process relied on two core elements: hope and forgiveness. With this paper, I aim to discuss these two necessary ingredients which assist in the processes of communities moving beyond conflict and the lessons we can learn.

3. On Forgiveness

In a 2004 paper Kelly Oliver draws on the work of both Hegel and Kristeva to outline four types of forgiveness: Hegelian, sovereign, psychoanalytic and social.[7] It is within this fourth type of forgiveness that Oliver discusses the notion of a 'heroic particularity,' where specific desires of the individual are redeemed and meaning is created. In this process of asking for forgiveness, we hold ourselves responsible for both our actions, as well as our desires. Here forgiveness moves in both the realms of the conscious and unconscious.

Oliver's argument is that forgiveness exists as meaning rather than absolution or even exoneration. That is, meaning is created in the very *act* or *process* of forgiveness. In the process, a sense of forgiveness constitutes the subject as 'both individual and belonging to a community'[8] as the subject simultaneously acknowledges the individual as sovereign while still remaining connected with others. Hence, forgiveness is a social dynamic that enables both sovereignty and agency to emerge.

This active process of forgiving, I argue, is one that creates a sense agency for the wronged individual. Such an active move is echoed in the works of both Elisabeth Gedge[9] and Richard Kyte[10] in this volume. Gedge attempts to fuse radical forgiveness and feminist theology, and describes just such an act of agency when discussing the need to rebuild relations of trust in any process of moral repair. [11] These must not, however, compromise the personal dignity, political solidarity or hope of vindication of those who have been wronged. While the type of forgiveness discussed in this chapter is secular, the overlap with the divine vindication that Gedge describes revolves around both the processes and acts of forgiving.

This agency is also evident in Kyte's aptly named chapter 'The Art of Forgiving.' Amongst other elements of Kyte's 'art,' is the need for of a 'certain type of preliminary work that effects an emotional transformation in the person who has been injured.'[12] This process requires the wronged to purposefully alter their view or perception of those who have perpetrated the wrong, something that is not possible by passively accepting what has occurred.

Furthermore, Kelly Oliver argues that one dimension of the meaning created in the act of forgiveness is the acknowledgement of both our unique individuality as well as our shared humanity.[13] The point here, is that to actively forgive is to see the other as someone we can relate to while accepting his/her difference.

To succeed, forgiveness is also a reciprocated process. Like a handshake or a greeting, it must be both instigated and returned. Such a procedure makes us vulnerable since we are never sure if our desire for forgiveness will be returned.[14] This practice of asking for and accepting forgiveness constructs two further meanings. The first is a sense of reciprocated desire to interact beyond a single set of deeds. Further, this desire to interact establishes the foundations of an authentic community. As will be discussed below, this 'desire' is important in maintaining a community. That is, an authentic community does not simply rely on a common thread such as location, religion or language, but a desire for it. Additionally, a sense of agency is created as the pursuit of this desire must be an informed decision by each individual.

In contrast, without forgiveness we are never released from the consequences of past deeds. This, according to Hannah Arendt, means our capacity to act is limited by a single endeavour that confines our actions.[15] Without the ability to forgive, we deny the humanity of others along with their subjectivity and agency. Importantly, as Malika Rebai Maamri argues elsewhere in this volume, to forgive in not to condone, but to reconcile what has happened.[16]

Forgiveness then highlights a complex interplay between a shared humanity, unique individuality, sovereignty and agency. To ask for and accept forgiveness is a process that allows us to acknowledge, accept and reciprocate an offer that can be conceptualised in what Rosalyn Diprose describes as 'a hand of friendship.'[17] This is not, according to Diprose, an act of friendship in the common conceptualisation, but a desire to live together in peace and harmony. As such it is not an invitation to dinner, but a desire to embrace a shared humanity of irreducible difference. It is this sense of forgiveness that was present in the workshops I facilitated in Bougainville. It was evident in the process of acknowledging the actions perpetrated by oneself and others, accompanied by a sense of shared humanity and a desire to move beyond such deeds. At no stage did this process condone what had occurred, but it was rather an attempt to reconcile past actions. For this process to be effective, however such a desire must also be shared with a belief that the agency we are promoting means a better world is possible through our actions. Such a vision that a better world is possible and is defined by a sense of hope.

4. On Hope

Hope is underscored by a belief that a better world is possible and exists on both a personal and societal level. Alphonso Lingis argues that hope involves a vision that is outside oneself.[18] In secular societies, hope is faith without certainties. Importantly, hope is not passive: it emerges in our actions, not in sitting around and waiting for a better world to emerge. As such, hope emerges in struggles for justice and political activity.[19]

In 'decent' societies, we witness a surplus and abundant distribution of hope. According to Ghassan Hage,

> The key to a decent society is above all this capacity to distribute…opportunities for self-realization, which are none other than what we have been calling societal hope.[20]

Hope, like forgiveness for that matter, becomes abundant when openly distributed. That is, unlike a glass of water or a chocolate bar which diminish when consumed, both hope and forgiveness actually expand the more we share them. In this way, through a process of reciprocated interactions, both hope and forgiveness continue to grow.

In the absence of hope, such a vision of a shared and better world quickly diminishes. And according to Mary Zournazi, a lack of hope leads to a focus on individualism and competition.[21] This is a *negative* hope that creates a sense of uncertainty, insecurity and competition, as we feel hope will be consumed by others and disappear. Here hope is not reciprocated but withheld, breaking the potential cycle of shared desire.

To make this point, Michael Taussig argues that in a commodified world, hope slowly 'masquerades as envy' as it is overtaken materialism.[22] When a community becomes focused on competing rather than imagining that a better world is possible, Taussig believes hope is displaced, changed or even undone and becomes something else – possibly resentment and greed.

In Bougainville, the establishment of the mine and the displacement of the population meant that the underlying sense was one of survival. The abundance of food and land commons were replaced by a single commodity, cash. This came in the form of payment for labouring in the mines as well as limited royalties to the 'land owners.' In such an environment, competition for the increasingly limited resources replaced the shared sense of hope.

The re-establishment of hope underscored the interaction of the ex-combatants in the workshops that formed part of the project. This was not something that was created by the workshops, but what made the workshops possible. The participants began to forgive and overcome past injustices because of hope, or this belief that a better world was possible through their very actions. This promoted a sense of agency, identity and desire for an authentic community.

5. On Community

The concept of community is something that crosses all political divides: conservative, reactionary, progressive and radical groups all invoke the concept of community.[23] For example, Thomas Friedman argues that through economic globalisation and the free market, we are witnessing the formation of a 'global community.' Those who oppose the 'free market' also summon community arguing that such policies undermine local communities.[24] That is, free market based on the international movement of capital has no loyalty towards local communities and once it takes what is materially valuable, moves on, a process that often devastates local communities. Programs managed by both government and non-government agencies promote community as a key 'ingredient' that leads to harmony.

Jeremy Brent states that community is something that is invoked when social problems emerge though it is something that is rarely defined.[25] In a similar vein, Zygmunt Bauman believes our craving for community is 'like a roof under which we shelter in heavy rain, like a fireplace which we warm our hands on a frosty day.'[26] In many ways then, community is like our need for oxygen. When it is there, we rarely think about it, but when it lacks, we begin to see the consequences.

Despite such a longing for the stability and warmth of community, we need to see it as a double-edged sword: it can produce cooperation and mutuality, but can also be divisive and create conflict. In Australia, for example, the population pulled together to assist bushfire victims from fires that ravaged south-eastern forests in Victoria in 2009. In contrast, community was also evoked as an excuse to attack 'outsiders' during race riots in the picturesque beach of Cronulla in 2004.

Theoretically, there are two broad conceptions about community formation which I have detailed elsewhere.[27] The first revolves around 'recognition' and the concept that there exist 'natural communities' based on the concept that we form communities with those we 'recognize' as being 'like us.'[28] This is the dominant conceptualisation of community defining the concept through ideas of natural formation, relying on a shared identity arising out of mutual beliefs, understandings and practices – all seen to create a stable sense of identity.[29]

Various theorists have criticized this position, noting that this concept of natural communities formed around people 'like us' has the real potential to become exclusionary.[30] Fundamental to such criticisms is the concern about defining what 'like us' means: those with the same religion, colour skin, eye colour or language?

The alternative perspective is that community only forms through a sense of both difference and desire: that is, you have to 'want' to form a community with someone and this may require hard work and understanding. Rather than seeking others 'like us,' we want to be seen as individuals and have this individuality appreciated. Here, community is something that is not neat and easily defined by a common feature, but something complicated. Consequently, community is formed both through this sense of difference and a desire to accept and be accepted.[31] This community is based on a sense of reciprocity: I want you to be part of my community and you want me to be part of yours, so we work at establishing and maintaining it.

In this way, an 'authentic' community is composed of unique individuals who might not necessarily understand each other's subjectivity, but rather possess reciprocal desires to establish and maintain community. This conceptualisation of community is formed through the desire for alterity, subjectivity and agency between another and me, an alterity advanced not repressed. This promotes a heterogeneous community as individuals are never reduced to uniform beings.

This desire for a reciprocated exchange of both hope and forgiveness is essential in establishing and promoting this sense of community, for as Anna M. Szczepan-Wojnarska argues in her chapter, there is a 'collective experience of hope in forgiveness.'[32] Both hope and forgiveness promote agency and sovereignty as well as a sense of solidarity.

It is here that we find a sense of justice that is not limited in time or space, but rather only our sense of desire. That is, both community and justice are not temporal. Rather, our sense of justice and community can cross generations and not be limited by location. In this way, our demands for justice are not limited to those with which we share a common language or culture.

6. On the Search for an Authentic Community

Bougainville is, unfortunately, only one of the many societies that have emerged from conflict since the turn of the century, while many others remain in conflict. The yearning for peace and rebuilding is underscored by the interwoven desire for hope and forgiveness. This desire, as stated above, is an active process built on a sense of agency. Furthermore, it is this sense of desire and agency which assists the emergence of authentic communities.

The aforementioned project was part of a broader peace process that required ex-combatants to acknowledge their past actions, but not have their future limited by these. It is a peace process that continues today and still relies on hope and forgiveness. For those of us working within community confronting challenges of racism, violence, exclusion and lack of hope, there are a number of implications that we need to consider.

The first is that to overcome a fracturing, a community relies on a sense of agency – meaning our actions can make a difference. If individuals feel that their own actions are pointless, then they are unlikely to participate in any communal interactions beyond those of self-interest. This agency is fundamental in any form of active and engaged citizenship.

Further, communities that cross both location and time can be built. In other words, both forgiveness and hope, and the desire for a reciprocated exchange of these are not anchored by any specific location or time period. The deeds of the past are not forgotten but form part of the present and those affected are acknowledged even if they are no longer present.

This takes us to the third implication which is that community is not a stale notion that exists separate from our actions. Rather, community is a dynamic phenomenon that requires work and effort. Communities change and are often under threat from unforeseen circumstances. Such threats and challenges can be overcome with a sense of desire. Hope and forgiveness are two fundamental efforts to ensure that communities do not fracture.

These are the lessons to learn within our own communities – even if unaffected by civil conflict. To ensure that communities remain authentic, viable and inclusive, we must ensure that we continue to strive for both hope and forgiveness.

Notes

[1] The causes of any conflict are always complex and multi-dimensional. The assertion here is that the Panguna mine was the most significant trigger for the conflict. See Alastair McIntosh, 'The Bougainville Crisis: A South Pacific Crofters' War,' *Radical* 44 (1990): 18-22.

[2] Ibid., 19.

[3] Ibid., 18.

[4] See Naomi Sharp, *Blood on Our Hands in Bougainville: Australia's Role in PNG's War*, Sydney, Aid/Watch, 1997. As the conflict progressed the military aims changed, from re-opening the mine to stopping the emergence of a succession movement. See Sean Dorney, *The Sandline Affair* (Sydney: ABC Enterprises, 1998).

[5] Dorney, 23-27.

[6] For a detailed discussion, see Anthony J. Regan, 'Towards Peace for Bougainville?' *Asia-Pacific Magazine* 9.10 (1998): 12-16.

[7] Kelly Oliver, 'Forgiveness and Community', *Journal of Southern Philosophy* 42 Supplement (2004): 1-15.

[8] Ibid., 1.

[9] Elisabeth Gedge, 'Radical Forgiveness and Feminist Theology,' in *A Journey through Forgiveness*, edited by Malika Rebai Maamri, Nehama Verbin and Everett L. Worthington, Jr. (Oxford: Inter-Disciplinary Press, 2010), accessed January 11, 2011, http://www.inter-disciplinary.net/publishing/id-press/ebooks/a-journey-throu gh-forgiveness/, 69-78.

[10] Richard Kyte, 'The Art of Forgiving: Conditions of Perspective and Transformation', in *A Journey through Forgiveness*, edited by Malika Rebai Maamri, Nehama Verbin and Everett L. Worthington, Jr. (Oxford: Inter-Disciplinary Press, 2010), accessed February 9, 2011, http://www.inter-disciplinary.net/publishing/id-press/ebooks/a-journey-through-forgiveness/, 79-86.

[11] Gedge, 70.

[12] Kyte, 89.

[13] Oliver, 1.

[14] For a detailed discussion of the metaphor of the 'handshake,' see Rosalyn Diprose, 'Communities written in Blood,' *Cultural Studies Review* 9.1 (2003): 35.

[15] Hannah Arendt, *The Human Condition* (Chicago: University of Chicago Press, 1959), 213.

[16] Malika Rebai Maamri, 'Algerian President's Peace Plan: Political and Psychological Perspectives of Forgiveness,' in *A Journey through Forgiveness*, edited by Malika Rebai Maamri, Nehama Verbin and Everett L. Worthington, Jr. (Oxford: Inter-Disciplinary Press, 2010), accessed February 9, 2011, http://www.inter-disciplinary.net/publishing/id-press/ebooks/a-journey-through-forgiveness/, 141-148.

[17] Diprose, 36.

[18] Alphonso Lingis, 'Murmurs of Life', in Mary Zournazi, ed., *Hope* (Annandale: Pluto Press, 2002), 34.

[19] Mary Zournazi, *Hope*, 3.

[20] Ghassan Hage, *Against Paranoid Nationalism: Searching for Hope in a Shrinking Society* (Sydney: Pluto Press, 2003), 16.

[21] Zounazi, 33.

[22] Michael Taussig, 'Carnival of the Senses', in Mary Zournazi, ed., *Hope* (Annandale: Pluto Press, 2002), 63.

[23] Thomas L. Friedman, *The World is Flat* (New York: Farrar, Straus & Giroux, 2005), 236.

[24] James Goodman and Paul James, *Nationalism and Global Solidarities* (New York: Routledge, 2007), 187.

[25] Jeremy Brent, 'The Desire for Community: Illusion, Confusion and Paradox', *Community Development Journal* 39.3 (2004): 214.

[26] Zygmunt Bauman, *Community: Seeking Safety in an Insecure World* (Cambridge: Polity Press, 2001), 1.

[27] I have discussed elsewhere and at great length the debates over the meaning of community. See James Arvanitakis, *The Cultural Commons of Hope* (Germany: VDM, 2007), 174-202.

[28] Kelly Oliver, *Witnessing: Beyond Recognition* (Minneapolis and London: University of Minnesota Press, 2001), 25.

[29] One example here is Charles Taylor, 'The Politics of Recognition', in *Multiculturalism: Examining the Politics of Recognition*, edited by A. Gutmann (Princeton: Princeton University Press, 1994), 25-73.

[30] See Diprose, 40.

[31] Brent, 3.

[32] Anna M. Szczepan-Wojnarska, 'Poetry as a Medium of Forgiveness in the Light of Czesław Miłosz's Oeuvre,' in *A Journey through Forgiveness*, edited by Malika Rebai Maamri, Nehama Verbin and Everett L. Worthington, Jr. (Oxford: Inter-Disciplinary Press, 2010), accessed February 9, 2011, http://www.inter-disciplinary.net/publishing/id-press/ebooks/a-journey-through-forgiveness/, 201-208.

Bibliography

Arendt, Hannah. *The Human Condition*. Chicago: University of Chicago Press, 1959.

Arvanitakis, James. *The Cultural Commons of Hope*. Germany: VDM, 2007.

Bauman, Zygmunt. *Community: Seeking Safety in an Insecure World*. Cambridge: Polity Press, 2001.

Brent, Jeremy. 'The Desire for Community: Illusion, Confusion and Paradox'. *Community Development Journal* 39.3 (2004): 213-223.

Diprose, Rosalyn. 'Communities written in Blood'. *Cultural Studies Review* 9.1 (2003): 35-50.

Dorney, Sean. *The Sandline Affair*. Sydney: ABC Enterprises, 1998.

Friedman, Thomas.L. *The World is Flat*. New York: Farrar, Straus & Giroux, 2005.

Gedge, Elisabeth. 'Radical Forgiveness and Feminist Theology'. In *A Journey through Forgiveness*, edited by Malika Rebai Maamri, Nehama Verbin and Everett L. Worthington, Jr. (Oxford: Inter-Disciplinary Press, 2010), accessed February 9, 2011, http://www.inter-disciplinary.net/publishing/id-press/ebooks/a-journey-through-forgiveness/.

Goodman, James and Paul James. *Nationalism and Global Solidarities*. New York: Routledge, 2007.

Hage, Ghassan. 'The Incredible Shrinking Society'. *Weekend Review: Australian Financial Review*, 7 September 2001, 4-5.

————. *Against Paranoid Nationalism: Searching for Hope in a Shrinking Society*. Sydney: Pluto Press, 2003.

Kyte, Richard. 'The Art of Forgiving: Conditions of Perspective and Transformation'. In *A Journey through Forgiveness*, edited by Malika Rebai Maamri, Nehama Verbin and Everett L. Worthington, Jr. (Oxford: Inter-Disciplinary Press, 2010), accessed February 9, 2011, http://www.inter-disciplinary.net/publishing/id-press/ebooks/a-journey-through-forgiveness/.

Lingis, Alphonso. 'Murmurs of Life'. In *Hope*, edited by M. Zournazi, 22-41. Annandale: Pluto Press, 2002.

McIntosh, Alistair. 'The Bougainville Crisis: A South Pacific Crofters' War'. *Radical* 44 (1990): 18-22.

Oliver, Kelly. *Witnessing: Beyond Recognition*. Minneapolis and London: University of Minnesota Press, 2001.

Oliver, Kelly. 'Forgiveness and Community'. *Journal of Southern Philosophy* 42 Supplement (2004): 1-15.

Rebai Maamri, Malika. 'Algerian President's Peace Plan: Political and Psychological Perspectives of Forgiveness'. In *A Journey through Forgiveness*, edited by Malika Rebai Maamri, Nehama Verbin and Everett L. Worthington, Jr. (Oxford: Inter-Disciplinary Press, 2010), accessed February 9, 2011, http://www.inter-disciplinary.net/publishing/id-press/ebooks/a-journey-through-forgiveness/.

Regan, Anthony J. 'Towards Peace for Bougainville?' *Asia-Pacific Magazine* 9, no. 10, 1998: 12-16.

Sharp, Naomi. *Blood on Our Hands in Bougainville: Australia's Role in PNG's War.* Sydney: Aid/Watch, 1997.

Szczepan-Wojnarska, Anna.M. 'Poetry as a Medium of Forgiveness in the Light of Czesław Miłosz's Oeuvre'. In In *A Journey through Forgiveness*, edited by Malika Rebai Maamri, Nehama Verbin and Everett L. Worthington, Jr. (Oxford: Inter-Disciplinary Press, 2010), accessed February 9, 2011, http://www.inter-disciplinary.net/publishing/id-press/ebooks/a-journey-through-forgiveness/.

Taussig, Michael. 'Carnival of the Senses'. In *Hope*, edited by M. Zournazi, 42-63. Annandale: Pluto Press, 2002.

Taylor, Charles. 'The Politics of Recognition'. In *Multiculturalism: Examining the Politics of Recognition*, edited by A. Gutmann, 25-73. Princeton: Princeton University Press, 1994.

Zournazi, Mary. *Hope*. Annandale: Pluto Press, 2002.

James Arvanitakis is a former economist and banker. He is now an activist-academic based at the Centre for Cultural Research at the University of Western Sydney.

Part 4:

Interpretations of Forgiveness in Literary Studies

Poetry as a Medium of Forgiveness in the Light of Czesław Miłosz's Oeuvre

Anna M. Szczepan-Wojnarska

Abstract

Czesław Miłosz presents how complicated and multilayered is the relation between poetry and history, and between a poet as a citizen and member of a national community and his own oeuvre. His verses also appear as a medium for the examination of forgiveness. Miłosz's masterpieces had been struck off the list of prohibited books by the communist censorship in Poland. His visit in the country in 1981, which coincided with the rise of Solidarity's political importance, culminated in the symbolic act of the engraving of the following lines from one of his formerly censored poems upon the pedestal of a newly erected monument commemorating the shipyard strikers fallen in the riots of 1970:

> Do not feel safe. The poet remembers.
> You can kill one, but another is born.
> The words are written down, the deed, the date. [1]

Next to Lech Wałęsa and Jean Paul II, in the perception of the Poles, Miłosz gained the status of a significant historical figure and an authority. Involuntarily, he became inscribed into the myth of a champion-of-national-freedom, and eventually came to be known and represented as a national seer-poet. Yet it is precisely from these roles that Miłosz wished to distance himself, as paradoxically expressed in the poem quoted above. A poet as a concrete human being is of no importance for the universal discourse. Writing that 'the poet remembers,' Miłosz pointed out that a concrete single human being, either a victim or a witness, has an ability and credibility to express and to record existence of the world in all its manifestations. Poetry in Miłosz's perspective thus takes over the meaning of remembrance and gains significance as it remains. Miłosz would consistently ask questions concerning the role of literature in the historical process, the essence of which he perceived in terms of the accumulation of wrongs and reconciliations. His oeuvre uncovers both the power and the helplessness of poetry in the face of iniquity and evil. The proposed analysis seeks to demonstrate that, according to Miłosz, poetry has the capacity to mediate forgiveness without bleeding into it. More than anything else, poetry is a form of penance.

Key Words: Czesław Miłosz, poetry, forgiveness, penance.

*****

1. Introduction

Miłosz was born in Szetejnie in 1911 and belonged to the world that vanished after World War II, a multicultural, multinational community of coexisting nations within Poland's Republic before 1939. The poet was of Polish landed gentry in Czarist Russia and was educated in Wilno, one of the most unique cities for the encounter of the Eastern and Western worlds. This city is also known for the famous University of Stefan Batory which was established much earlier than Harvard and nurtured a young generation with knowledge and tradition of tolerance and coexistence. Miłosz also lived in Warsaw during the Nazi and Soviet occupations. He became a diplomat of Communist Poland but defected, inspiring suspicion on both sides. He left Poland in 1951 and lived in France and the USA. He came to like America, after an initial revulsion, while teaching as a Professor at Berkeley. He then returned to Poland and settled in Cracow where he spent the last few years of his life. Thus, as his life story shows Miłosz was immersed in many cultures. He made significant political decisions and did not hesitate to change them. The lesson learned from his experience was that a poet needs to be very humble and refrain from preaching people.

Moreover, Miłosz distanced himself from any party and any influential literary societies of his times. His pre-Second World War poetry was marked by an apocalyptic pessimism. In his later work, he presented highly formal sophistication and a belief that poetry could overcome evil, or at least go through it without inspiring hopelessness. By this poetic belief, Miłosz instigated the light of hope and optimism even through dark and depressing narratives, in order to showcase hope in the long run. He has been considered (especially from the American perspective) as a leftist but without sympathy for the regime, and a classic, but without any respect for the canon. At the same time, he has been regarded as a thinker deeply engaged in spirituality but with no connection to socio-religious forms of life.

As a poet, novelist, translator, critic, Professor of literature at Berkeley University, and the author of the collection of essays, *Captive Mind*, he consequently emphasized the difference between the poet's self and the self of the narrative voice(s). Miłosz also demonstrated awareness that as a poet, he gained ascendency over people however like anyone else, he was a fallible hence his reluctance to give directions on how to live in his verses. Nevertheless Milosz tried to present a kind of hierarchy of values and disseminated directions to follow. His greatest concern was the fact that he can also mislead the others unwillingly. Miłosz's concern goes beyond the issue of a writer's responsibility only in moral terms. A poet is the one who helps the process of coming to terms with forgiveness, and who expects to be forgiven as well. Miłosz's conception of poetry is rooted in paradoxical aspects of his poetry, the versified power, powerlessness, and the quality and form of poetic penance.

2. The Power of Poetry

Poetry is powerful in that it may call for evidence which ruins the sense of safety and impunity of wrongdoers. It witnesses history, accommodates the knowledge about the victims and their perpetrators. Giving evidence to past actions as if they did not have any consequence means recording them, evaluating them in an arbitrary manner and at the same time, sealing them as complete and foregone. Such evidence does not disturb the perpetrator because it places him also in the foregone past. One of the main goals of poetry Milosz highlights is to make people feel unsafe. There is no distance, no sense of compassion as a poet is also not authorized to judge or offer mercy. Perhaps it is a peculiar sense of a poet's humbleness. As such structure does not imply the poet's moral superiority nor suggest that a poet belongs to the oppressed and victimized to be their representative. There is a very strong tension between witnessing and remaining beyond judgment. A poet as a witness knows the protagonists of national history not directly, and may get fascinated with them hence be uncritical. However, criticizing national heroes might be perceived as betrayal of the nation. Laurie Vickroy, who developed the trauma theory in literature, believes that when we learn about the characters' suffering and trauma, we often take their side for as readers, we are in a certain distance to the traumatic event, cannot help adjusting this distance and therefore feel compassion and pity. Nevertheless, trauma 'forces us to face difficult human issues such as vulnerability and our capacity for evil, bearing witness to horrible events and taking sides between victims and perpetrators. We often take the perpetrator's side, because it is easier to forget or to preserve our deeply held views of normality than to share the victim's horribly alienating memories.'[2] In my opinion, Miłosz was deeply aware of the multilayered complexity of a witness-position.

Miłosz does not argue for a special status of a poet whose figure serves more as a tool of history than as an independent and totally free creator. Considering that a poet is not in charge of disseminating forgiveness, one may think that putting a poet in the role of an accuser is equally inadequate. Moreover a poet is not protected from the influence of the events, but is exposed to them even if poetry is taken as being deprived of the human factor, as an unavoidable human experience whose subjectivity utterly depends on a specific witness-position or victim-position. Besides, observation from the witness-position entails a variety of emotional approaches to the victim and his/her situation. One may as well feel a mix of compassion and doubt while others, coming from a non-traumatized position, may patronize both victim and perpetrator.

On the other hand, forgiveness may be granted only to the one who is aware of the wrong done and asks for forgiveness, realizing that his world also collapsed after the crime had been committed. Such an attitude has been reciprocally presented in Miłosz's poetry. Therefore, poetry which arouses anxiety means more than a formal accusation based on a specific provision of law. Paradoxically, it situates the wrongdoer primarily as the one who has to realize his/her own loss. Poetry becomes a form of existence of the loss and actualizes a sense of guilt. In a way, such change of attitude recalls a Levinasian way of understanding forgiveness as discussed in Canan Savkay's chapter.[3]

Perhaps such great expectations towards poetry will never be fulfilled successfully. Miłosz seems close to Hannah Arendt, and does not believe in the so-called history lessons or in ascribing to poetry the role of a catalyst of historical experience to warn future generations. Rather, he had been interested in the question of how the past may be actualized, or experienced now, asking about consequences, concrete things which we may and should handle. History is not ontologically separated from literature, therefore cannot be taken as a background order only to bring a new historicism and dimensions for analysis and interpretation. This is also what Miłosz regarded as the most important role of poetry – making the past manifest. Miłosz recognized poetic art not as a narrative recollecting history and evaluating it, but as a reflection of effects, consequences, influences of past events for each individual in the human here-and-now. Poetry gradually resolves itself from being an account only and becomes more an inspiration for a subject to analyse one's self-explanatory procedures. It forces reader and poet alike to discover the strategies of laying and hiding the truth to oneself for various reasons. However, there is no longer a direction for prophecy either. Miłosz clearly explained this in his *Charles Eliot Norton lectures* at Harvard University in 1982: 'Humanity will increasingly be turning back to itself, increasingly contemplating its entire past, searching for a key to its own enigma, and penetrating, through empathy, the soul of bygone generations of whole civilizations.'[4]

The aim of poetry goes beyond traditional expectations in Miłosz's view. Poetry looks into individual entities, so it does not absolve too easily, does not excuse by saying that they were a mere cog in the machine of evil and only followed orders. This would be a very comfortable explanation, particularly in reference to the times of war and the communist regime. In Miłosz's major work of political analysis, *The Captive Mind*, the poet diagnosed various ways that Polish intellectuals adapted hesitantly to communism towards passing judgments on them and he refused to recall this book in later years. Many a times, the poet kept highlighting that only those who passed through Marxism, atheism and other deviations were able to share his language. Nevertheless, the poet's words, which celebrate subjectivity, cannot at the same time deny it. As a result, the price of subjectivity is responsibility, which entails a sense of guilt. Miłosz never refused to speak about how easy is to be mesmerized by ideas, and dictatorship. Perhaps the most beautiful expression of this problem can be found in the 17th stanza of his *Treaty on Theology*:

I was not innocent, I wanted to be innocent but I could not.
Misfortune that was sent me I endured, without blaspheming
against God, since I learned not to blaspheme against God for
the fact that He created me such a man rather than someone
else.[5]

Temptation cannot be identified with compulsion and it is all too easy to accuse
someone, or ourselves. It is not enough to want to be innocent, since temptation
equated with compulsion is a prospect of a self-created hell. Neither is it enough to
be just a victim, a subject to whom some misfortune happens. This does not
absolve nor does it make one innocent.

It is moreover difficult to assign the need of forgiveness only to moral and
religious areas. As evidenced in the poem quoted above, the goal of being innocent
appears unachievable, originating from the very act of creation. Two reasons for
blaspheming God had been identified: the act of creation itself and the unavoidable
misfortunes that may happen to the created. Who then, needs to be forgiven? How
should the reader understand the meaning of blaspheming? In the given context
and in the original Polish version of the poem, blasphemy is directly connected
with accusation. If God is not officially accused, but presented as the one who
needs forgiveness and simultaneously a human being is depicted as being deprived
of innocence by Him, then, there is a good example in Miłosz's discussion of
forgiveness gathering contradictions that are hardly noticeable at first glance. First,
misfortunes are no longer treated as a form of penalty; therefore experienced
suffering is not an indirect evidence of one's guilt. This strongly suggests the
innocence of the speaking subject. Second, the subject proved his virtues by
enduring misfortunes and does so because of an initial will to be innocent. Third,
he 'learned not to blaspheme against God,' which suggests he made an effort to
maintain his relationship with God. Fourth, if God created such a fallible and
imperfect being is Thou[6] spared misfortunes and suffering?

Summing up these gradually intertwined factors, I would conclude that Miłosz
emphasizes the role of psychodynamic relations between God and human being.
Forgiveness without interpersonal context becomes just another term. The
'narrative self,' based on the psychology of interpersonal behaviour, tries to
communicate forgiveness and to avoid a need to be forgiven as analysed by
Maryam Farahani in her chapter, 'Felicia Hemans, Psychodynamic Hope and
Trend Forgiveness.'[7]

In this vision of humanity, suffering, with its complexity and mystery, is one
basic element for human life. It is more than just a foundation for moral
qualifications and evaluations. It is the task of poetry and its power to raise this
kind of awareness. Poetry reveals multilayered dimensions of being human and at
the same time, it is one of them, something one may call experience in progress.

3. Powerlessness of Poetry

Poetry is powerless in that it neither prevents evils nor metes out justice. A question arises about the significance of poetry, which according to Miłosz is always written for someone and addressed to someone. Miłosz already asked this question in one of his 'Dedication' poems in his first post-war *Rescue* volume. His enquiry itself involves the question of poetry's address and apostrophe; for whom it is written and to whom it is read. I argue that these questions clearly correspond to Theodor Adorno's reflections about the poem after Auschwitz and this correspondence generates a means of poetic interpersonal behaviour.

> You whom I could not save,
> Listen to me. [...]
>
> What is poetry which does not save
> Nations or people?
> A connivance with official lies,
> A song of drunkards whose throats will be cut in a moment,
> Readings for sophomore girls.
>
> That I wanted good poetry without knowing it,
> That I discovered, late, its salutary aim,
> In this and only this I find salvation.[8]

This sense of powerlessness reveals at the same time the belief in the power of poetry which has other tasks than mimesis or expression of feelings. You may feel powerless only if you know the sense of power and know that real salvation is more than just the preservation of your own protein structure. Neither is salvation transference into an extraterrestrial, theological sphere. The poet clearly locates it in the worldly dimension, exploiting the distinction between rescue and salvation. Verses do not go on well with bullets; nevertheless, it is a comforting dream that a verse may stop gunfire. Miłosz does not go in this direction, relating such feelings to immature 'sophomore girls' whose dreams about the heroes are naive. Bizarrely enough the fighters become real heroes trying to imitate the pure simplicity of poetry and having faith in the beauty of self-sacrifice for values.

Continuing this strand of reflections, we should state that the order of poetry will not accommodate compensation. It will not tolerate asking for forgiveness or forgiving through poetry. To treat poetry in such a way would be nothing more than a rhetorical gesture, a form devoid of any important message, even bordering on the grotesque in the context of the World War II experience. Miłosz consistently avoids consolatory usurpations, being aware that he could not apologize or forgive on anyone's behalf. He may describe his own sense of helplessness and pain, a sense of guilt about *loneliness of the dying*.[9] Instead of too easy explanations, simplifications and distortions, he would rather propose quite an ostentatious understanding, ultimately understood as an affirmation of life. This involves searching for agreement, after all, and maintaining distance. Rather than justifying the guilty, poetry demonstrates humbleness and self-restraint in passing judgment. Its power of powerlessness demonstrates dignity and at the same time evokes the sense of irony captured in William Blake's *Songs of Innocence and Experience.* A poem cannot be regarded as a document. Its significance is limited to possible influence on the others only as it will never be taken as a document and therefore metaphorically it will never be accepted and welcomed in 'the real' world.

Another dimension of poetry's helplessness is its entanglement in language. Poetry addresses the overwhelming experience of disintegration of not only the dreams of the Tower of Babel, but also the basic principles of communication. When words lose their meaning, although spoken and 'uttered by lips that perish,'[10] writing becomes a metaphor of the mystery that leads one out of death's darkness. This metaphorical utterance evokes M. Blanchot's reflections about Orpheus and Eurydice.[11] Miłosz lays 'little bowls of colours' as his 'Faithful Mother Tongue' to encourage the sense of return to some form of interpersonal relationship, be it in speech. The loss of language becomes equated with loss of life and legitimacy to live, too. Language appears as a form of life and as a living form itself. Perhaps that situation refers to the very sense of relation between experience and the process of experiencing itself. Language becomes a medium of being and a particular aspect of this medium is poetry. Miłosz's exploration of the limits of the representational power of poetry leads the reader to be aware that these limits are not determined by circumstances and external factors as in censorship, for example. These limits are under the high pressure of a quest for meaning starting with a basic meaning of the 'I.'

> If only the stars contained me.
> If only everything kept happening in such way
> that so-called world opposed the so-called flesh.
> Were I at least not contradictory. Alas.[12]

Therefore to forgive and to be forgiven becomes a multilayered problem of structure. To sum up, poetry's helplessness in relation to forgiveness covers several dimensions: self-referential helplessness; helplessness directed to the outside in the face of language and contextual strategies of articulation and expression; helplessness directed to the inside in the face of events that happen. Poetry cannot substitute personal encounter between the victim and the executioner.

Poetry's powerlessness cannot be reduced to failed communication. Miłosz recounted a few more important factors such as:

The separation of the poet from the great human family; the progressing subjectivization that becomes manifest when we are imprisoned in the melancholy of our individual transience; the automatism of literary structures, or simply a fashion – all this undoubtedly has weight. Yet if I declare myself for realism as the poet conscious or unconscious longing, I should pay what is due to a sober assessment of our predicament.[13]

4. Poetry as a Form of Penance

Miłosz raised a question about the meaning of poetry in the post-war world quite different from the one Theodor Adorno asked. Miłosz suggests that the power of poetry involves the ability to mediate forgiveness, without however becoming identified with it or replacing it. Rather, poetry is penance, as Tomas Venclova put it. Penance consists of admitting the guilt and carrying out tasks by putting some effort into compensating the unwanted results of the committed crime. If poetry is in charge of fulfilling such demands, the poet, most likely, will struggle with the paradox of being imprisoned by words alone. Admitting guilt in poetry may be understood as disseminating the knowledge of the committed crimes, hence unwillingly spreading evil or unwanted information to the world. Silence is not an alternative either. There is also a third dimension of penance, wherein the consciousness of penance's mechanism enacts in its mere presentation and through the multifaceted structure of human experience of trauma. Perhaps, all three factors indirectly build Miłosz's sense of poetic realism. The author of the 'Song of the End of World' considers realism not only as a view focused on data, but also on spirituality and ideas, on feelings, emotions, in addition to those that are denied and suppressed, which to Miłosz are equally as real as a piece of land or bread is.

Josif Brodski, on the other hand, pointed out to an important aspect of the poet's work, the 'acquisition' of the world:

> Czesław Miłosz is perfectly aware that language is not a tool for cognition but for acquisition of the world, which seems quite hostile – unless language is used by poetry, which alone attempts to conquer it in its own game and, by this, came as close as possible to true knowledge. Shortening, and rather entangling the analytical process, Miłosz's poetry releases the reader from many psychological and purely linguistic traps, because it does not answer the question 'how to live?' but 'what to live for?' The poet seems to proclaim a certain, extremely sober, version of stoicism, which does not ignore reality, even incredibly absurd and horrendous, but accepts it as a new standard which a human being must externalize, without resigning from values, undermined by many compromises.[14]

As already mentioned, Miłosz always writes for someone and to someone. I agree with Brodski that one of the key issues for the poet was to answer the question: 'What to live for?' What actually gives meaning to his work is the search for the reason here and now, not the justification. If the poet had assumed the role of a master providing advice on 'how to live,' this would have been anachronistic and inconsistent. The poet has no right for superiority or for speaking on behalf of the nation or society. He rather identifies himself with (guilty) average people who, having lost everything, also lost the faith in justice and their own innocence. Putting himself into the same category as the executors, the category of the uncircumcised, the poet attempts to find his own place through poetry, and tries to acquire the world in which he happened to live for himself. A re-categorization of reality and reconstitution of norms bring about reconstruction at the expense of placing the self in undesired positions. Although for Miłosz the need of order wins both realistically and in poetic form, there is an inflexible sensibility in his want of achieving compromise.

> And how could he do it? Knowing what we know
> About his life, every day aware
> Of harm he did to others. I think he was aware.
> Just not concerned, he promised his soul to Hell,
> provided that his work remained clear and pure.[15]

Poetry, then in his view, is a process of acquiring the world as it is, an experience in progression and embedded in different physical, psychological, and historical directions. Poetry, as he writes and knows, is the experience entangled in the process of experience. It is also a reconstitution of the world of lost values, a voice creating a space of contact, the proof of struggling and clarification. Finally, his poetry operates as a rescue which may not be understood in the literal, physical sense, but as a deliverance from death or oblivion. This form of poetic deliverance engenders in the first place, a preservation of accepted values, not only in the historical and hierarchical order, but also in the individual domain. Second, it is a form of penance, admitting to helplessness. Third, it achieves compensation, even though forgiveness seems impossible.

The power of poetry may thus lead us astray, making us treat it as a means to an end, always subject to some ideology. Therefore, teleology's invasion into the domain of poetry, irrespective of the level of poetic temptation, proves to be dangerous if it makes an exhibition of verse as a form of rhymed politics.

The weakness of poetry may ultimately create a space for possible forgiveness. For Miłosz, that so called 'pure art' was pointless as writing and reading poetry was, for him, an effort to remain human and to restore dignity to the human being. As G. Agamben explains, the problem with the concept of guilt is not in marking with evil. It is the release of evil in the victim or witness-position that horrid victory avails. It is also directly a matter of position; to know if the position one experiences is between or rather *beyond good and evil*. This conception prevails upon the structure and position of expressions in Milosz's poetry. His verse cannot lead to agreement between opposite forces, but it can sanction and validate the missing position; the one at which we fail to act, eventually causing evil to respond to evil. A failure to give such a response, that is, the failure to do evil, does not amount to doing good and is not yet evil, even though it admits evil without preventing it.

Such a state requires penance, therefore purification, and this purification process assumes the form of poetry. The poet struggles not only against conventions, language, artistic method, but also against death and nothingness. By the end of WWII, he tried to commemorate the innocent rather than the innocent victim. This is a recalling of the innocent who were victims but also those victims who were not necessarily in the innocent-position. Through this poetic interpersonal connection, Milosz endeavours to restore communication with all sides and positions and tries to find *the* language for this kind of communication. The poet is the tongue that bridges history and eternity, guilt and forgiveness. He is, then, a tireless messenger

> who runs and runs
> through interstellar fields,
> through the revolving galaxies,
> and calls out, protests, screams.[16]

Notes

[1] Czesław Miłosz, 'You who Wronged', in *New and Collected Poems 1931-2001*, trans. Czesław Miłosz and Robert Hass (London: Penguin Classics, 2005), 103.

[2] Laurie Vicroy, *Trauma and Survival in Contemporary Fiction* (Charlottesville: University of Virginia Press, 2002), 18-19.

[3] Canan Savkay, 'Levinasian Ethics and a Failure to Forgive', in *A Journey through Forgiveness*, edited by Malika Rebai Maamri, Nehama Verbin and Everett L. Worthington, Jr. (Oxford: Inter-Disciplinary Press, 2010), accessed February 9, 2011, http://www.inter-disciplinary.net/publishing/id-press/ebooks/a-journey-through-forgiveness/.

[4] Czesław Miłosz, 'On Hope', In *Poetry in Theory: An Anthology 1900-2000*, ed. Jon Cook (Oxford: Blackwell Publishing, 2004), 498.

[5] Czesław Miłosz, 'Traktat teologiczny', in *Collected Works*, Vol. 5 (Kraków: Znak, 2009), 237. Translation mine.

[6] There is a tradition in religious writings to refer to God in that way.

[7] Maryam Farahani, 'Felicia Hemans, Psychodynamic Hope and Trend Forgiveness', in *A Journey through Forgiveness*, edited by Malika Rebai Maamri,

Nehama Verbin and Everett L. Worthington, Jr. (Oxford: Inter-Disciplinary Press, 2010), accessed February 9, 2011, http://www.inter-disciplinary.net/publishing/id-press/ebooks/a-journey-through-forgiveness/.
[8] Czesław Miłosz, 'Dedication', in *New and Collected Poems 1931-2001*, trans. Czesław Miłosz and Robert Pinsky (London: Penguin Classics, 2005), 77.
[9] Czesław Miłosz, 'Campo dei Fiori', in *New and Collected Poems, 1931-2001*, trans. David Brooks and Louis Iribarne (London: Penguin Classics, 2005), 33.
[10] Czesław Miłosz, 'Meaning', in *New and Collected Poems 1931-2001*, trans. Czesław Miłosz and Robert Hass (London: Penguin Classics, 2005), 569.
[11] For the role of 'lack of presence' in communication see Maurice Blanchot, *The Infinite Conversation* (Minneapolis, 1992).
[12] Czesław Miłosz, 'What does it Mean', in *New and Collected Poems 1931-2001*, trans. Czesław Miłosz and Robert Hass (London: Penguin Classics, 2005), 164.
[13] Czesław Miłosz, 'On Hope', In *Poetry in Theory: An Anthology 1900-2000*, ed. by Jon Cook (Oxford: Blackwell Publishing, 2004), 502.
[14] Josif Brodski, 'Wytrwałość bólu', *Apokryf*, June 9, 1999, 5.
[15] Czesław Miłosz, 'Biography of An Artist', in *New and Collected Poems 1931-2001*, trans. Czesław Miłosz and Robert Hass (London: Penguin Classics, 2005), 604.
[16] Czesław Miłosz, 'Meaning', in *New and Collected Poems 1931-2001*, trans. Czesław Miłosz and Robert Hass (London: Penguin Classics, 2005), 569.

Bibliography

Bieńkowska, Ewa. *W ogrodzie ziemskim. Książka o Miłoszu.* Warszawa: Wyd. Sic!, 2004.

Błoński, Jan. *Miłosz jak świat.* Kraków: Znak,1999.

Brodski, Josif. 'Wytrwałość bólu'. *Apokryf,* June 9,1999, 5.

Farahani, Maryam. 'Felicia Hemans, Psychodynamic Hope and Trend Forgiveness'. In *A Journey through Forgiveness*, edited by Malika Rebai Maamri, Nehama Verbin and Everett L. Worthington, Jr. (Oxford: Inter-Disciplinary Press, 2010), accessed February 9, 2011, http://www.inter-disciplinary.net/publishing/id-press/ebooks/a-journey-through-forgiveness/.

Fiut, Aleksander. *W stronę Miłosza.* Kraków: WL, 2003.

Miłosz, Czesław. *New and Collected Poems 1931-2001.* Translated by Czesław Miłosz and Robert Hass. London: Penguin Classics, 2005.

————. 'Traktat teologiczny'. *Collected Works*. Vol. 5. Kraków: Znak, 2009.

Savkay, Canan. 'Levinasian Ethics and a Failure to Forgive'. In *A Journey through Forgiveness*, edited by Malika Rebai Maamri, Nehama Verbin and Everett L. Worthington, Jr. (Oxford: Inter-Disciplinary Press, 2010), accessed February 9, 2011, http://www.inter-disciplinary.net/publishing/id-press/ebooks/a-journey-throu gh-forgiveness/.

Vicroy, Laurie. *Trauma and Survival in Contemporary Fiction*. Charlottesville :U of Virginia P, 2002.

Zaleski, Marek. *Zamiast. O twórczości Czesława Miłosza*. Kraków: WL, 2005.

Anna M. Szczepan-Wojnarska is an Assistant Professor of literature studies at Cardinal Wyszynski University, Warsaw, Poland. Her research interests include literary anthropology transcultural literary criticism, and relations between literature and religion. She published: *You Will Get Married to the Fire, Experience of Transcendence in Life and Poetry of Jerzy Liebert* and *To Forgive God: A Figure of Job in the Literature Related to WWII*.

Hemans Hosting the Poetic Absolution in 'Anguish with Delight'

Maryam Farahani

Abstract
The dialogue of joy and suffering is fundamental to Felicia Hemans's verse narratives and lyrics. To transfer the affective dimension of texts for the sake of meaningful contentment in life and to be transferred by means of pain is the essential string that forms the poetical fabric of Hemans's texts. In a more particular sense, the encounter of two opposites as joy and pain in Hemans's poetry develops beyond the question of aesthetic co-relation between these two concepts. What male-authored poetry during the Romantic era put forward in painful narratives as awe-inspiring suggests gloom, unhappiness, and immensity as cognate states of the sublime. Hemans, on the other hand, portrays a more complex paradigm of this aesthetic term, which reaches out to the beautiful and breaks, if not the constructs, the dark contours of the male-authored Romantic sublime by way of actively versifying positive emotions. Hope is an integral part in Hemans's characterization of the sublime, which helps host absolution in suffering, harmoniously entwined with joy. How Hemans achieves this juxtaposition of 'anguish with delight' is the major theme of this chapter. Although other Romantic female poets' works bear some resemblance to Hemans's definition of the sublime, I argue that her poetry provides a means of showcasing (un)forgiveness as a step towards understanding the sublime, the self, and the origin of sublimity. Through psychological perspectives introduced by Julie Exline (2010) and Michael McCullough et al. (2007), I elaborate on the wider scope of Hemans's attention to forgiveness regarding the presence of God and others. I also offer an exploration of Hemans's narrative self through literary debates by reading Anna M. Szczepan-Wojnarska (2010), Elisabeth Gedge (2010), and Adam Potkay (2007). In the light of this cross-disciplinary study, I aim to propose the expansion of the Romantic sublime through Hemans's verse.[1]

Key Words: Destruction, absolution, transformation, joy, sublime, forgiveness, melancholy, self, anguish.

*****

1. The Poetical Fabric beyond 'Indian Woman's Death-Song'
As the most widely read female-authored verse [2] in nineteenth- century Britain, Felicia Hemans's poetry (1793-1835) is marked by seemingly paradoxical terms, whose combination often transforms the affective dimension of hope in texts and its aesthetics of the sublime. In *Hemans's Poetical Works* (1881), we encounter a poetical fabric woven with threads of joy and anguish, designing hope while generating complex forms of literary and aesthetic transformation. Hemans's

poetics of forgiveness are, in particular, composed by layers of this poetical fabric that rears textual diversity and conceptual complexity of the Romantic sublime. Depending on the intensity of specific affects (emotions) that are paradoxically and intensely juxtaposed, Hemans's poetical fabric presents different forms of transformation in the narrating self, the conversant personae, and the sublime origin. The psychodynamics of hope, interestingly, remains a major subject in Hemans's poetic vocation.

On the other hand, melancholy and the sublime defined by male philosophers and endorsed by male poets in the eighteenth and nineteenth centuries are considerably distinguished due to the negative attributes of these literary and philosophical concepts as comprehended by the post-Enlightenment intellectual man.[3] During this period women's texts were often criticized for being emotional rather than intellectual, while female characters in prose fiction frequently appeared with bouts of fainting and fits of weeping or narrated as hysterical figures, a literary tradition that was well followed into the literature of the early twentieth century.[4] One reason is that the Romantic-era poetry not only witnessed war and conflict, but also used these incidents as a means of celebrating 'both the fallen heroes of the wars and the less famous survivors who managed to return to Britain.'[5] But today, we know that the majority of Romantic female poets neither negotiated, nor did they define the sublime and melancholy by focusing on affective negativity and destruction so much as their male counterparts indulged in gloom.[6]

Hemans, for example, openly questioned the aesthetic categorization of women and men in one of her conversational lyrics entitled 'Man and Woman,' to which I will return in due course.[7] Unjust criticism and misinterpretation of women's prose and verse was not limited to conceptual facts, but rather extended to their textual shortcomings. Many female intellectuals objected not only to the oppression that was disturbing their personal lives, but also to the discrimination that was somehow pressed upon their literary productions. Catharine Upton[8] – about whom little is known – and Mary Wollstonecraft were among those women, who directly disapproved and rejected the anguished masculine gloom. Stephen Behrendt's reading of Upton reveals that she was aware and responsive to the so-called male intellectual criticism of women's verse.[9] Behrendt quotes Upton:

> [S]ome critics finding fault with my Poem entitled [sic] The Siege of Gibraltar, induce me to say a few words in my own defence. One gentleman said it was not English; another avowed the versification was bad, as one line in it was a syllable too long.

> . . . Errors like these (if they can be called such) are forgiven in great Poets and learned men, but not in a *woman*, who pretends to no learning at all. Their observations put me in mind of what

> Dean Swift says of critics, whose utmost ingenuity lies in scanning the verses of others on their fingers [sic] ends, without being able to make a tolerable rhyme themselves during the course of their lives.[10]

Upton's distrustful tone is in fact an outright expression of anger towards the offensive male critics whose manner of literary judgement exhausted Upton's affective endurance. Later we realize that Upton claims poetical potential and aesthetic capability in composition of verse for the hope of improving the lives of her children – perhaps metaphorically pointing to the next generation of women – rather than transforming her own image as a feminine-poetic icon in the public domain. She thus continues:

> If my accusers expect me to write better than Dryden or Pope, they assign me a strange task indeed! But I have done with these, and with much more pleasure address myself to the candid part of mankind. Far be such vanity from me to suppose that my Miscellany contains no faults; but my avocation as a Governess, will, I hope, plead my excuse! I have but little time to write, or *correct* what I write, and shall ingenuously confess, that I send the following sheets into the world, with view to *support my children*, not to extend my own fame.[11]

At a time when women suffered due to national and international conflict, female poets also struggled to protect their literary productions and vocations as well as their husbands, children, and siblings.[12] Felicia Hemans's brothers whose bravery and suffering became a subject to inspire Hemans's key poems during early stages of her poetic career including her 1808 'Melancholy,' served in the Peninsular War (1807-1814). Hemans also wrote a series of miscellaneous poems including the subject of war in a notebook (1810-1814) dedicated to Miss Maynard, one of her friends.[13] A few decades earlier, Mary Robinson, Anna Seward, and Charlotte Smith composed various series of elegies, all of which pointed to conflict and the serious anguish caused by wars.[14] International and domestic anxieties were implicitly portrayed in the works of such poets as Hemans, and the consequences were poetically dealt with. But how could women forgive the wars? And how did Felicia Hemans define the sublime rather than being merely destructive, a matter of delight through an affective and poetic fusion of the positive with hopelessness and darkness?

By connecting two opposites such as 'delight with anguish' through narratives and lyrics, Hemans negotiates the complexity of the sublime by showcasing (un)forgiveness as a step towards neutralizing the masculine-destructive sublimity. To forgive and to be forgiven in hope, to delay forgiveness and expect absolution in depths of pain and joy, is a central path in demonstrating interpersonal behaviour in times of conflict. It is also a theological indicator to the origin of sublimity, e.g. God. The conceptual tension that Hemans creates in her poetry underlines the fact that the presence of single negative affects or a group of similar affects does not cause melancholy nor does it prove effective in engendering the sublime. Rather than following examples of pure anguish in male-authored poetry, Hemans hosts the debate of absolution in the interplay between joy and suffering, through which she achieves a different definition of sublimity; the actively delightful sublime. [15]

In Hemans's poetry, the interface between forgiveness and absolution opens up the pathway to the dynamics of romantic and non-romantic hope. It is in the interest of her nineteenth-century feminist perspective that she draws a border line between these two varieties of dismissal regarding wrongdoings. In 'The Abencerrage' (1819) Hemans writes, 'I may forgive, but not at will the heart / can bid its dark remembrance depart.' [16] Absolution as 'the action of delivering words' and 'dismissal' [17] is completely forbidden in this poem, although there are hints of forgiveness as pardoning sins in different cantos of 'The Abencerrage'. This verse narrative is set upon a fictive-historical background which dramatizes the encounter of the East with the West. Without proposing or pretending a positive greeting between these two cultural and geographical spheres, Hemans portrays women's objective position in the public and private domains by discussing traditional attributes of sublimity and masculinity in destruction.

The poetical fabric in 'The Abencerrage' is woven by the joy in the love-story of Hamet and Zayda with the darkness in the destruction that clouds the lives of Catholics and Muslims in conflict. Both 'In the historic and public level of Abdallah and Aixa and the fictional and private sphere of Hamet and Zayda,' Diego Saglia notes that 'the feminine raises its voice to condemn a code of masculine values that is ultimately bankrupt and only capable of bringing death and destruction.' [18] This line of enquiry regarding the masculinity of melancholy and the sublime is followed throughout in Hemans's poetic career. In another verse narrative, 'Night-Scene in Genoa,' Hemans repeats the complexity of forgiveness and humanity's weakness in forgetting and dismissing transgressions. Unlike the narrative of 'Indian Woman's Death-Song,' [19] which spreads the news of the Indian woman's sufferings, in 'Night-Scene in Genoa,' the anguish of a melancholy warrior after the end of war in Genoa is portrayed. Looking back to the masculine destruction and reflecting on the sublimity of God by declaring the 'strife by mutual wrong' of the two human sides in the war, the warrior is left desolate and lonely, though it seems that he speaks for troops on each side and also with God.

The same strategy of struggle with forgiveness is applied in 'Night-Scene in Genoa,' which also clearly describes 'Indian Woman's Death-Song' and 'The Abencerrage.' The warrior, finding humanity's misconduct beyond endurance, and therefore himself alone in understanding sin, yet partaking in transgressions, addresses God – perhaps for forgiveness:

Father! Not thus the wounds may close
Indicted by eternal foes.
Deem'st thou thy mandate can efface
The dread volcano's burning trace?
Or bid the earthquake's ravaged scene
Be smiling, as it once hath been?
No! For the deeds the sword hath done
Forgiveness is not lightly won;
The words, by hatred spoke, may not
Be, as a summer breeze forgot!
Tis vain, we deem the war-feud's rage
A portion of our heritage.[20]

As the warrior in 'Night-Scene in Genoa' admits to the affective dimension of transgressions in 'rage' and claims it to be part of humanity's 'heritage,' so does the woman in 'Indian Woman's Death-Song.' The problem is that what male characters achieve through conflict in fictive-historical spaces is described by heroism, even if their actions can be utterly destructive. But Hemans cuts through this masculine bravery and heroism and its designated sublimity by leaving the warrior entirely desolate. More specifically, through the self-annihilation of the woman and the murder of her infant daughter in 'Indian Woman's Death-Song,' Hemans stops this kind of hereditary rage from being born into the forthcoming generation(s); thereby ending the dark and masculine heritage of rage and revenge by killing the woman in nature.

In the 'Night-Scene in Genoa,' the joy in this type of desolation is ingrained in the warrior's anguish while confessing to God. Experiencing pain and loneliness, the warrior cries to God for purification of his sinful share in the war. This joy, according to Adam Potkay's comparative study of *Robinson Crusoe* may be that of self-preservation. By surviving in the war, the warrior recalls that he needs to protect his narrative self and maintain hopefulness, although he admits to rage. Potkay observes, 'that Crusoe's progress of the passions is, finally, an arc from common joy in self-preservation to spiritual joy in deliverance from sin as well as from the island – although, as a sign of God's favour and by dint of his own prevalence, Crusoe gets to keep the island *in absentia*.'[21] In Hemans's depiction, however, the warrior's spiritual joy experienced with anguish points towards God without being given any part of the land where he fought. As the origin of sublimity, God in Hemans's poem shows no such remorse for the warrior to grant him part of the earth. The poetic sublime achieved through this plea for forgiveness is higher in might and grandeur than the sublime understood by humanity. It may be that the warrior soothes his own anguish by calling to God as well as feeling forgiven, but whether he is gifted with God's absolution is a matter of question.

From the earthly perspective, the warrior neither asks for humanity's forgiveness nor does he consult other poetic personae regarding the case of humanity's 'rage.' What he mostly desires is absolution, yet how can he hear God's words of forgiveness and comprehend his dismissal? The case is similar to 'Indian Woman's Death-Song,' who liberates her narrative self from oppression. Besides in forbidding any future possibility of rage to be born as heritage through womanhood, she also kills her infant daughter simultaneously with her own suicide. Her joy, however, is altogether in higher grounds as she addresses God in the position of the offended by the male infidel who not only admits to inheriting rage, but also indulges in the darkness of revenge.

Hope for forgiveness is enforced through confessions by poetic personae in Hemans's poetical fabric of joy and anguish. Hosting the poetic absolution and the desire for deliverance from sin, and transgression is Hemans's major attempt in her poetics of conflict and forgiveness; however, it is up to the readers to decide whether absolution is offered. In effect, without hearing the voice of God, Hemans's poetic personae maintain this hope through their communication with voices that symbolize the sublimity and beauty of God's kingdom on earth. Interestingly, the voice of nature stands for such Biblical aesthetics in Hemans's narrative verses and lyrics. Nature itself is often referred to as feminine and somehow uncivilised. 'Thus, the nature-feminine principle is associated with the primitive rather than the civilised' and it is connected, as Peter Hay puts, 'with the realm of necessity rather than freedom and high-mindedness, with carnality rather than discipline, with associative, "non-rigorous" thought rather than rationality, and so on.'[22] But Hemans joins two paradoxical entities (feminine and masculine) through two affective concepts (joy and anguish). In this process, she transforms the incomplete masculine sublime to the unified sublimity which indirectly and poetically attests to the complexity and diversity of God's absolution.

2. 'The Suliote Mother' and the Narrative Self

Hemans's depiction of woman, anguish, and delight in 'Indian Woman's Death-Song' appears elsewhere in 'The Suliote Mother.' The domestic conflict in the former takes on a public domain by narrating the story of an international war in 'The Suliote Mother.' This verse narrative portrays the consequences of conflict for the Balkans, when they were 'subjected to ravages of the provincial notable Ali Pasha, who acted independently of the central Ottoman authority.'[23] It is believed that upon the advancement of Ali Pasha, the Christian Suliote women escaped to the hilltop near the monastery of Zalongo[24] and collectively committed suicide by jumping off the hilltop. In this process, they also killed their own children in order to save themselves from slavery in harems of the Ottoman Turks.

In the narrative of 'The Suliote Mother,' Hemans draws on the anguish and delight of one Suliote woman who kills her son along with herself. Unlike the group-image of women in Ary Scheffer's painting of *The Suliote Women* (1827),[25]

Hemans reflects on the personalised consequences of conflict. Besides, instead of repeating the same scenario of 'Indian Woman's Death-Song,' Hemans relocates the scene on a hilltop. If the Indian woman killed herself and her daughter in depth of waters down a waterfall, the Suliote woman goes high up to the mountain with her infant son, instead of giving control to the water to lead her on to death.

Similar to 'Indian Woman's Death-Song', the narrative starts with the words of an unknown observer who then leaves the rest of the poem to the narrative self of the Suliote woman. The narrator in 'The Suliote Mother'[26] sings parallel lines to those read by the narrator in 'Indian Woman's Death-Song': 'She stood upon the loftiest peak / Amidst the clear blue sky' and yet the Suliote woman is described as mysteriously delighted and anguished as the Indian woman, 'A bitter smile was on her cheek / and a dark flash in her eyes.'[27] Further into the scene, while standing on the hilltop, the Suliote woman cries in a one-sided conversation with her son:

> Dost thou see them, boy? Through the dusky pines
> Dost thou see where the foeman's armour shines?
> Hast thou caught the gleam of the conqueror's crest?
> My babe, that I cradled on my breast!
> Woudst thou spring from thy mother's arm with joy?
> That sight hath cost thee a father, my boy![28]

In this process of designing the Suliote woman's fate within the poetical fabric, Hemans immediately attacks the attraction of rage for the masculine symbolics of the sublime.

The shining armour, which is a metaphor for the sublime destruction, is an object of interest for the little boy. But the Suliote woman warns her son that this shining armour has a glow only through the dark and shadowy pine trees. In aesthetic terms, Hemans states that the sublime in the armour destroys, even though it brings temporary joy for the male observer, but the pines in the heart of nature do not destroy while they seem dark and dusky. Here, we note that another metaphor for destruction takes form. Angela Leighton analyses a comparative case in Shelley's application of the pine as a metaphor for the sublime. Leighton argues that 'The trees seem to represent the imagination's last foothold before the abyss, and their music that poetry which would still express something in the face of emptiness.'[29] The armour, therefore, signifies not only the masculine definition of the sublime but also the abyss of emptiness that is created by this aesthetic understanding.

In the midst of this troubling scene, we note Hemans's idea of delight repeatedly. This joy has several and varied dimensions. On the one hand, cradling the child on a mother's breast is a deeply passionate and joyful process. On the other, the woman recognizes the masculine joy, and aims to protect her son from future despair and desolation, perhaps of a kind which is documented as depressingly haunting for the warrior in 'Night-Scene in Genoa.' In a more specific sense, the Suliote woman forbids absolution for the masculine sublime because firstly she aims to preserve her son's eternal glory. Secondly, her murder of the male child prohibits future violation of other women. Perhaps if the Suliote woman did not commit this crime, she would have become a slave and her son would have consequently been trained by the Ottoman Turks for future transgression.

This earthly joy of self-preservation with its complex affective paradigm reaches out to the theological joy by the Suliote woman's manner of communication on the mountain edge. Akin to Dante, Hemans does not necessarily propose 'the slightest gratification'[30] to the peak of the mountain, and where she announces joy in the mountainous areas, her positive affects are those of refreshment in nature. But by placing the woman on the mountain top, Hemans rearranges the gender-specific characterisation of Biblical joy on the peak of mountains. We know that by the late seventeenth century, 'poets continued to turn back to the Bible for mountain drama. More melodramatic than any contemporary scientific account was the drama according to Moses or the Fathers: mountains had risen by miracle, making a joyful noise before the Lord.'[31] The post-1700s poetry did not so much reorganise the presence of joyful and destructive male figures on hilltops. Hemans, however, manages to break through those established geographical spaces for men by presenting women instead. Besides, the joyful noise is not that of the miracle of the mountain, but a peaceful and unforgiving song heard from the Suliote woman.

In addition to the Suliote woman's lamenting voice, the poem constitutes another complex notion of joy and anguish which is juxtaposed by the sorrow for 'the mountain hearth and home!'[32] The advancing troops play a music that again attracts the boy's attention. The Suliote woman, similar to her disapproval of the shining armour, rejects the sublime in the music of enemy. She sings:

> Hark! They bring music, my joyous child!
> What saith the trumpet to Suli's wild!
> Doth it light thine eye with so quick a fire,
> as if at a glance of thine armed sire?
> Still! Be thou still! There are brave men low
> thou wouldst not smile couldst thou see him now![33]

If the little boy's fascination with the enemy's armour and music is a light and agreeable scene in the narrative, paradoxically it also identifies a horrid recalling of the beautiful childhood innocence imprisoned within the shackles of the grown-up masculine sinfulness. The Suliote woman not only reveals this reality, but she also climbs to the mountain-top to seek absolution for her action of murder including both self-annihilation and killing the boy who symbolically is the future sinful man. By hosting this poetic absolution, rather than following the ethics of a comprehensively Christian joy, Hemans turns to Shaftesbury's idea of joy, wherein he 'opposed a Christian ethics of obedience to a God (or monarch) who punishes the breach of His revealed laws or, more fundamentally, lack of proper faith in His saving grace.'[34] In this perspective, as Potkay puts it, 'Joy serves as a sanction, in short, for anything that contributes to the general happiness, properly understood. Joy is the point and proof of one's insertion into a unified and meaningful order of nature.'[35] Hemans, thus, unifies the narrative self (the Suliote woman) with the origin of sublimity (God) and the others (the boy and nature).

The question of forgiveness in this process is again similar to that of 'Indian Woman's Death-Song.' In this instance, however, the Suliote woman announces the presence of the unforgiving narrative self with regard to the other – the future man in the little boy. By contrast, the Indian woman represents the unforgiving narrative self in opposition to the future woman in her infant daughter, thereby rejecting the self. Both verse narratives have a technically similar design and coherent poetical fabric, yet they open up different aesthetic and psychological pathways. While 'Indian Woman's Death-Song' leads us to the rejection of the female narrative self, 'The Suliote Mother' closes up on the masculine self. And why do the narrative female personae in Hemans's poetics of forgiveness and conflict showcase (un)forgiveness?

According to Anna M. Szczepan-Wojnarska, there is a certain anxiety in forgiveness; one of its own kind, one that most specifically regulates the presentation of the narrative self. In her reading of the Polish Nobel Prize winner, Czesław Miłosz, Szczepan-Wojnarska hints to the psychological consequences of great responsibility, by the provocative prolongation of which one becomes overtly self-conscious, and thereby attempts to distance oneself.[36] Hemans communicates the image of a distanced self from the human and earthly sublime. As a mother, the Suliote woman shares, in her affective and aesthetic understanding, similarities with the Indian woman, at the centre of which hope is to be heard. They also both share in the immensity of motherhood as a duty. And they both react to transgression in the same way.

This interpersonal behaviour, based on the fact that women's need for companionship is not actively met, takes on a solitary path. Unlike the music of enemy, which stems from the male group and transforms into a collective and harrowing noise, the voices of the Indian and Suliote woman remain single. Although the Indian woman's lack of time for reflection on the possibility of forgiveness is due to her willingness in speeding the process of suicide by letting the river take control of her destiny, the Suliote woman does not even get a chance of contemplation as the enemy advances. Not only does trend forgiveness, in these two cases, slowly fade, but the matter of God's absolution altogether remains in the domain of Hemans's hosting of the subject.

Within the final moments of the Suliote woman's suicide, a glimpse of eternal joy can be noticed. The woman cries to her son, 'Freedom, young Suliote! For thee and me!'[37] Likewise, in 'Indian Woman's Death-Song,' we hear the reassuring words of the mother to her daughter, 'Smile! To that wasting of the heart, my own! I leave thee not.'[38] This complex joy derives its power from transforming the imprisonment that may affectively be felt upon forgiving a transgression. By means of transforming the aesthetics of the sublime – here, the probable slavery and oppression of Suliote women – through suicide, the narrative self is liberated. Hemans, however, manages to break through established geographical spaces for men by presenting women instead. Besides, the joyful noise is not that of the miracle of the mountain, but a peaceful and unforgiving song heard from the Suliote woman.

The expression of 'freedom' symbolically signals the poetic absolution of the narrative self in verse. The narrator of the poem appears in the end, restating the liberties achieved in this process of self-annihilation:

> And from the arrowy peak she sprung,
> And fast the fair child bore:
> a veil upon the wind was flung,
> A cry and all was o'er![39]

As it stands, finally the narrator ends the poem in the heart of nature and within a downward flight from the peak of the mountain. The spectator of the previous joyful process of liberation may, however, doubt the continuation of this delight within anguish, as merely 'A cry' forms the last part of the narrative.

3. Aesthetic Rage: Reconstruction of Love

In her exhaustive analysis of gender and the sublime, Anne Mellor argues that for women poets of the Romantic era 'Nature is not an overwhelming power, not even an all-bountiful mother. Instead nature is a *female friend*, a sister, with whom they share their most intimate experiences.'[40] In the poems already discussed, such female friendship does not provide an active means of inspiration for poetic forgiveness. Instead, Hemans's poetic women try to distance themselves from nature by removing the narrative self from physical contact with nature. The Indian woman's manner of drowning proposes a momentary detachment from the top of the waterfall and then fall into the water again. Likewise, the Suliote woman detaches herself by jumping from the mountain, the majesty of which is synonymous with the masculine and dark sublime.

Hemans's women experience loneliness prior to suicide and also during the process. That is why forgiveness becomes a more difficult task than suicide. They reach, however, the origin of sublimity by death through this lonely process. Mellor's view that 'the experience of the sublime for this tradition of women writers [Sydney Owenson, Susan Ferrier, and Helen Maria Williams, who portray the sublime landscape as locations of blissful childhood] is rarely solitary'[41] does not work in Hemans's poetry. Rather by juxtaposing anguish with delight, Hemans hosts the poetic absolution, of whose theological details we are not informed. The last line in 'The Suliote Mother' likewise hosts 'A cry,' but there is no solid justification as to decide whether this cry is that of the child, the mother, a human spectator, or even the cry of absolution by God. And yet this kind of cry will always be a matter of doubt as whether it is a cry of forgiveness, fear, joy or anguish.

What remains archetypal in this process is the significance of hopeful rage as human heritage, which in 'The Suliote Mother' is shaped through the pleasure of the armour for the boy or in the complaints of the Suliote woman and her ironical warning of the child. On the one hand, rage belongs to the aesthetics of the sublime and melancholy by presenting masculine discontentment in life, horror, and darkness of the mind. Besides, this aesthetic paradigm is rooted in human love. John Donne's 'A Hymn to Christ, at the Author's Last Going into Germany' communicates this concept poetically as he sings, 'Though thou with clouds of anger do disguise / [...] / In winter, in my winter now I go, / where none but thee, th' eternal root,' one that is 'Of true love I may know.'[42] Hemans shows us that women's love for the continuation of their beloveds' joy is somehow troubled by the egotistical categorisation of the sublime; that men inherit rage by defining joy only within the sphere of the beautiful, thereby reclaiming masculinity and power in the sublime which for them is devoid of delight.

This inherited rage has also a part to do with anger towards God. According to Julie Exline, 'recent research in psychology clarifies that people can experience anger toward impersonal forces such as tornadoes or cancer cells, suggesting the possibility of anger toward an impersonal divine force.'[43] In both Hemans's 'The Suliote Mother' and 'Indian Woman's Death-Song,' one notes this type of anger in the poetic personae's rage towards the symbolics of sublimity. By flying off the mountain peak or drowning the narrative self in the depths of waters, the poetic personae directly object to the masculinity assigned to these natural elements. Furthermore, by preventing the little boy from attraction to the shining armour, for example, the Suliote woman not only detaches the boy from the metaphor of violence and destruction, but also presents her anger toward this symbolic object. And by jumping off the hilltop, she communicates her anger toward God as the origin of sublimity, the action wherein lies her delight.

Considering the importance of Judeo-Christian ethics in Hemans's poetry, we may as well see her moral restructuring of forgiveness. As Elisabeth Gedge notes, 'Forgiveness, as a moral phenomenon, aims at moral repair, a restructuring of moral relation.'[44] It is 'in forgiving' that 'we abandon expressions of anger, mistrust, reproach or punishment which are no longer appropriate after we have forgiven.'[45] But Hemans's women consider male-imposed transgressions as a connection to God's punishment, for which they struggle to abandon their frustration and anger. These poetic personae not only detach themselves from the source of sublimity, but also they morally restructure their new attachment with God by the joy and delight in the heights of anguish and pain.

4. Neutralization of the Sublime

Hemans's idea of liberation is not limited to women's rights.[46] In her poetry, by means of symbolic and metaphorical examples, the writer liberates the masculine definition of the sublime from destruction. Neutralization as 'The action or process of rendering something or someone harmless or inconsequential, esp. by violent or coercive means'[47] is what can be applied to Hemans's process of disentangling the Romantic masculine sublime. The action of self-annihilation by female poetic personae drives the poetical fabric to transformation; to the neutralization of the Romantic egotistical and masculine sublime. In 'Man and Woman,' Hemans argues that although suffering is a major part of women's lives, their aesthetic classification is contradictory.[48] This poetical objection to the subjectivity of women begins by questioning the destruction defined in the masculine sublime:

> Warrior! Whose image on thy tomb,
> With shield and crested head,
> sleeps proudly in the purple gloom
> by the stain'd window shed;
> the records of thy name and race
> Have faded from the stone,
> yet thou a cloud of years I trace
> what thou hast been and done.[49]

In the above stanza, the concept of destruction as a result of humanity's egotism and inherited rage is symbolized in the warrior's shield and crested head, but his race's name has long been faded from tombs. However, the narrator attacks the shadow and cloud of darkness and gloom in this sublimity which continue to bring anguish and nothingness. In the next stanzas, the narrator outlines the belongings of the warrior by pointing to his 'lofty place where leaders sate,' 'An arm that bravely bore the lance,' 'A haughty heart and kingly glance,' and 'A name that drew a prouder tone,' yet what of it? His reward is nothingness in death.

Turning towards the woman, the narrator enquires, 'What was thy tale? Oh, gentle mate / of him the bold and free,' and 'What bard hath sung of *thee*?'[50] It is then confirmed by the narrative that the woman's part is only in endless anguish and pain:

> He woo'd a bright and burning star;
> thine was the void, the gloom,
> the straining eye that follow'd far
> his oft-receding plume;

the heart-sick listening while his steed
sent echoes on the breeze;
the pang— but when did fame take heed
of griefs obscure as these?

Thy silent and secluded hours,
through many a lonely day
while bending o'er thy broider'd flowers,
with spirit far away;
thy weeping midnight prayers for him
tho fought on Syrian plains;
thy watchings till the torch grew dim,—
these fill no minstrel strains.[51]

The woman's life, in comparison with the warrior's, is filled with its own anxieties. It also beholds its own lack of contentment and grim hope. It is hard to judge who has suffered more, but by the face of this narrative, one finds the lengthy lines in the second part rather foreboding and heart-sickening. If the woman is the aesthetic metaphor for beauty, her share in life is the sublimity of the void and destructive gloom. Hemans does not equip the narrator with inspirational moments in the woman's prayers and sleepless nights of agony for her beloved. Rather, she reaches to silence and seclusion, which from a psychological perspective not only leads to rage and revenge, but relates to depression. For example, 'Depression is our way of shrinking in the physical and emotional size to silence the rage we feel for existing. We hide from others, including ourselves.'[52] The woman cannot share these sufferings thus, she remains helpless with regard to what we know as trend forgiveness, a type of temporary forgiveness as the basic step towards complete forgiveness.[53]

Joy in this metaphorical anguish is only achieved through reconstructing the sublime by reaching to the greatest origin of sublimity. That is why the last stanza creates a sense of ending the woman's life, and so connecting her with God. It is also a cry for absolution, perhaps sung by the woman herself to God for the deliverance of her husband's sins committed in battles. Thus the closing reads:

A still sad life was thine! long years.
With tasks unguerdon'd fraught,
Deep, quiet love, submissive tears,
Vigils of anxious thought;
Prayers at the cross in fervour pour'd
Alms to the pilgrims given;
O happy, happier than thy lord,
In that lone path to heaven![54]

The textual and poetical fabric of 'Man and Woman' is such that the 'lord' in the last stanza represents 'man,' but may well be interpreted as God. The delight in the woman's lonely path towards the origin of sublimity is full of hope, which itself is indicated in the woman's vigil prayers. The extent to which the woman's happiness stretches is beyond humanity's and God's delight. This final moment is overjoyed with the fact that the woman can pray and suffer, hope and wait, love and hate, and reach to the heart of sublimity. The man and God, on the other hand, do not share in the same complex experience. Therefore, Hemans's idea of the woman's happiness, far beyond the man's, expands the aesthetics of the sublime towards neutralization of this concept by showing the other side of sublimity, the actively prayerful, hopeful, and joyful sublime.

This contextual neutralization of the sublime in 'Man and Woman' resonates within a textual grandeur which is superior with regard to poetical dimension. The first three stanzas replicate the destruction of the masculine sublime, whereas the other four discuss the female anguish and joy by relocating the definition of the sublime in the encounter of man, woman, and God, wherein the poetic absolution is hosted.

5. Affective Pathways to Transcendence

'In glorifying the ethics of female self-sacrifice and linking it in many poems (particularly later in her career) with the heroic deaths of women as sacrifices to the domestic ideal,' Anthony Harding observes that 'Hemans delivers a new version of the Romantic hunger for transcendence, a version that purports to compensate women for their unpaid labour and the relative obscurity of their lives as nurturers and caregivers.'[55] During the early to middle stages of her poetic career, Hemans proposed the international aspect of this perspective, the most important example of which is her *Records of Woman* (1828). Besides, Hemans's skill in translating poetry plays a crucial role in identifying a type of transcendence which spans different religious, cultural, and geographical domains. The lyrical poems of Luis de Camões (1524-1580), one of Portugal's greatest poets (also known as Camoens) translated into English by Hemans offers one such example.

Quoting a lyrical narrative written by Camoens, Hemans translates the idea of 'anguish with delight' central to which a sense of forgiveness and consequently a profound relation to transcendence is hidden. Within the domestic realm of love, a man narrates the parting story of his beloved. He says, 'Amidst the bitter tears that fell / In anguish at my last farewell / Oh! Who would dream that joy could dwell'[56] The narrative which is opened by the man is a depiction of woman's suffering and death whose final words reassure the man of her love for him. These words poured out in the final moment of the woman's life create a passionate delight for the man in lowest point of distress. Thus he explains the scene:

It was, when Hope, oppress'd with woes,
Seem'd her dim eyes in death to close.
That rapture's brightest beam arose
In sorrow's darkest night.
Thus if my soul survive that hour,
Tis that my fate o'ercame the power
Of anguish with delight.

For oh! her love, so long unknown,
She *then* confest, was all my own,
And in that parting hour alone
Reveal'd it to my sight.
And now what pangs will rend my soul,
Should fortune still, with stern control,
Forbid me this delight.[57]

One may hardly know if these intense moments 'Of anguish with delight' remark the woman's self-sacrifice, self-annihilation, or natural death. For if this final moment, as the man recites, characterizes the only occasion that the woman confessed her love for him, a love 'so long unknown' there will be some doubt over the manner of the woman's death. The man's narrative remains, however, sensational. Here, paradoxes of joy and suffering are rather nicely mingled with the confession of human love, so much so that rage and anger toward God leave the poetic space. The sublime is at the heart of this paradox, as the man admits to the possibility of helplessness in overcoming the power of the paradoxes in juxtaposition.

Equally, we may wonder whether the woman's confession of love is the only stirring point in sustaining the man's delight. And if this late-confessed love is all that he cares for to remain elated and buoyant, does this lyric not display man's inherited rage and egotism; hence compensate? The woman and the Romantic hunger for transcendence. As the poem ends, we note that the man regrets the lost beauty and sublimity in a mighty arena, where the blooming nature aggravates his agony as well as his joy. He cries:

I know not if my bliss were vain,
For all the force of parting pain
Forbade suspicious doubts to reign,
When exiled from her sight;
Yet now what double woe for me,
Just at the close of eve, to see
The day-spring of delight.[58]

The man himself derives a great sense of transcendence from this double sorrow which metaphorically puts forgiveness in the heart of nature. The flourishing trees and blossoming flowers after the melancholy season, similar to the blooming of every new day beyond the darkest of nights, captures a symbol of absolution through the continuity of creation, despite human agony.

The poetic hosting of absolution, thereby, can help shape a fictive space for Hemans and the readers in order to transform agony into delight in their own lives. It creates a 'Double religious belonging;' one that as Ursula King puts it, 'can be spiritually sustaining and helpful for one's life.'[59] On the other hand, neutralization of the sublime in women's Romantic poetry communicates the poetic personae's belonging to the realm of the absolved, beyond traditional gender roles. If the Romantic masculine sublime contains meaning and glory, so does the aesthetics of the female sublime on all together higher grounds; the only reason being that women Romantic poets transformed the masculinity of destruction to eternal joy. And there is meaning in life if there is meaning in suffering. Viktor Emil Frankl (1905-1997) has splendidly explained this concept in 'The Will to Meaning,' remembering the Shoah. He notes:

> . . . I remember, it seemed to me that I would die in the near future. In this critical situation, however, my concern was different from that of most of my comrades. Their question was, "Will we survive the camp? For, if not, all this suffering has no meaning." The question which beset me was, "Has all this suffering, this dying around us, a meaning? For, if not, then ultimately there is no meaning to survival; for a life whose meaning depends upon such happenstance – as whether one escapes or not – ultimately would not be worth living at all." [60]

And Hemans precisely puts the necessity for neutralization of the sublime destruction into words, asserting that forgiveness, if not always simply possible or contextually accessible, is nevertheless an inseparable enclosure to the meaning of life. Thus 'anguish with delight' unfolds and

> . . . in the face of death, whose shadowy arm
> Comes dim between us, to regard th' exchange
> Of our tried hearts' forgiveness,— Who are they,
> That in one path have journey'd, needing not
> Forgiveness at its close? [61]

Notes

[1] Emma Mason has advised on my literary analysis of joy in relation to the Romantic narratives of hope, introducing Adam Potkay's *Story of Joy*. Jill Rudd has guided on the Romantic aesthetics of the sublime. Greg Lynall has offered a discussion of psychological perspectives on the Romantic male-authored texts and Ian Schermbrucker suggested a reading of the psychology of faith, forgiveness, and hope through Viktor Emil Frankl (1905-1997) and Dietrich Bonhoeffer (1906-1945). Maureen Watry has kindly offered help with a series of Felicia Hemans's manuscripts in the Sydney Jones Library at the University of Liverpool and Rachel Ben-Itzhak's views on male-authored Romantic poetry including the works of John Keats have been significant in helping provide comparative analysis. Editors, specifically Malika Rebai Maamri have offered thorough readings. I am grateful to all and dedicate this chapter to Professor Sue Owen in gratitude for her teachings of Early Modern Women's Writings.

[2] Simon Bainbridge, *British Poetry and the Revolutionary and Napoleonic Wars: Visions of Conflict* (Oxford: Oxford University Press, 2003), 150.

[3] Patricia Yaeger and Elizabeth Kowaleski-Wallace, 1989; Juliana Schiesari, 1992; Anne Mellor, 1993; and Catherine Maxwell, 2001 are examples of literary critics who have challenged gendered views of the sublime.

[4] Samuel Richardson (1689-1761) and Jane Austen (1775-1817) among others produced examples of this kind.

[5] Stephen Behrendt, *British Women Poets and the Romantic Writing Community* (Baltimore: The John Hopkins University, 2009), 80.

[6] The case of melancholy in Samuel Johnson (1709-84) is an example of such indulgence during the eighteenth century, which was often criticized by Hannah More (1745-1833). For further details, see Annette Meakin, *Hannah More: A Bibliographical Study* (London: Smith, Elder, and Co., 1911), 202-4.

[7] Felicia Hemans, *The Poetical Works of Felicia Hemans, Complete with a Critical Preface* (New York: American Book Exchange, 1881), 239.

[8] Examples of less well-known poets such as Upton can be found in Robyn Bolam, *Eliza's Babes: Four Centuries of Women's Poetry in English, c. 1500-1900* (Northumberland: Bloodaxe, 2005).

[9] Behrendt, *British Women Poets*, 88.

[10] Ibid.

[11] Ibid., 89.

[12] For example, Charlotte Smith's son died away from home. See Behrendt, *British Women Poets*, 84.

[13] Felicia Hemans, Notebook (1810-1814) written at Bronwhilfa, St Asaph, Denbighshire, MS/28/3/2/1, Special Collections and Archives, Sydney Jones Library, University of Liverpool, England.

[14] Behrendt, *British Women Poets*, 85.

[15] Joy and delight are different concepts compared to temporary and sudden 'pleasure.' For a comprehensive study of such terms see Maryam Farahani, 'The Psychology of Melancholy Aesthetics: A Study of Romantic Verse Narratives of Hannah More (1745-1833) and Felicia Hemans (1793-135)' (PhD diss., University of Liverpool, 2011).

[16] Hemans, *Poetical Works*, 34.

[17] 'Absolution, n', *The Oxford English Dictionary*, 3rd ed., 2009 in *OED Online*, Viewed 4 February 2011, http://www.oed.com.ezproxy.liv.ac.uk/Entry/682.

[18] Diego Saglia, 'The Moor's Last Sigh: Spanish-Moorish Exoticism and the Gender of History in British Romantic Poetry', *Journal of English Studies* 3 (2001-2): 202.

[19] Hemans, *Poetical Works*, 166-7.

[20] Ibid., ll. 94-105, 52.

[21] Adam Potkay, *The Story of Joy: From Bible to Late Romanticism* (Cambridge: Cambridge University Press, 2007), 93.

[22] Peter Hay, *Main Currents in Western Environmental Thought* (Sydney: University of New South Wales Press, 2002), 75.

[23] Albert Boime, *Art in an Age of Counterrevolution, 1815-1848* (Chicago: The Chicago University Press, 2004), 221.

[24] Ibid.

[25] Ary Scheffer (1795-1858), *The Suliote Women* (1827), Viewed 10 August 2010, http://www.artrenewal.org/pages/artwork.php?artworkid=3461&size=large.

[26] Hemans, *Poetical Works*, 266.

[27] Ibid., ll. 1-4.

[28] Ibid., ll. 5-10.

[29] Angela Leighton, *Shelley and the Sublime: An Interpretation of the Major Poems* (Cambridge: Cambridge University Press, 1984), 157.

[30] Marjorie Hope Nicolson, *Mountain Gloom and Mountain Glory: The Development of the Aesthetics of the Infinite* (Washington: University of Washington Press, 1997), 48.

[31] Ibid., 159.

[32] Hemans, *Poetical Works*, 266.

[33] Ibid., ll. 25-30.

[34] Potkay, *Story of Joy*, 96.

[35] Ibid.

[36] Anna Szczepan-Wojnarska, 'Poetry as a Medium of Forgiveness in the Light of Czesław Miłosz's Oeuvre', in *A Journey through Forgiveness* edited by Malika Rebai Maamri, Nehama Verbin and Everett L. Washington, Jr (Oxford: Inter-Disciplinary Press, 2010), viewed 10 March 2011, http://www.inter-

disciplinary.net/wp-content/uploads/2011/01/forgiveness3ever19122010.pdf/, 201.

[37] Hemans, *Poetical Works*, 266.

[38] Ibid, l. 37, 166-7.

[39] Ibid, ll. 41-44, 266.

[40] Anne Mellor, *Romanticism and Gender*, 97.

[41] Ibid.

[42] See the two beginning stanzas in Paul Negri, ed., *Metaphysical Poetry: an Anthology* (Devon: Dover Publications, 2002), 54.

[43] Julie J. Exline, 'Anger toward God: A New Frontier in the Study of Forgiveness', in *Journey through Forgiveness*, ed. Malika Rebai Maamri, Nehama Verbin and Everett L. Washington, Jr (Oxford: Inter-Disciplinary Press, 2010), viewed 10 April 2011, http://www.inter-disciplinary.net/wp-ontent/uploads/2011/01/forgive ness3ever19122010.pdf/, 30.

[44] Elisabeth Gedge, 'Radical Forgiveness and Feminist Theology', in *Journey through Forgiveness*, ed. Malika Rebai Maamri, Nehama Verbin and Everett L. Washington, Jr (Oxford: Inter-Disciplinary Press, 2010), viewed 15 March 2011, http://www.inter-disciplinary.net/wpcontent/uploads/2011/01/forgiveness3ever191 22010.pdf/, 70.

[45] Ibid.

[46] For an example of women's liberation, see Emma Mason and Jonathan Roberts, 'Felicia Hemans's *Sonnets on Female Characters of Scripture*,' in *The Yearbook of English Studies: Literature and Religion* 39 (2009): 72-83.

[47] 'Neutralization, n.', n. 8, *The Oxford English Dictionary*, 3rd ed., 2009 in *OED Online*, Viewed 15 January 2011, http://www.oed.com.ezproxy.liv.ac.uk/Entry/ 126462.

[48] Hemans, *Poetical Works*, 234.

[49] Ibid., ll. 1-8.

[50] Ibid., ll. 29-32.

[51] Ibid., ll. 33-48.

[52] Ruth King, *Healing Rage: Women Making Inner Peace Possible* (Berkeley: Gotham, 2007), 74.

[53] For a study of poetical trend forgiveness, see Maryam Farahani, 'Felicia Hemans, the Psychodynamics of Hope and trend Forgiveness', in *Journey through Forgiveness*, ed. Malika Rebai Maamri, Nehama Verbin and Everett L. Worthington, Jr (Oxford: Inter-Disciplinary Press, 2010), 220-222.

[54] Hemans, *Poetical Works*, ll. 49-56, 234.

[55] Anthony Harding, 'Felicia Hemans and the Effacement of Woman', in *Romantic Women Writers: Voices and Countervoices*, ed. Paula R. Feldman and Theresa M. Kelley (Hanover: University Press of New England, 1995), 139.

[56] Hemans, *Poetical Works*, ll. 1-3, 59.
[57] Ibid., ll. 8-21.
[58] Ibid., ll. 22-28.
[59] Ursula King, *The Search for Spirituality: Our Global Quest for Meaning and Fulfilment* (Norwich: Canterbury Press, 2009), 62.
[60] See Frankl's excerpt from 'The Will to Meaning', in Francis S. Collins, ed., *Belief: Readings on the Reason for Faith* (New York: HarperOne, 2010), 251-258, 258.
[61] 'The Siege of Valencia' (1812) in Hemans, *Poetical Works*, ll. 250-254, 120.

Bibliography

Bainbridge, Simon. *British Poetry and the Revolutionary and Napoleonic Wars: Visions of Conflict*. Oxford: Oxford University Press, 2003.

Behrendt, Stephen. *British Women Poets and the Romantic Writing Community*. Baltimore: The John Hopkins University, 2009.

Boime, Albert. *Art in an Age of Counterrevolution, 1815-1848*. Chicago: The Chicago University Press, 2004.

Bolam, Robyn. *Eliza's Babes: Four Centuries of Women's Poetry in English, c. 1500-1900*. Northumberland: Bloodaxe, 2005.

Burke, Edmund. *Philosophical Enquiry into the Origin of Our Ideas of the Sublime and the Beautiful*. Edited by Abraham Mills. New York: Harper and Brothers, 1844.

Exline, Julie. 'Anger toward God: A New Frontier in the Study of Forgiveness'. in *A Journey through Forgiveness*, edited by Malika Rebai Maamri, Nehama Verbin and Everett L. Worthington, Jr. (Oxford: Inter-Disciplinary Press, 2010), accessed February 9, 2011, http://www.inter-disciplinary.net/publishing/id-press/ebooks/a-journey-through-forgiveness/.

Farahani, Maryam. 'The Psychology of Melancholy Aesthetics: A Study of Romantic Verse Narratives of Hannah More (1745-1833) and Felicia Hemans (1793-1835)'. PhD diss., University of Liverpool, 2011.

Farahani, Maryam. 'Felicia Hemans, the Psychodynamics of Hope and Trend Forgiveness'. In *A Journey through Forgiveness*, edited by Malika Rebai Maamri, Nehama Verbin and Everett L. Worthington, Jr. (Oxford: Inter-Disciplinary Press, 2010), accessed February 9, 2011, http://www.inter-disciplinary.net/publishing/id-press/ebooks/a-journey-through-forgiveness/.

Feldman, Paula R., and Theresa M. Kelley, eds. *Romantic Women Writers: Voices and Countervoices*. Hanover: University Press of New England, 1995.

Frankl, Viktor Emil. 'The Will to Meaning.' In *Belief: Readings on the Reason for Faith*, edited by Francis S. Collins, 251-258. New York: HarperOne, 2010.

Gedge, Elisabeth. 'Radical Forgiveness and Feminist Theology'. in *A Journey through Forgiveness*, edited by Malika Rebai Maamri, Nehama Verbin and Everett L. Worthington, Jr. (Oxford: Inter-Disciplinary Press, 2010), accessed February 9, 2011, http://www.inter-disciplinary.net/publishing/id-press/ebooks/a-journey-through-forgiveness/.

Harding, Anthony. 'Felicia Hemans and the Effacement of Woman'. In *Romantic Women Writers: Voices and Countervoices*, edited by Paula R. Feldman and Theresa M. Kelley. Hanover: University Press of New England, 1995.

Hay, Peter. *Main Currents in Western Environmental Thought*. Sydney: University of New South Wales Press, 2002.

Hemans, Felicia. *Notebook (1810-1814) Written at Bronwhilfa, St Asaph, Denbighshire*. MS/28/3/2/1. England: Special Collections and Archives at Sydney Jones Library, University of Liverpool, 2010.

———. *Poems*. Liverpool: T. Cadell, 1808.

———. *Records of Woman, With Other Poems*. 2nd edn. Edinburgh: W. Blackwood; London: T. Cadell, 1828.

———. *The Poetical Works of Felicia Hemans, Complete with a Critical Preface*. New York: American Book Exchange, 1881.

Kelly, Gary, ed. *Felicia Hemans: Selected Poems, Prose, and Letters*. New York: Broadview Press, 1998.

King, Ruth. *Healing Rage: Women Making Inner Peace Possible.* Berkeley: Gotham, 2007.

King, Ursula. *The Search for Spirituality: Our Global Quest for Meaning and Fulfilment.* Norwich: Canterbury Press, 2009.

Kowaleski-Wallace, Elizabeth. *Their Fathers' Daughters: Hannah More, Maria Edgeworth, and Patriarchal Complicity.* New York: Oxford University Press, 1991.

Leighton, Angela. *Shelley and the Sublime: An Interpretation of the Major Poems.* Cambridge: Cambridge University Press, 1984.

Mason, Emma. *Women Poets of the Nineteenth Century.* Devon: Northcote House, 2006.

————. Sensibility into Sense: Barbauld, Hemans and Religious Commitment'. In *Spiritual Identities, Literature and the Post-Secular Imagination*, edited by Jo Carruthers and Andrew Tate, 79-96. New York: Peter Lang, 2009.

Mason, Emma, and Jonathan Roberts, 'Felicia Hemans's *Sonnets on Female Characters of Scripture'. The Yearbook of English Studies: Literature and Religion* 39 (2009): 72-83.

Maxwell, Catherine. *The Female Sublime from Milton to Swinburne: Bearing Blindness.* Basingstoke: Palgrave Macmillan, 2001.

McCullough, M., Fincham, F., and J. Tsang. 'Forgiveness, Forbearance, and Time: The Temporal Unfolding of Transgression-Related Interpersonal Motivations'. *Journal of Personality and Social Psychology* 84 (2003): 540-557.

McCullough, M., Bono, G., and L. Root. 'Rumination, Emotion, and Forgiveness: Three Longitudinal Studies'. *Journal of Personality and Social Psychology* 92 (2007): 490-505.

Meakin, Annette. *Hannah More: a Bibliographical Study.* London: Smith, Elder, and Co., 1911.

Mellor, Anne K. *Romanticism and Feminism.* Bloomington and Indianapolis: Indiana University Press, 1988.

————. '*Romanticism and Gender*. New York: Routledge, 1993.

Negri, Paul, ed. *Metaphysical Poetry: An Anthology*. Devon: Dover Publications, 2002.

Nicolson, Marjorie Hope. *Mountain Gloom and Mountain Glory: The Development of the Aesthetics of the Infinite*. Washington: University of Washington Press, 1997.

OED Online. *The Oxford English Dictionary*. 3rd ed., 2009. <http://www.oed.com. ezproxy.liv.ac.uk/Entry/126462>.

OED Online. *The Oxford English Dictionary*, 3rd ed., 2009. <http://www.oed.com. ezproxy.liv.ac.uk/Entry/682>.

Potkay, Adam. *The Story of Joy: From Bible to Late Romanticism*. Cambridge: Cambridge University Press, 2007.

Saglia, Diego. 'The Moor's Last Sigh: Spanish-Moorish Exoticism and the Gender of History in British Romantic Poetry'. *Journal of English Studies* 3 (2001-2): 193-215.

Scheffer, Ary. *The Suliote Women* (1827). In Art Renewal Centre Online. 2010. http://www.artrenewal.org/pages/artwork.php?artworkid=3461&size=large.

Schiesari, Juliana. *The Gendering of Melancholia: Feminism, Psychoanalysis, and the Symbolics of Loss in Renaissance Literature*. Ithaca: Cornell University Press, 1992.

Shaw, Philip. *The Sublime*. Oxon: Routledge, 2006.

Szczepan-Wojnarska, Anna M. 'Poetry as a Medium of Forgiveness in the Light of Czesław Miłosz's Oeuvre'. In *A Journey through Forgiveness*, edited by Malika Rebai Maamri, Nehama Verbin and Everett L. Worthington, Jr. (Oxford: Inter-Disciplinary Press, 2010), accessed February 9, 2011, http://www.inter-disciplinary.net/publishing/id-press/ebooks/a-journey-through-forgiveness/.

Tsang, J., M. McCullough and F. Fincham. 'The Longitudinal Association Between Forgiveness and Relationship Closeness and Commitment'. *Journal of Social and Clinical Psychology* 25 (2006): 448-472.

Wolfson, Susan, ed. *Felicia Hemans: Selected Poems, Letters, Reception Materials.* Princeton: Princeton University Press, 2000.

Yaegar, Patricia. 'Toward A Female Sublime'. In *Gender and Theory: Dialogues on Feminist Criticism.* edited by Linda Kauffman. Oxford: Blackwell, 1989.

Žižek, Slavoj. *The Sublime Object of Ideology.* New York: Verso, 1989.

Maryam Farahani is a research member of *Personalised* and *Global Health Research Networks* at the University of Liverpool with expertise in women's post-Enlightenment literature, social psychology and feminist perspectives. Her current work includes a monograph on the psychology of melancholy aesthetics, entitled *Melancholy, Myth, and Mirth: The Romantic Women Poets, 1773-1835* and co-authoring of two books: *Conflict and Affect: A Century of Catholic Women's Poetry,* with Ian Schermbrucker (School of Psychology) and *Hay Ibn Yaqzan; or, The Awakening of the Soul* with Nick Davis (School of English) at the University of Liverpool.

Levinasian Ethics and the Failure to Forgive in Jean-Paul Sartre's *The Flies*

Canan Şavkay

Abstract

Jean Paul Sartre rewrote *The Oresteia*, Aeschylus's ancient tragedy which revolves around the question of revenge and justice during the German occupation of France. Therefore *The Flies* has often been regarded as a disguised appeal to resist the German oppressors. Yet Sartre's depiction of Orestes' murderous acts reveals his concern with the problematic nature of revenge. In the Greek tragedy, Orestes is not faced with the alternative of forgiveness, whereas in *The Flies,* Orestes is continuously asked to leave Argos. Leaving Argos, however, implies that the father's murder is not going to be avenged by the son. As many critics have pointed out, the use of dual opposites in the Greek version functions to justify Orestes' murder, for the protagonist is thus put under the obligation to take revenge in order to maintain his father's order. Philosopher Emmanuel Levinas claims that forgiveness absolves the offender and thus allows him or her to go back in time, pretending that the offence never happened. In Levinas's terms, Orestes's forgiveness would entail the betrayal of his father's order. The possibility of forgiveness therefore appears to belong to a different order, one in which the traditionally established dualisms no longer work. According to Levinas, the act of revenge belongs to the order of what he terms 'the same,' implying a view that evaluates events from one's own perspective. Forgiveness, on the other hand, constitutes a response to the other. In *The Flies*, Sartre carves out an ethical space in which forgiveness remains a possibility and is intricately linked with a different kind of representation. Orestes is asked to leave without committing the murderous deed. Exploring Orestes' decision in favour of revenge, this chapter aims to show that Orestes's failure to forgive stems from the fact that forgiveness belongs to an order that is different from his father's.

Key Words: Forgiveness, *The Flies*, Jean-Paul Sartre, Emmanuel Levinas, ethics, the dwelling, the feminine.

*****

In 1942, Jean-Paul Sartre rewrote Aeschylus's ancient tragedy, *The Oresteia*, in which he remained at large faithful to the original plot version, yet gave Orestes the chance to leave Argos without committing the crime, whereas in the original version, Orestes is strictly required to avenge his father's murder. The choice between revenge and forgiveness is closely connected with the use of binary oppositions both plays employ, though in quite distinct ways.

The *Oresteia* is an attempt to question the nature of justice and therefore focuses on the problem of revenge because each act of revenge requires a renewed call for revenge and thus, represents a vicious circle that has to be broken. This conflict, however, is solved in *The Oresteia* through the sacrifice of the maternal function that is taken over by father.

The play revolves around the question whether it is right to murder Clytemnestra, who killed her husband Agamemnon. God Apollo believes that it is right, for he demands of Orestes to kill his mother. However, when Orestes obeys Apollo and kills his mother, he is pursued by the Eumenides because he violated the ancient law that forbids the killing of one's kin. The question whether Orestes was right in killing his mother or whether he committed a grave sin by killing her, is finally resolved at the expense of the function of the mother. Claiming that the mother is not the true parent of the child but merely a vessel for the man who impregnates her, Apollo convinces the jury that Orestes has not sinned against the law that forbids the killing of one's own kin. Apollo addresses the jury proclaiming:

> The mother is not the true parent of the child which is
> called hers. She is a nurse who tends the growth of
> young seed planted by its true parent, the male. So,
> if Fate spares the child, she keeps it, as one might Keep
> for some friend a growing plant. And of this truth, that
> father without mother may beget, we have present, as proof,
> the daughter of Olympian Zeus: One never nursed in the dark
> cradle of the womb; Yet such a being no god will beget again.[1]

Apollo thus severs the bond between the mother and her children and instead subordinates the mother to the authority of her husband. Luce Irigaray believes that Aeschylus's *The Oresteia* illustrates the establishment of the patriarchal order, claiming that Freud's focus on the myth of Oedipus hides the truth of a more archaic murder, namely the murder of the mother. Irigaray states:

> When Freud describes and theorizes, notably in *Totem and Taboo*, the murder of the father as founding the primal horde, he forgets a more archaic murder, that of the mother, necessitated by the establishment of a certain order in the polis.[2]

Although neither Agamemnon, nor Orestes is depicted as an innocent character, the play nevertheless sides with them against Clytemnestra who, in the end is portrayed as deserving punishment. Irigaray points at the injustice of the play's outcome, stating that Clytemnestra has her reasons for wanting to kill Agamemnon when he returns to Argos. Irigaray writes:

Clytemnestra, for her part has taken a lover. But she had heard nothing from her husband for so long that she thought he was dead. So she kills Agamemnon when he returns in glory with his mistress. She kills him out of jealousy, out of fear perhaps, and because she has been unsatisfied and frustrated for so long. She also kills him because he sacrificed their daughter to conflicts between men, a motive which is often forgotten by the tragedians.[3]

The misogynist character of the play is underscored when at the end Orestes, the murderer of his mother, becomes the new founder of the social order because this system subordinates motherhood to a masculine order and is based on violence and subjection.

In this vein, David Cohen argues that the order established in *The Oresteia* is neither moral, nor just, but rather based on force[4] and this is mainly emphasized in the scene when at the beginning of the tragedy the chorus remembers an incident that took place shortly before the Greek troops set out on their journey to Troy. Observing the sight of two eagles devouring a pregnant hare, the priests interpret it as a sign of the goddess Artemis's anger; for they believe that the two eagles symbolize the two kings, Agamemnon and Menelaus. Goddess Artemis turns against the Greek expedition because as the protector of pregnancy, she naturally loathes the killing of the pregnant hare. As a result, Artemis calms down the winds and demands an impossible sacrifice, that of Iphigenia, Agamemnon's own daughter. Cohen argues that Artemis's demand is not cruel, but rather aims at protecting the innocent victims of the war. He states: 'Artemis, the goddess who protects the young and the helpless, pities the future victims of the eagles and demands an impossible sacrifice to turn them back.'[5] Nevertheless, Agamemnon opts for the sacrifice of his daughter and thus commits a crime that is justified throughout the play. When Clytmemnestra, Agamemnon's murderer, tries to save her life by trying to remind her son Orestes – determined to avenge his father's death – that Agamemnon was a sinner too, Orestes replies 'He spent himself in battle, you sat at home.'[6] The fact that at the end of the play Orestes is acquitted and becomes the founder of a new social order underscores the play's upholding of force and violence.

Sartre's *The Flies*, however, differs in its attitude towards violence and revenge. In Aeschylus' *The Oresteia*, forgiveness is never an option, because those who forgive are said to share the sinner's guilt.[7] This implies that if Orestes forgave his mother, he would side with her against his father, which would be unacceptable considering the patriarchal context of the play. In *The Oresteia*, the possibility to forgive does not exist, for the chorus explicitly states:

> The gods are deaf to every prayer;
> if pity lights a human eye,
> pity by Justice' law must share
> the sinner's guilt, and with the sinner die.[8]

Nathaniel Wade and Julia Kidwell, who explore the role of forgiveness in the lives of religious people, argue that religious commitment helps victims to forgive because most of the world's religions encourage forgiveness;[9] yet the religious order ruled by Zeus in *The Oresteia* is characterized by its complicity with force and violence and therefore rules out any possibility for forgiveness. *The Flies*, however, which reflects the basic aspects of Sartre's existentialist philosophy, widely differs from Aeschylus's notion of justice.

A superficial reading of *The Flies* might reveal that the play also advocates revenge; however, a more thorough reading shows that Sartre's text is much more complex and actually distances itself from revenge. A major difference between the two plays lies in the description of Orestes. In *The Flies*, for example, Orestes is incessantly told by several characters to leave Argos without committing the murder, whereas for Orestes in the original version no such choice ever exists. The philosopher Emmanuel Levinas believes that forgiveness 'permits the subject who had committed himself in a past instant to be as though that instant had not past on, to be as though he had not committed himself.'[10] Forgiveness, however, must not be confused with the act of forgetting, for Levinas states that 'Active in a stronger sense than forgetting, which does not concern the reality of the event forgotten, pardon acts upon the past, somehow repeats the event, purifying it.'[11] This idea is closely connected with Levinas's concept of time, for he believes that forgetting nullifies the past, whereas forgiveness conserves the past in a purified present.[12]

Orestes' inability to live in the present, which stems from his sense of homelessness, leads to his decision to kill his mother. His profound desire to overcome his rootlessness bears close parallels with Levinas's concept of the dwelling and hospitality, which he describes in feminine terms. Levinas states 'the primary hospitable welcome which describes the field of intimacy is the Woman. The woman is the condition for recollection, the interiority of the Home, and inhabitation.'[13] When Levinas elaborates on his idea of the dwelling, he associates it with a feminine welcome, yet he makes it clear that the feminine is used as a trope and refers to attributes inherent in all human beings. In *Ethics and Infinity* he writes:

> Perhaps...all these allusions to the ontological differences between the masculine and the feminine would appear less archaic if, instead of dividing humanity into two species... they would signify that the participation in the masculine and the feminine were the attribute of every human being.[14]

Levinas's idea of hospitality and the dwelling views the self as a home that provides a shelter for the other person because the dwelling is 'a retreat home with oneself as in a land of refuge, which answers to a hospitality, an expectancy, a human welcome.'[15] The sense of belonging is thus severed from place and:

> What is human is inscribed ... in the break with every private locale... or homeland...The human, or the nomad, has left without reserves... his mind made up by hearing the summons of the other man.[16]

Viewed from the perspective of the concept of the dwelling, Orestes's inability to establish a psychic space in which he feels at home and at ease with his environment leads him to act violently, for he fails to establish a connection with the sides in him that are traditionally associated with the feminine. Orestes's association with feminine aspects is emphasized at the beginning of the play, for unlike the mythological hero, Orestes in *The Flies* bears mainly feminine features. His sister Electra, for instance, describes him having a 'kind, girlish face,'[17] which underscores the fact that at the beginning of the play he had the opportunity to remain faithful to his more gentle and compliant side, yet because his idea of home is already tainted with a sense of domination, he tends to side with his father.

In *The Flies*, revenge is associated with masculine aspects and the parallel between Sartre's portrayal of the vengeful Orestes and Levinas's view of a philosophy devoid of ethics bears a striking resemblance. Levinas describes a relation that does not take into account the otherness of the other as 'hard and cold...it neither clothes those who are naked nor feeds those who are hungry... spirit in its masculine existence... *lives outdoors*.'[18] This sense of alienation 'results from the very masculinity of the universal and conquering logos'[19] and is evident in Orestes' feeling of homelessness, for aligning himself with the father and the logos, he is unable to create a spiritual home in which he might feel being welcome.

Jacques Derrida's view of evil and forgiveness underscores the destructive nature of Orestes's deed. Derrida claims:

> But in order for evil to emerge, 'radical evil' and perhaps worse again, the unforgiveable evil, the only one which would make the question of forgiveness emerge, it is necessary that at the most intimate of that intimacy an absolute hatred would come to interrupt the peace. This destructive hostility can only aim at what Levinas calls the 'face' of the Other, the similar other, the closest neighbour, between the Bosnians and Serbs, for example, within the same quarter, the same house, sometimes in the same family.[20]

Disregarding the fact that Orestes has not seen his mother for years, he turns against his closest kin when he decides to murder his mother. To Orestes, his mother has committed an 'unforgiveable evil' not only by depriving him of his father, but also of maternal care – because after the murder, she sent the young Orestes away to be raised by strangers. Derrida, however, notes that unforgiveable evil is the only situation where forgiveness gains its value and force. Viewed under this perspective, Orestes fails to forgive the unforgiveable.

Sartre takes up the binary oppositions employed in *The Oresteia,* yet whereas the audience in *The Oresteia* is made to side with the avenger, Sartre regards the nature of revenge from a different angle. In *The Flies,* he identifies revenge with masculine characteristics and endows forgiveness with traits that are generally regarded as feminine. Revenge in *The Flies* represents a view that believes in the existence of only one right and one truth and is based on force and violence, and consequently does not acknowledge the position of the other. Forgiveness, on the other hand, represents a state of being which feels at home with his/her environment, has come to terms with the fragility and mortality of existence, acknowledges passivity and is therefore open to an encounter with the other. As Richard A. Cohen points out, 'Levinas takes the key to embodiment to lie in its vulnerability, a vulnerability that opens the human to the suffering of others.'[21] Because Orestes is not at ease with his fragile existence, he is not able to empathize with Clytemnestra and leaves her to come to terms with her own sense of guilt.

The play clearly states that Orestes could have opted for forgiveness and not for revenge, but already at the beginning of the play it becomes evident that Orestes has an essentially oedipal problem and is therefore going to side with his father against his mother. For example, when he meets Electra for the first time, he does not reveal to her his true identity. He omits to tell her that he came from Athens where he was actually raised, but tells her that he is Pilebus from Corinth, 'which... recalls Oedipus, who was adopted by Polybus, King of Corinth.'[22] Keeping in mind that psychoanalysis describes the oedipal conflict as a phase during which the boy overcomes his rivalry with the father and consequently identifies with him, Orestes's link with Oedipus underscores his desire to side with his father against his mother. Thus despite all the appeals that try to prevent him from killing his mother, Orestes sides with his father, just like the mythical Orestes. O'Donohoe notes that the murder of his mother even becomes 'his rite of passage to adulthood and freedom.'[23] Orestes in *The Flies* remains deaf to the possibility of forgiveness, sides with his father and thus loses all his feminine attributes, which leads to the loss of his humanity.

Although Orestes at once, seemed to be reluctant to kill his mother, the fact that already at the beginning of the play there was something wrong with his sense of belonging makes it evident that he would finally opt for revenge and not for forgiveness. Orestes's sense of belonging is not based on a natural bond between the individual and his/her environment, but is expressed in terms associated with violence and suppression. When Orestes laments his lack of memories regarding his hometown Argos, he states that 'memories are luxuries reserved for people who own houses, cattle, fields, and servants. Whereas I-! I'm free as air.'[24]

After his resolution to kill his mother, Orestes once more expresses the close connection between violence and his sense of belonging when he tells his sister:

> Even the slave bent beneath his load, dropping with fatigue and staring dully at the ground a foot in front of him – why, even that poor slave can say he's in his town, as a tree is in a forest, or a leaf upon the tree.[25]

Only after having come to terms with the implicit violence within him does Orestes decide to take possession of his heritage, for then, just before he murders his mother, he suddenly appears to be possessive of both his hometown and his sister. He addresses Electra and tells her 'You are *my* sister, Electra, and that city is *my* city. *My* sister.'[26] He then makes it explicit that in order to take over his city, he has to act: 'I must take a burden on my shoulders, a load of guilt so heavy as to drag me down, right down into the abyss of Argos.'[27] After killing his mother, Orestes actually becomes the slave he wanted to be in order to relieve himself of his sense of isolation.

His violent deed, however, cuts him off even further from his hometown and his sister. At the end of the play, he ironically assumes the role of the hero who liberates Argos and burdens himself with its guilt. Orestes's transformation from the gentle young man he was at the beginning into the fierce hero of Electra's dreams questions the nature of Orestes's freedom of choice which he proclaims to possess at the end of the play. Sartre's 'use of 'extreme' situations produces a brutal illumination,'[28] for Orestes' decision to take action may appear at first glance as an act in which Orestes recognizes his individual freedom, yet it turns out to be a cloak for his underlying desire for violence.

The thought of revenge does not only isolate Orestes, but also kills the loving and gentle part in him, for after his resolution to kill his mother, his eyes become 'dull and smoldering.'[29] This transformation had already been foreshadowed earlier when Clytemnestra rebuked Electra for her stubbornness and told her that she sees her own likeness in the hateful looks of her daughter. Addressing Electra, Clytemnestra tells her:

> Only too well I see you are determined to bring ruin on yourself, and on us all. Yet who am I to counsel you, I who ruined my whole life in a single morning? You hate me, my child, but what disturbs me more is your likeness to me, as I was once.[30]

After Clytemnestra's murder, Orestes looks at Electra and cries out:

> Where, now, have I seen dead eyes like those? Electra – you are
> like *her*. Like Clytemnestra. What use, then was it killing her?
> When I see my crime in those eyes, it revolts me.[31]

Thus both children, whose aim was to restore justice, lose their connection with life and come to resemble the criminal they wanted to punish. The two children's inability to forgive their mother reflects Steven J. Sandage and Peter J. Jankowski's description of the psychological effects of victimization. They argue that offence often leads to the victim distancing him/herself from the other, thus drawing impermeable boundaries. Forgiveness, they claim, poses a solution to the resulting sense of isolation, because it allows the victim to open a space for the other.[32] It should be noted that opening a space for the other is an act that is often associated with the maternal and it is exactly this feature which the two children lose when they kill their mother as a result of siding with their father.

In his chapter on 'The Art of Forgiving: Conditions of Perspective and Transformation,' Richard Kyte also claims that injuries of various kinds lead to the victim isolating him/herself from others and consequently, forgiveness takes on the function of a healing process whereby the victim is given the opportunity to love again and to re-establish social relationships. Kyte argues that forgiveness cannot be accomplished by a mere act of will and points out that it is often difficult to come to terms with severe injuries that have been inflicted on one's person. Accordingly, art can be used as a device to confront and come to terms with pain and injury.

Kyte's argument concerning art can be well applied to *The Flies* because the audience is made to reflect on the rightfulness of revenge. Terry Eagleton's attitude to *The Oresteia* clearly emphasizes Kyte's point, because Eagleton draws attention to the fact that the characters in *The Oresteia* do not learn anything, and this foregrounds the fact that the play is actually addressed to its audience. Eagleton claims that '[t]ragedy is commonly supposed to teach wisdom through suffering, as the Chorus chants in Aeschylus's *Agamemnon*. Yet nobody in *The Oresteia* really learns from his suffering, last of all Agamemnon.'[33] Although the characters may not have learnt anything, the audience, nevertheless, does. At the end of *The Oresteia* it gets to know about Zeus's moral order and that the act of forgiveness is necessary in order to stop the vicious circle of revenge. Needless to say that the solution is completely misogyn.

Emphasizing the play's engagement with violence, Philip Velacott draws attention to the fact that Agamemnon causes his own murder when he kills his daughter and thereby puts Orestes under the obligation to kill his mother. Velacott states:

Orestes is bound by immemorial tradition to exact vengeance for
his murdered father; but his deed, even by the primitive standards
of the old religion, is a still worse crime than that which he has
avenged. In the end reconciliation is achieved… Thus out of sin
and struggle, revenge and atonement, there appears at last a new
phase in man's quest for justice.[34]

Although the new order is based on forgiveness, it is nevertheless not just, as
forgiveness is not granted to everybody, but to the male offender. The killing of
Clytemnestra is justified in the play.

In *The Flies*, however, there is no forgiveness at the end because the only
opportunity for forgiveness is forfeited when Orestes decides to kill his mother.
After this act, Orestes defies any sense of guilt and as a consequence claims not to
need any forgiveness. This, however, underscores the cruelty of his deed. He
neither shows compassion for his murder, nor does he seem to have learnt anything
from his family's cruel history and this shows that he lacks those two features
which Charlotte van Oyen Witvliet regards as essential for the successful
accomplishment of the act of forgiveness. Witvliet distinguishes between two
kinds of forgiveness: forgiveness that shows compassion for the offender,
emphasizing his/her humanity, and on the other hand, a kind of forgiveness arising
out of awareness that the offence can be viewed as an opportunity for growth and
self-understanding.[35] Viewed under Witvliet's concept of compassion-based
forgiveness, Electra and Orestes's stance towards their mother clearly indicates
their lack of compassion, because Clytemnestra's dead eyes are proof that she has
lost a vital part of her self when she committed the murder, yet despite this fact, her
children never acknowledge her as a victim. Consequently, they do not treat her
with compassion.

After Orestes loses his soft and gentle nature and kills his mother, Electra in
despair of her guilt, accuses Orestes and tells him that he should have preserved his
mildness, because then he would not have joined Electra in her hatred. [36]
Consequently, their mother would not have been murdered, as Electra would never
have attempted the murder on her own. However, when at the beginning, Orestes
asked Electra to leave Argos with him, she declined the offer precisely because she
did not want to abandon her hatred and leave her hometown without revenge. Thus
both children aligned themselves with their father and consequently killed their
mother, which emphasizes their failure to create a dwelling for each other, to
borrow Levinasian terms. Ignoring the part within them which might create a place
of welcome for each other, they fail to understand and forgive their mother,
although, as mentioned above, Clytemnestra's dead eyes should have been a
warning to both of them. As a mother, she avenged her child, yet this deed killed
her spirit and she now represents death in life. Concurrently, she lost all her

feminine aspects and significantly, she treated her other daughter, Electra, as a servant, having lost all motherly feelings.

As such, Clytemnestra has turned into the victimizer she punished. She initially wanted to kill her husband, because he brutally sacrificed their daughter for a war between men. She therefore acted out of maternal instinct and was appalled that the men should sacrifice her daughter for a mere war. However, once she uses violence against her husband, she becomes like him and so she loses her feminine and maternal side, underscored by the fact that the bond with her remaining two children is severed. Orestes is raised in another city and Electra is treated like a stepdaughter. Hence, she becomes as cruel as her husband Agamemnon.

The different treatment of revenge and forgiveness in the two plays is mainly emphasized in the representation of Clytemnestra's dilemma. Because justice in *The Oresteia* is based on masculine force and violence, Clytemnestra is expected to forgive her husband. The reason why she is expected to forgive him, however, stems from the fact that she is supposed to give in to his decisions because he represents masculine authority. The demand to forgive therefore bears no moral force and merely relies on her inferior position as a woman. It is clear at the beginning of the play that the chorus condemns Agamemnon's decision to sacrifice his daughter rather than to retreat from the expedition against Troy. Describing Agamemnon's determination to kill his daughter, the chorus sings:

> The doubtful tempest of his soul
> veered, and his prayer was turned to blasphemy,
> his offering to impiety.[37]

Despite the fact that the chorus condemns the deed, it still expects Clytemnestra not to act against her husband, but not out of a belief that forgiveness is better than revenge. As already stated above, in *The Oresteia* forgiveness does not bear any force as a religious command, because the religious order itself is based on revenge. The chorus explicitly underlines Zeus's order of punishment when it sings: The scale of Justice falls in equity/ the killer will be killed.[38]

The chorus's demand of Clytemnestra to leave the past alone is therefore devoid of any moral ethics, but rather relies on the fact that Agamemnon now returns home as a victor. Representing male strength and victory, the chorus expects her to relent to her husband's will and as such, it represents the problematic attitude which Elizabeth Gedge discusses in relation to the feminist mystic Beverly Lanzetta's view on women's victimization and the problem of forgiveness,[39] for although forgiveness may be an act of healing, she points out that in the case of women, forgiveness poses a grave problem. If radical forgiveness is a renunciation of ultimate vindication, does forgiveness not represent a reinforcement of traditional patterns of behaviour for women, Gedge asks. In

Clytemnestra's case, the chorus's expectation of Clytemnestra to renounce her wish for revenge is proof of just such a case.

In *The Flies*, however, Clytemnestra's position is different, for emphasizing the loss of the vital part of her self, Sartre's play suggests that the option to forgive would have saved Clytemnestra and as such, it would have been a moral action. Gedge's description of radical forgiveness and feminist theology supports the view that an active engagement with forgiveness would have saved Clytemnestra. Drawing her argument from Lanzetta's concept of feminist theology, Gedge states that women's oppression stems from their internalization of traditionally established binary oppositions that identify them with the body as opposed to the spirit. In the system of dualistic hierarchies, the body is regarded as inferior to the mind. Therefore, Gedge argues, women's spiritual practice must be able to deconstruct these oppositions in order to affirm women's worth and address the denigration of embodiment.

The Oresteia is a typical example of a work that reinforces these stereotypical patterns, especially in the case where Apollo justifies Orestes's murder of Clytemnestra. Stating that 'The mother is not the true parent of the child', but merely 'a nurse who tends the growth/of young seed planted by its true parent, the male,' Apollo reduces woman to passive matter and associates the father with creative energy. If Clytemnestra actively engaged with forgiveness, she would have been able to maintain her feminine and maternal side. Rejecting the chorus's demand that adheres to the traditional norms of society and requires of women to remain passive, Clytemnestra opted for revenge. The act of revenge, however, turned her into another victimizer just like her dead husband, for she allowed her daughter to be maltreated by her new husband and left her own son to live a life in exile. In Levinas's terms, then, she loses those aspects that Levinas's associates with the feminine because she is no longer at home with herself, but alienated. As such, she is not able to represent hospitality and the welcome and this leads to her estrangement both from life and her own children.

Whereas *The Oresteia* is an attempt to break up the vicious circle of revenge by finally cleansing Orestes from the guilt of having murdered his mother, *The Flies* maintains a much more ambivalent attitude towards Orestes's deed. As has been stated above, revenge, in both plays, is associated with masculine force and violence. At the beginning of *The Flies*, Argos appears to be a place where the inhabitants cannot feel safe and at home and as such, Argos seems to be a city devoid of maternal aspects. This is mainly emphasized at the start of the play when Orestes arrives at Argos and is confronted with an old woman who talks about the repenting citizens of Argos. Zeus argues that Argos's repentance is a mere hypocrisy because it only uses repentance as a self-justification. He further explains to Orestes that they feel guilty because they did not warn Agamemnon against his wife, and because they actually wanted to see a violent death. However, their desire to see Agamemnon dead has nothing to do with their wish for revenge. On the contrary, Zeus explains:

> Agamemnon was a worthy man, you know, but he made one great mistake. He put a ban on public executions. That was a pity. A good hanging now and then - that entertains folk in the provinces and robs death of its glamour... So the people here held their tongues; they looked forward to seeing, for once, a violent death. They still kept silent when they saw their King entering by the city gates... Yet at that moment a word, a single word, might have sufficed. But no one said it; each was gloating in imagination over the picture of a huge corpse with a shattered face.[40]

According to Zeus's explanation, the people's motive has been the desire to witness a violent death and as such, their desires do not overlap with Clytemnestra's wish to kill her husband because Clytemnestra committed the deed out of revenge. However, the silence of Argos people illustrates the affinity they share with Levinas's description of the dwelling and hospitality. As already described above, Levinas believes that an ethical relationship with the other can only be accomplished if the desire for violence and control is abandoned, and the essential passivity and fragility of human existence is accepted. Only such a stance allows the individual to respond to the other. The people of Argos therefore appear to possess an immoral character. In contrast to Clytemnestra, who had a personal reason for revenge, these people merely desired to witness a spectacular death. This wish stemmed from a deep-seated fear of death and as such, the people appear to deny the vulnerable state of man advocated by Levinas. As Zeus explained in the aforementioned quote: 'A good hanging... robs death of its glamour,'[41] because in the case of executions, man enjoys the power over death and life and this gives man the pleasing, but illusionary notion that he is in control over death.

The old woman's reaction to Orestes further underscores that Argos is a place devoid of any maternal features. It should first be noted that it is not a place characterized by Levinas's idea of the dwelling and the welcome, because no inhabitant of the place actually *feels at home* there. Nobody welcomes Orestes when he arrives at Argos and when he asks for the way, he does not even get a reply. When Zeus finally forces an old woman to speak and asks her whether she repents like everyone else, she replies:

> Oh. Sir, I do repent, most heartily I repent. If you only knew how I repent, and my daughter too, and my son-in-law offers up a heifer every year, and my little grandson has been brought up in a spirit of repentance. He's a pretty lad, with flaxen hair, and he

always behaves as good as gold. Though he's only seven, he never plays or laughs, for thinking of his original sin.[42]

The fact that the old woman describes the younger generation as rejecting the joys of life underscores the life-denying stance of Argos. The maternal is traditionally associated with life and fulfillment; the people's behaviour reveals the absence of maternal aspects in the city. When Orestes therefore kills his mother, who has already undergone a transformation and represents, just like the old woman, death in life, he merely repeats a pattern that is antagonistic to the maternal and therefore devoid of ethics.

In *The Flies*, therefore, forgiveness would have been a valid solution for both Clytemnestra and Orestes, but it would be wrong to state that *The Flies* is Sartre's appeal for forgiveness, especially when the date of its first performance, which was during the German occupation of France, is considered. Critics, such as Jon Bartley Stewart, believe that the play was an appeal to take action against the German oppressors,[43] yet this would diametrically oppose Sartre's view of writing. One of the most prominent points he stresses is the reader's freedom. In his book *What is Literature*, Sartre expounds on his concept of writing:

> If I appeal to my readers so that we may carry the enterprise which I have begun to a successful conclusion, it is self-evident that I consider him as a pure freedom, as an unconditioned activity; thus, in no case can I address myself to his passiveness, that is, try to affect him, to communicate to him, from the very first, emotions of fear, desire, or anger.[44]

Sartre's aim is therefore, to engage the reader in a critical response to the dilemma he proposes in his play. In this sense, Suzanne Guerlac points out that 'Sartre explicitly distinguishes literature from the restricted or utilitarian economy of means-ends relations.'[45] It is obvious that Sartre does not impose on the reader any form of message in *The Flies,* and it would be wrong to consider the play as a plead to take action against the Nazis because this view totally ignores those aspects of the play that question the nature of revenge, especially when viewed against its historical background. In an interview, Sartre expresses his ambivalent relation to the Resistance that launched various attacks on members of the occupying forces because the Germans reacted to each attack by executing a greater number of mostly innocent, hostages.[46]

In *The Flies,* Sartre's response to the German occupation of France and the atrocities of the Nazis reflects Anna M. Szczepan-Wojnarska's discussion of Czeslaw Milosz's poetry.[47] Szczepan-Wojnarska argues that Milosz's poetry addresses the problem of human helplessness in the face of evil, claiming that Milosz's poems validate the position where we do not act because any further

_y lead to further evil. Szczepan-Wojnarska states that the failure to
_. not good in itself, yet it is not evil either, even though it admits evil. Art
_s becomes a form of penance and purification for the artist who is faced with an
unresolved dilemma.

This dilemma represents the crucial point in *The Flies* and this is why the play
remains essentially ambivalent both towards revenge and forgiveness. Rhiannon
Goldthorpe regards the play as 'morally ambiguous,'[48] and Benedict O'Donohoe
shares this view. The latter claims that Orestes's valedictory speech remains
unconvincing. O'Donohoe also points out that Orestes merely acts out a mythically
prescribed pattern when he avenges his father's murder, concluding that Orestes's
freedom of choice would have been more plausible, if Sartre departed from legend
and changed the end of the plot. Choosing to kill his father's murderer, Orestes
obeys 'impulses which are manifestly those of a son avenging his father by slaying
his *ersatz*, and retrospectively rationalizing it as an ethical and political act.'[49]
O'Donohoe thus concludes that Argos is Orestes's alibi.[50]

The ambivalent position of Orestes's act is essential to the play's concern. A
superficial reading of *The Flies* may mistakenly lead to regarding Orestes's final
decision to avenge his father as his recognition of an existential freedom; yet this
kind of reading, as Allan Stoekl points out, overlooks the fascist traits combined in
Orestes who is 'a lonely, elite hero, breaking brutally with the past, showing
nothing but contempt for accepted morality, willingly commits a crime universally
judged indecent, monstrous.'[51] This fascist trait is further underscored by Stoekl
when he cites the Nazi Himmler, who proclaimed in 1943:

> To have endured this sight [the sight of hundreds of corpses] and
> at the same time to remain a decent person [...] this has made us
> tough, and is a page of glory never mentioned and never to be
> mentioned [...].'[52]

From this point of view, the parallel between Himmler's fascist hero and Orestes is
obvious.

It should be further noted that Orestes shows no interest at all for the effect his
action has on the community of Argos. Compared with Malika Rebai Maamri's
and James Arvanitakis's engagement with the necessity to forgive in order to
restore a community's health, Orestes's indifference appears to be evident. Maamri
argues that if social groups desire to live peacefully after traumatic events,
reconciliation and the establishment of mutual trust are indispensable and this can
only be achieved through forgiveness.[53] James Arvanitakis, on the other hand,
points out that forgiveness is a reciprocated process and therefore involves two
sides. According to Arvanitakis, hope and forgiveness are of prime importance if
social fracture is to be avoided after trauma.[54] Orestes, however, is not concerned
at all with the effects on the community on Argos. From an existentialist point of

view he certainly liberates the people from an oppressive regime that has controlled them by indoctrinating them with a sense of guilt. Burdening himself with their guilt, he grants them the opportunity to lead their lives according to their own wishes. On the other hand, Orestes's disregard for the reaction of the people of Argos leaves the audience dissatisfied. At the end of the play, he tells the people: 'Farewell, my people. Try to reshape your lives. All here is new, all must begin anew. And for me, too, a new life is beginning.'[55] Orestes then continues to tell them the story of the Pied Piper in which he himself appears to impersonate the piper who frees the city of a plague. He takes out a flute and starts playing and in this case, it is not the rats that follow him out of the city, but the flies. The fact that Orestes becomes a parody of the Pied Piper further underscores the ambivalent character of his position, because the conflation of his heroic position with a fairy tale does not allow the audience to take seriously Orestes's seemingly heroic act. His unwillingness to engage with the social community which has to heal the wounds of the past thus appears even more an act of selfishness.

Forgiveness in *The Flies* appears to be a valid solution to the problem of revenge and a close look at the way Sartre employs binary oppositions reveals that revenge is associated with the masculine order which relies on the logos and values only one truth and is therefore life-denying. Forgiveness, on the other hand, is associated with feminine aspects such as the recognition of the standpoint of the other. Nevertheless, considering Levinas's famous statement concerning the philosopher Heidegger highlights Levinas's own problems with forgiveness and the difficulty of such an act. Levinas admired Heidegger and was extremely disappointed when he had to see that Heidegger revealed signs of sympathy with the Nazi ideology. Commenting on Heidegger and the problem of forgiveness, Levinas states: 'One can forgive many Germans, but there are some Germans it is difficult to forgive. It is difficult to forgive Heidegger.'[56]

Notes

[1] Aeschylus, *The Oresteian Trilogy* (London: Penguin, 1959), 169.
[2] Luce Irigaray, *The Irigaray Reader* (Oxford: Blackwell, 1995), 36.
[3] Ibid., 37.
[4] David Cohen, 'The Theodicy of Aeschylus: Justice and Tyranny in *The Oresteia*', in *Greek Tragedy*, eds. Ian McAuslan and Peter Walcot (Oxford: Oxford University Press, 1993), 45.
[5] Ibid., 48.
[6] Aeschylus, *The Oresteian Trilogy*, 137.
[7] Ibid., 56.
[8] Ibid.

[9] Nathanial Wade & Julia Kidwell, 'Understanding Forgiveness in the Lives of Religious People: The Role of Sacred and Secular Elements', in *A Journey Through Forgiveness*, edited by Malika Rebai Maamri, Nehama Verbin and Everett L. Worthington, Jr. (Oxford: Inter-Disciplinary Press, 2010), accessed February 2nd 2011, http://www.inter-disciplinary.net/publishing/id-press/ebooks/a-journey-through-forgiveness/, 39-48.

[10] Emmanuel Levinas, *Totality and Infinity* (Pittsburgh: Duquesne University Press, 2008), 283.

[11] Ibid.

[12] Ibid.

[13] Ibid., 155.

[14] Quoted in Stella Sandford, 'Masculine Mothers? Maternity in Levinas and Plato', in *Feminist Interpretations of Emmanuel Levinas*, ed. Tina Chanter (University Park: Pennsylvania University Press, 2001), 185.

[15] Emmanuel Levinas, *Totality and Infinity*, 156.

[16] Catherine Chalier, 'The Exteriority of the Feminine', in *Feminist Interpretations of Emmanuel Levinas*, ed. Tina Chanter (University Park: Pennsylvania University Press, 2001), 171-2.

[17] Jean-Paul Sartre, *'The Flies'*, in *No Exit and Three Other Plays* (New York: Vintage, 1989), 84.

[18] Quoted in Stella Sandford, 'Masculine Mothers? Maternity in Levinas and Plato', 184.

[19] Ibid., 184.

[20] Jacques Derrida, *On Cosmopolitanism and Forgiveness* (London: Routledge, 2002), 49-50.

[21] Richard A. Cohen, ed., Introduction to *Humanism of the Other* (Urbana: University of Illinois Press, 2006), xxxiii.

[22] Johan Callens, *Double Binds: Existentialist Inspiration and Generic Experimentation in the Early Work of Jack Richardson* (Amsterdam: Rodopi, 1993),161.

[23] Benedict O'Donohoe, 'Fraternity: Liberty Or Inequality? Incest in Sartre's Drama', *French Studies* 50.1 (1996): 59.

[24] Sartre, *The Flies*, 59.

[25] Ibid., 88-9.

[26] Ibid., 90.

[27] Ibid., 91.

[28] Robert Champigny, 'Comedian and Martyr: *Le Diable et le bon Dieu*', in *Jean-Paul Sartre*, ed. Harold Bloom (Philadelphia: Chelsea House Publishers, 2001), 20.

[29] Sartre, *The Flies*, 91.

[30] Ibid., 67.

[31] Ibid., 110

[32] Steven J. Sandage and Peter J. Jankowski, 'Forgiveness, Differentiation of Self and Mental Health', in *A Journey Through Forgiveness*, edited by Malika Rebai Maamri, Nehama Verbin and Everett L. Worthington, Jr. (Oxford: Inter-Disciplinary Press, 2010), accessed February 2nd 2011, http://www.inter-disciplinary.net/publishing/id-press/ebooks/a-journey-through-forgiveness/, 87-98.

[33] Terry Eagleton, *Sweet Violence: The Idea of the Tragic* (Oxford: Blackwell Publishers, 2003), 31.

[34] Philip Vellacott, 'Introduction', in *The Oresteian Trilogy*, 23.

[35] Charlotte van Oyen Witvliet, 'Understanding and Approaching Forgiveness as Altruism: Relationships with Rumination, Self-Control and a Gratitude-Based Strategy', in *A Journey Through Forgiveness*, edited by Malika Rebai Maamri, Nehama Verbin and Everett L. Worthington, Jr. (Oxford: Inter-Disciplinary Press, 2010), accessed February 2nd 2011, http://www.inter-disciplinary.net/publishing/id-press/ebooks/a-journey-through-forgiveness/,

[36] Jean-Paul Sartre, *The Flies*, 120.

[37] Aeschylus, The Oresteian Trilogy, 50.

[38] Ibid., 51.

[39] Elizabeth Gedge, 'Radical Forgiveness and Feminist Theology', in *A Journey Through Forgiveness*, edited by Malika Rebai Maamri, Nehama Verbin and Everett L. Worthington, Jr. (Oxford: Inter-Disciplinary Press, 2010), accessed February 2nd 2011, http://www.inter-disciplinary.net/publishing/id-press/ebooks/a-journey-through-forgiveness/, 69-78.

[40] Sartre, *The Flies*, 52.

[41] Ibid.

[42] Ibid., 54.

[43] Jon B. Stewart, 'Introduction', in *The Debate between Sartre and Merleau-Ponty: Studies in Phenomenology and Existential Philosophy*, ed. Jon B. Stewart (Evanston: Northwestern University Press, 1998), xx.

[44] Jean-Paul Sartre, *What Is Literature?* (Guildford: Methuen, 1978), 32.

[45] Suzanne Guerlac, *Literary Polemics: Bataille, Sartre, Valéry, Breton* (Stanford: Stanford University Press, 1997), 71.

[46] Ian H. Birchall, *Sartre against Stalinism* (Oxford: Berghahn Books, 2004), 43.

[47] Anna M. Szczepan-Wojnarska, 'Poetry as a Medium of Forgiveness in the Light of Czeslaw Milosz's Oeuvre', in *A Journey Through Forgiveness*, edited by Malika Rebai Maamri, Nehama Verbin and Everett L. Worthington, Jr. (Oxford: Inter-Disciplinary Press, 2010), accessed February 2nd 2011, http://www.inter-disciplinary.net/publishing/id-press/ebooks/a-journey-through-forgiveness/, 201-208.

[48] Rhiannon Goldthorpe, *Sartre: Literature and Theory* (Cambridge: Cambridge University Press, 1986), 82.
[49] Benedict O'Donohoe, 'Sartre's Melodrama: *Les Mouches*, or The Stepson's Revenge', *French Studies Bulletin* 20(1999): 8.
[50] Ibid.
[51] Allan Stoekl, 'What the Nazis Saw: *Les Mouches* in Occupied Paris', *SubStance* 32.3 (2003): 83.
[52] Ibid., 84.
[53] Malika Rebai Maamri, 'Algerian President's Peace Plan: Political and Psychological Perspectives of Forgiveness', in *A Journey Through Forgiveness*, edited by Malika Rebai Maamri, Nehama Verbin and Everett L. Worthington, Jr. (Oxford: Inter-Disciplinary Press, 2010), accessed February 2nd 2011, http://www.inter-disciplinary.net/publishing/id-press/ebooks/a-journey-through-forgiveness/, 141-148.
[54] James Arvanitakis, 'On Forgiveness, Hope and Community: or theFine Line Step between Authentic and Fractured Communities', in *A Journey Through Forgiveness*, edited by Malika Rebai Maamri, Nehama Verbin and Everett L. Worthington, Jr. (Oxford: Inter-Disciplinary Press, 2010), 149-158.
[55] Sartre, *The Flies*, 123.
[56] Emmanuel Levinas, *Nine Talmudic Readings* (Indiana: Indiana University Press, 1994), 25.

Bibliography

Aeschylus. *The Oresteian Trilogy*. London: Penguin, 1959.

Birchall, Ian H. *Sartre Against Stalinism*. Oxford: Berghahn Books, 2004.

Callens, Johan. *Double Binds: Existentialist Inspiration and Generic Experimentation in the Early Work of Jack Richardson*. Amsterdam Rodopi, 1993.

Chalier, Catherine. 'The Exteriority of the Feminine'. In *Feminist Interpretations of Emmanuel Levinas*, edited by Tina Chanter, 171-179. University Park: Pennsylvania University Press, 2001.

Champigny, Robert. 'Comedian and Martyr: *Le Diable et le bon Dieu*'. In *Jean-Paul Sartre*, edited by Harold Bloom, 3-22. Philadelphia: Chelsea House Publishers, 2001.

Cohen, David. 'The Theodicy of Aeschylus: Justice and Tyranny in *The Oresteia*'. In *Greek Tragedy*, edited by Ian McAuslan and Peter Walcot, 45-57. Oxford: Oxford University Press, 1993.

Cohen, Richard A. Introduction to *Humanism of the Other*, by Emmanuel Levinas. Translated by Nidra Poller, vii-xliv. Urbana: University of Illinois Press, 2006.

Derrida, Jacques. *Cosmopolitanism and Forgiveness*. Translated by Mark Dooley and Michael Hughes. London: Routledge, 2001.

Eagleton, Terry. *Sweet Violence: The Idea of the Tragic*. Oxford: Blackwell Publishers, 2003.

Goldthorpe, Rhiannon. *Sartre: Literature and Theory*. Cambridge: Cambridge University Press, 1986.

Guerlac, Suzanne. *Literary Polemics: Bataille, Sartre, Valéry, Breton*. Stanford: Stanford University Press, 1997.

Irigaray, Luce. *The Irigaray Reader*, edited by Margaret Whitford. Oxford: Blackwell, 1995.

Levinas, Emmanuel. *Totality and Infinity*. Translated by Alphonso Lingis. Pittsburgh: Duquesne University Press, 2008.

Levinas, Emmanuel. *Nine Talmudic Readings*. Translated by Annette Aronowicz. Bloomington: Indiana University Press, 1994.

O'Donohoe, Benedict. 'Fraternity: Liberty or Inequality? Incest in Sartre's Drama'. *French Studies* 50.1 (1996): 54-65.

O'Donohoe, Benedict. 'Sartre's Melodrama: *Les Mouches*, or The Stepson's Revenge'. *French Studies Bulletin* 20 (1999): 6-8.

Sandford, Stella. 'Masculine Mothers? Maternity in Levinas and Plato'. In *Feminist Interpretations of Emmanuel Levinas*, edited by Tina Chanter, 180-202. University Park: Pennsylvania University Press, 2001.

Sartre, Jean-Paul. *No Exit and Three Other Plays*. New York: Vintage, 1989.

Sartre, Jean-Paul. *What Is Literature?* Guildford: Methuen, 1978.

Stewart, Jon B. 'Introduction'. In *The Debate between Sartre and Merleau-Ponty: Studies in Phenomenology and Existential Philosophy*, edited by Jon B. Stewart, xiii-xl. Evanston: Northwestern University Press, 1998.

Stoekl, Allan. 'What the Nazis Saw: *Les Mouches* in Occupied Paris'. *SubStance* 32.3 (2003): 78-91.

Vellacott, Philip. Introduction to *The Oresteian Trilogy*, by Aeschylus. Translated by Phillip Vellacott, 9-37. London: Penguin, 1959.

Canan Şavkay is Assistant Professor at the Department of English Language and Literature at Istanbul University, Turkey. She has published various articles on women's writing and the postmodern novel and is interested in the study of the interrelation between philosophy and literature.

Mapping Forgiveness: Conclusion

Malika Rebai Maamri

While the topic of forgiveness deserves further attention, I would like to close this volume by expressing my deep gratitude to the contributors for their patience and support, and most significant contribution to the growing body of literature on a subject of enormous relevance to our troubled world. I would like also to thank the ID editorial team for giving me the opportunity to collaborate in this 'raising awareness' project.

What are the lessons we learned from these insights and comments on the issue of forgiveness and its power of healing the individual and whole communities? These profound insights certainly helped us gain entrée into the most recesses of our hearts. This book, which resulted from a wonderful international co-operation and dedication to the promotion of dialogue through cultures, explored forgiveness in interpersonal relationships, the individual and society relationship and international relations through the lenses of a wide range of disciplines. Traditionally thought of as the preserve of religion, the concepts of forgiveness and reconciliation have been examined through an academic lens by investigating their emotional, religious, cultural, philosophical and political constituents. The contributors offered some penetrating concepts and practical ideas on how to deal with those offences through forgiveness. Although the authors of this collection revealed how long and painful the road to forgiveness is, they all embrace forgiveness as part of the healing process.

Through this wide range of papers, the process of the 'globalisation' of forgiveness proliferates. We have seen this fostering of tolerance and forgiveness. Forgiveness as a response to past wrong constrains the forgiver's future acts, ruling out revenge. It is both a gift for the offender and for the offended. Moreover, the very word forgiveness, built on the root word 'give,' does not mean surrender, but a conscious decision to cease brooding over grudges. Forgiveness is not forgetfulness either but involves accepting the promise that the future can be more than dwelling on memories of past injury. It is a creative act that liberates people from their painful past. In effect, it cleanses our system of the poison that would surely fester and cause illness and continued misery if not released. By embracing forgiveness, we embrace peace, hope, gratitude and joy.

Moreover, the relationship between anger, revenge, and forgiveness is particularly important in understanding the role of forgiveness in reconstructing post- conflict societies. When members of a community become aware of their inextricable link with others, then they realize that individual misdeeds have repercussions on the whole community. We have also come to the understanding that the individual healing process entwined with the larger global community needs to move toward forgiveness in order to reorganize life with a new wisdom and deeper understanding of how to live in unity. Reconciliation and forgiveness are indeed imperative processes for restoration and normalisation after any period of violence and war.

The concept of forgiveness is interwoven with justice, apology, truth, and reconciliation. Forgiveness is shown to be a must, a necessity, as it gives rise to social harmony. It builds a sense of solidarity and fellow-feeling. It is important to note that no matter how much a group promotes or supports a climate for reconciliation and healing, it is the capacity for forgiveness that lies within each individual that arguably influences the long term success of these efforts.

Crucial to forgiveness is learning to identify, to empathize with others. An 'us' and 'them' approach to relationships will never allow individuals to experience themselves as forgiving people. More importantly, in forgiveness, one should not await any reward or put any term or condition upon it. Forgiveness reunites us with God, and brings us into unity with one another, and restores the integrity of our inner self. A number of studies attest to the beneficial effect that positive relationships and good social ties have on indices of physical health. Research has indeed shown that people who are deeply and unjustly hurt by others can heal emotionally and, in some cases, physically by forgiving their offender. Compassion is one of the key ingredients of forgiveness. Letting go of grudges and bitterness indeed makes way for compassion and peace. Forgiveness is thus the most important single process that brings peace to our soul and harmony to our life. For the last word on this hot subject, I would add that forgiveness takes great courage and assertiveness, for in forgiving, we embrace the possibility of a real change; hence, we endeavour to make our world a better place to live in. Such an agenda calls forth from us elaborate positive and creative energies.